Restyling Fa

News and current affairs, documentary and reality TV are part of a turbulent time in broadcasting as the boundaries between fact and fiction are pushed to the limits. *Restyling Factual TV* addresses the wide range of programmes that fall within the category of 'factuality', from politics, to natural history, to reality entertainment. It looks at ways viewers navigate their way through a busy, noisy and constantly changing factual television environment.

Focusing on contemporary trends in the world of television, primarily in Britain and Sweden (both countries with a public service tradition), but with reference to other countries such as the US, Annette Hill investigates complex issues such as genre evaluation, the truth claims of factual television, knowledge and learning, and fair treatment in factual programming. Audience research highlights how people engage with and reflect on various representations of reality and, by looking at factuality in this way, we can see how audiences are centre stage in the transformation of factual television.

Annette Hill is Professor of Media and Research Director of the School of Media, Arts and Design, University of Westminster. Her previous publications include *Reality TV: Audiences and Popular Factual Television* (2005), the *Television Studies Reader* (with Robert C. Allen, 2003), *TV Living: Television, Audiences and Everyday Life* (with David Gauntlett, 1999) and *Shocking Entertainment: Viewing Responses to Violent Movies* (1997). Her current research is on Spirit TV and media audiences.

Restyling Factual TV

Audiences and news, documentary and reality genres

Annette Hill

Routledge
Taylor & Francis Group

LONDON AND NEW YORK

First published 2007
by Routledge
2 Park Square, Milton Park, Abingdon, Oxon OX14 4RN

Simultaneously published in the USA and Canada
by Routledge
711 Third Ave, New York, NY 10017

*Routledge is an imprint of the Taylor & Francis Group, an informa
business*

© 2007 Annette Hill

Typeset in Garamond 3 by
RefineCatch Limited, Bungay, Suffolk
Printed and bound in Great Britain by
Antony Rowe Ltd, Chippenham, Wiltshire

British Library Cataloguing in Publication Data
A catalogue record for this book is available from the British
Library

Library of Congress Cataloging-in-Publication Data
A catalog record for this book has been requested

ISBN10: 0–415–37955–5 (hbk)
ISBN10: 0–415–37956–3 (pbk)
ISBN10: 0–203–09973–7 (ebk)

ISBN13: 978–0–415–37955–7 (hbk)
ISBN13: 978–0–415–37956–4 (pbk)
ISBN13: 978–0–203–09973–5 (ebk)

For Don, and all the lovely people in my life, thank you very much.

Contents

List of tables   viii
List of figures   ix
Acknowledgements   xi

1   Restyling factuality   1

2   Mapping factual TV   30

3   Public and popular   58

4   Genre work   84

5   Truth claims   112

6   Knowledge and learning   145

7   Participation   172

8   Containing factuality   212

Appendix   234
Bibliography   241
Index   251

Tables

2.1	British factual TV schedules	35
2.2	British factual TV top ten	36
2.3	Swedish factual and reality programming, 2003	38
2.4	Swedish factual TV schedules	41
2.5	Swedish factual TV top ten	42
3.1a	Regular viewing habits for factual and reality TV by age	66
3.1b	Regular viewing habits for factual and reality TV by gender	66
3.1c	Regular viewing habits for factual and reality TV by education	67
3.2a	Public value of factual and reality TV by age	71
3.2b	Public value of factual and reality TV by gender	72
3.2c	Public value of factual and reality TV by education	72

Figures

2.1	British factual TV schedules	34
2.2	Swedish factual TV schedules	40
3.1	Regular viewing habits for factual and reality TV in Britain and Sweden	63
3.2	Occasional viewing habits for factual and reality TV in Britain and Sweden	64
3.3	Public value of factual and reality TV in Britain and Sweden	69
3.4	Categorization of factual and reality TV as informative and entertaining in Britain and Sweden	74
5.1	Perception of factual and reality TV as 'true to life' in Britain and Sweden	120
5.2	Value of factual and reality TV as 'true to life' in Britain and Sweden	121
5.3	Perception and value of factual and reality TV as 'true to life' in Britain	122
5.4	Perception and value of factual and reality TV as 'true to life' in Sweden	122
5.5	Perception of performance in factual and reality TV in Britain and Sweden	125
5.6	Value of performance in factual and reality TV in Britain and Sweden	125
5.7	Perception of factual TV as 'true to life' in programmes from different countries	129
5.8	Perception of factual TV as 'true to life' in programmes from different countries by age	130
6.1	Opinion formation from factual and reality TV in Britain and Sweden	155
6.2	Amount of learning from factual and reality TV in Britain and Sweden	157
7.1	Attitudes towards fair treatment of social groups in news and reality TV in Britain	181

7.2 Importance of fair treatment of social groups in news and
     reality TV in Britain   182
7.3 Attitudes towards fair treatment of social groups in news
     and reality TV in Sweden   183
7.4 Importance of fair treatment of social groups in news and
     reality TV in Sweden   183

Acknowledgements

This research was funded in Britain by the former regulatory bodies the Independent Television Commission and Broadcasting Standards Commission, now the Office of Communications. I owe a great debt to Andrea Millwood Hargrave and Pam Hanley for supporting the quantitative research. Thanks must also go to Robin Blake and Alison Preston at Ofcom for their support in the analysis of the survey data. I would also like to thank Susanna Dinnage, Julian Dobinson, Claire Grimmond, Richard Paterson, Rosa Sebastian, Julia Rulf and John Willis for their advice during the design of the survey. The research was funded in Sweden by the Media Management and Transformation Centre at Jönköping International Business School, with a small grant from the Department of Journalism and Mass Communication, Göteborg University, and partly carried out in co-operation with the SOM Institute, Göteborg University. The research also benefited from the advice of media professionals working within SVT, TV4 and Kanal 5. In particular, thanks must go to Johan Linden, Markus Sterky, Eva Landahl, Thomas Linde, Cecilia Zadig, Johan Westman, Malte Andreasson, Göran Ellung and Tobias Egge. Advice was also most welcome from colleagues working within Jönköping International Business School, Stockholm University, Södertörn University College and Lund University.

I am indebted to Robert Picard for his wonderful invitation to study Swedish television audiences. The research could not have taken place without Lennart Weibull and Åsa Nilsson, and their generosity of spirit in helping me with the quantitative data. Much of the Swedish data has already been published in *Swedish Factual and Reality Television Audiences*, with Lennart Weibull and Åsa Nilsson, Jonkoping International Business School Research Reports No. 2005–4, and also *Synen på icke-fiction I TV: resultatredovising*, with Lennart Weibull and Åsa Nilsson, Arbetsrapport nr. 33, Göteborgs Universitet, Institutionen for Journalistiyk och Masskommunikation. The analysis of cultural trends in Chapter 3 also features in an article 'Public and Popular: British and Swedish Audience Trends in Factual Television', *Cultural Trends* (2007), in collaboration with Weibull and Nilsson.

My research assistant Inger Skalse provided excellent support in the

Swedish data design and collection, and her transcription and translation of the focus groups provided an invaluable insight into Swedish viewing responses for a non-native speaker. Sofia Johansson also provided excellent assistance with the focus groups, and in her analysis and translation of the open questions in the Swedish survey, and in Swedish language research publications. In terms of the British research, Caroline Dover helped enormously in the early stages of the work, and her scheduling, ratings, textual analysis and assistance with the survey design was as always invaluable. Sofia Johansson was an excellent recruiter, moderator and transcriber of the focus groups, and I am also thankful to Mascha Brichta for her assistance with the focus groups and transcription of the data.

I would like to thank everyone in the Communication and Media Research Institute for their support over the past few years, they are excellent colleagues to work with. In particular, I must thank Sally Feldman for being a great boss, and Peter Goodwin and Colin Sparks for making things happen. Rachel Groom and Erica Spindler have also made it possible for me to work on this book, and I am truly grateful for their efficient running of the Research Office. Many colleagues have offered invaluable advice on the material for the book, and my thanks goes to Robert Allen, John Ellis, Jane Roscoe, Gareth Palmer, Derek Paget, Jason Mittell, Michelle Hilmes, Sonia Livingstone, David Gauntlett, Vincent Porter, Ian Calcutt, Peter Dahlgren, Jan Ekecrantz. I would especially like to thank John Corner, Peter Lunt and Göran Bolin for their generous reading of the manuscript, and for improving it enormously through their detailed comments and advice. Finally, a great big thank you to everyone who participated in this project.

Chapter 1

Restyling factuality

'It seems that Reality TV, documentary, and news are all kind of mixed up.'

The Armstrongs (BBC 2006) is about Coventry's third largest double glazing business. It's the office Christmas party and the owners are wrapping presents which, amongst other everyday household items, include a frozen shepherd's pie. Mrs Armstrong is worried it might defrost and give someone food poisoning. 'Fuck em,' says her husband. An ominous bell tolls as the employees gather, the funereal sounds accompanied by distorted shots of the party in progress, the factory workers drinking flat beer from a water cooler. There are flashbacks to a previous party, a similarly bleak affair that is reinforced by the music from the film *A Nightmare before Christmas*. The Armstrongs are unbelievable. One time they go on a trip to France to sell do-it-yourself conservatories, but they don't speak French. They hire a motivational guru called Basil Meanie who alienates the staff. Mr Armstrong says baffling things like 'What was was, and now what is is. And is tomorrow a new day? Yes it is.' Surely this is made up. It's a clever mock documentary, like *The Office*, only about double glazing rather than paper suppliers. And yet it is real. After the first episode aired, the Armstrongs received over four thousand emails, many asking if the show was a spoof. They established their own website with official merchandise and a regular blog, they made radio and television appearances, and signed book deals. The Armstrongs became famous for being themselves on television. As Mrs Armstrong explained: 'This is the weirdest situation I have ever found myself in . . . and I thought the world of double glazing was exciting.'

This book is about the topsy turvy world of factual television. This is a world where things are not quite as they appear to be, where viewers constantly ask themselves 'is this real?' It is a space where familiar factual genres such as news, or documentary, take on properties common to other genres. It's a place where reality TV runs wild, crossing over into fiction and non-fiction territories, taking genre experimentation to the limit. In the world of factual television a newsreader can be the presenter in a reality gameshow set on a desert island. A celebrity chef can change government policy on children's school meals. A celebrity lookalike can win a celebrity reality gameshow. Producers can trick a group of people into thinking they are in space when really they are on a film set in Suffolk. Watching factual television can feel like a strange dream, where people agree to live in the Iron Age, go to a baby mindreader, undergo plastic surgery live on television. It can feel like being trapped between fact and fiction, where news footage of violent acts can be so difficult to comprehend that it seems unreal, and where fake footage of violent acts is passed off as real. Surrounded by factual programmes, viewers have to deal with the various ways programmes represent reality.

Restyling Factual TV is about understanding genres in relation to each other and in relation to popular audiences. It takes as a starting point the idea that factual television is being restyled, that various kinds of news, current affairs, documentary and popular factual genres are part of a turbulent time in broadcasting. Hybridity is now the distinctive feature of factuality. The boundaries between fact and fiction have been pushed to the limits in various popular factual formats that mix non-fiction and fiction genres. Popular factual genres are not self-contained, stable and knowable, they migrate, mutate and replicate. Significantly, they cross over into existing factual genres, with the cross-pollination of styles increasing the pace of change in news, current affairs or documentary.

Viewers do not experience factual genres in isolation but as part of a chaotic mix of factuality. The main research question is therefore one that asks what happens if we look at factual television from the position of the viewer? Using multimethod research with representative samples of British and Swedish audiences, a picture emerges of a viewer navigating their way through a busy, noisy and constantly changing factual television environment. As this viewer explains: 'the last couple of years or so, you know, reality TV is going towards a documentary kind of thing, and documentary is moving down to reality TV, and the news is just somewhere in between, so, none of them is actually factual.'

Viewing strategies show how audiences are dealing with the restyling of factuality. They classify factual genres so as to make them knowable and manageable, to make order out of chaos. Striking similarities between British and Swedish viewing practices highlight an overarching social and cultural order to factual genres, with public service genres at the top and popular genres at the bottom. Reality TV is off the factual scale and has been re-classified as reality entertainment. Another strategy for factuality is that of genre work. Genre work involves immersive and reflective modes of engagement with factual genres, allowing viewers to personally respond to programmes and themselves in conscious and unconscious ways, and often in contradictory ways. These viewing strategies highlight how audiences engage with and reflect on various representations of reality. Audiences are living in a cosmopolitan factual television environment, dealing with a mass of programmes

24 hours a day, finding various routes through the changes taking place in factuality.

Factuality

Factual television is a container for a variety of genres, sub-genres and hybrid genres. The term 'factual' is shorthand for non-fiction content. It is a useful term that instantly says this television programme is fact and not fiction. Factual is also a value laden term, and its association with truth, information and other conceptual values ensures it means different things to different people. The term 'factuality' refers to broader cultural production and reception processes. Factuality is understood as 'factual experiences, imagination, values, that provide settings within which media institutions operate, shaping the character of factual television processes and viewing practices' (adapted from Corner and Pels 2003: 3). Thus there are various interpretations of factual television commonly understood by audiences. Factual television is a container for non-fiction content; it signifies social and personal values for non fiction genres; and it is part of non-fiction production and reception practices. For most people factual television is concerned with knowledge about the real world; as this viewer explains, 'factual means that the programme will contain facts and no fiction. Programmes that are true and about real issues.' This is an idealized view of factual television, and the tensions between ideals and practices make the production and reception of factuality challenging and dynamic, as programme makers and audiences negotiate between what factual content ought to be and what it is on a day-to-day basis.

An overarching view of factual content as true and about real issues assumes that this content contains representations of reality. Audiences perform 'a series of mental operations in order to assess the reality status' of factual programmes (Grodal 2002: 68). Most audiences evaluate factual programmes by using a criterion of truth. In this sense, factual content is perceived as authentic and true to life, and audiences focus on the referential integrity of factual content. The other overarching view of factual content is that it contains facts and provides knowledge about the world. Knowledge signifies specific information about a subject, event or situation, and it can also mean knowledge gained through experience. Audiences evaluate the knowledge status of factual programmes by assessing the level of information provided, and how objective or impartial the facts are in a given situation. Assessments about the factual status of non-fiction content are therefore connected to attitudes towards truth and knowledge. Although factual is shorthand for non-fiction content, it is rarely used to define any kind of non-fiction, such as light entertainment, but instead tends to be used by audiences to signify non-fiction programmes that make truth claims and are based on facts.

The kinds of non-fiction content that typically would be classified as factual are based on established genres within television production. Television genre refers to specific types of content that can be categorized as similar in style and communicative modes of address. Television genres are constructed through production and reception processes (Mittell 2004). Programme makers draw on production traditions, referring to previous practices to construct a factual programme similar to, or a variation on, another type of programme; and audiences draw on their knowledge of previous programmes to recognize it as a distinctive genre. News is the most well-established and recognizable factual genre. In terms of broadcasting, it has always been an important genre in early radio and television production, and although it has changed over the years in style and content it nevertheless is firmly rooted in long-standing journalistic practices and in public service broadcasting traditions (Schudson 1995; Seaton 2005). For audiences, news is the first, and still the most familiar, factual television genre, and in many ways all other factual genres are evaluated alongside viewers' understanding and experience of news. Documentary is another genre that has a strong historical tradition within television production. The establishment of this genre as a way of documenting the world and observing people's real lives and experiences is part of the development of public service broadcasting (Winston 1995). Audiences have come to recognize documentary as a genre, and to classify different kinds of documentary as sub-genres, such as natural history, with distinctive modes of address. A huge variety of other kinds of factual genres work alongside news and documentary, some of which can be classified as hybrid genres, where one established factual genre has been merged with another fiction or non-fiction genre. According to Neale (2001), all television genres become mixed up with others, and in this sense all factual content is based on multiple generic participation. However, the development of a range of popular factual genres in the 1980s and 1990s has ensured audiences have come to expect hybrid factual genres to be associated with what is most commonly described as reality TV, a term that, like misdirection in a magic trick, is not quite what it claims to be (Hill 2005). Popular factual genres therefore sit at the margins of factuality.

The primary aim of this book is to compare different kinds of factual genres based on the understanding that audiences experience factuality 'in the round'. Corner describes something similar in his discussion of the fictionality of the factual and the factuality of the fictional (2006: 96). The term factual television stands for factual and reality programming, an understanding of the term that is taken directly from audiences and their classification of factuality. Whilst popular factual is located in border territory between factual and other non-fiction and fiction genres, it is nevertheless part of the story of contemporary factual television and needs to be included in any discussion of factual categories (see Kilborn 2003; Nichols 1994, amongst others). Factual television also includes television programmes with interactive elements, such as voting, and related websites or mobile content. The interactive and multiplatform elements of various factual television programmes are part of the story of the restyling of factuality. Whilst these various forms of factual content point to further diversification of factual genres, and future directions for segmented factual content to diverse audiences and users, these multiplatform elements are background to the primary experience of factual television. The focus on factual television programmes is derived from audience experiences and reflects the story of factuality at a specific moment in time.

Speaking in broad terms, there is a classification of factual content according to the specific genres of news, current affairs, documentary, and reality programmes, with further sub-genres applied within each of these categories. News is a category that encompasses regional, national and rolling news programmes. The major news programmes are often flagship productions, providing the main source of public information (Corner 1995). Current affairs and investigations is a broad category that encompasses both long form journalism, political debate, consumer-based stories, and investigative journalism (Turner 2006). Documentary is a category made up of different documentary modes (Nichols 2001). Selected documentary modes include specialist documentaries, observational documentaries and general documentaries, which can either be a strand or stand-alone documentaries on any number of topics. Reality TV, or popular factual, is a catch-all category for a variety of different one-off programmes, series and formats that follow real people and celebrities and their everyday or out of the ordinary experiences. Popular factual sub-categories include infotainment about crime or emergency services; docusoaps about institutions or groups of people; lifestyle, often about how to do gardening, or making over someone's home or personal appearance; life experiment programmes where people experiment with different social experiences; reality gameshows where a game element is introduced to a group of people in a controlled situation; reality talent shows where members of the public or celebrities audition for and perform music or other artistic endeavours; and the reality hoax, a mock situation that usually mocks those deceived by an elaborately staged set up (Hill 2005). There are other emergent categories within popular factual, such as reality business series like *The Apprentice*, and the wide range of hybrid genres shows how all encompassing this type of non-fiction content can be. The industry term 'reality event' sums up the scale and influence of hybrid genres such as *The X Factor*, that can run for up to twenty weeks, delivering a large audience share over a long period of time, and forcing competing genres to work hard to retain a place in the schedules. Popular factual is therefore a wide-ranging category that makes factual television top heavy with reality entertainment-led programming.

Factual and reality trends

In a report by the regulatory body the Office of Communications on British television in 2005, general factual (meaning all factual content that was not news or current affairs) was the largest growth genre. Across all five main channels there were more hours devoted to general factual content in peaktime than drama. For BBC2 and Channel 4, general factual was the dominant genre for peaktime schedules (46 per cent and 35 per cent, respectively). The BBC's digital channels were dominated by news, making up half of all output. The most dominant genre in daytime television across the five main channels was also news, followed by general factual. For example, for BBC1 28 per cent of all daytime content was news, and 24 per cent general factual; for ITV1 general factual was the largest single category, taking up 35 per cent of daytime content. For multichannel television a quarter of all broadcast hours were devoted to news and general factual.

In the top twenty British shows of 2005 were reality talent shows *I'm a Celebrity* . . . (ITV), *The X Factor* (ITV) and *Strictly Come Dancing* (BBC), with over ten million viewers and an audience share of 40 per cent. The BBC's *Ten O'Clock News* was the only other factual programme in the top twenty shows of the year (Reevell 2006). Other factual and reality shows that did well in 2005 included the CGI documentary *Supervolcano* (BBC, eight million viewers), *Big Brother* (Channel 4, seven million) and *Hell's Kitchen* (ITV, six million). In the top ten multichannel programmes dominated by sports, the reality football series *The Match* came number six, with almost two million viewers. Amongst the highest earning independent production companies of 2005 were Talkback Thames (£145 million), the makers of *Pop Idol* and *X Factor*, Endemol UK (£120 million), the makers of *Big Brother* and *Fame Academy*, and RDF Media (£64 million), who produce *Wife Swap* and *Faking It*.

The industry magazine *Broadcast* (2006) compiled a report on the most creative programmes, channels and genres of 2006, including programmes that either won or were nominated in 27 international award ceremonies, ranging from the British Academy Programme Awards, the Golden Globe Awards, to the Rose d'Or and the International Emmy Awards. The results indicate the growth genre of factual not only generates high ratings but also attracts international acclaim. News and reality entertainment are award-winning genres for commercial channels, and public service channels dominate all other factual genres. The best news coverage was awarded to Channel 4 news for the coverage of the leaked document from the Attorney General questioning the legality of the Iraq war; Sky News won best news channel, and ITN best news production company, showing the range of quality news provision on public service and commercial channels. The BBC won the award for best current affairs for their investigation into the Saudi royal family and their relationship with the USA; the BBC also won best current affairs channel, and best production company, highlighting the absence of commercial channels in this genre. For single documentary, *Children of Beslan* (BBC) won the top award, with a powerful account of the victims of the school massacre; Channel 4 won the channel award, and had three programmes in the top five documentaries; whilst the BBC won the production company award with their high end specialist documentaries. Most creative documentary series award went to *Jamie's School Dinners*, which took the critical issue of children's school meals and made it a government priority as a result of response to the series; the most creative channel was won by BBC2, and the production company Fresh One owned by Jamie Oliver, the star of the above documentary, won most creative company. For popular factual, *The Apprentice* got the top slot, with BBC2 winning the most creative channel, and Talkback Thames (producer of *The Apprentice* with Mark Burnett Productions) winning the production company award. The BBC also won hands down in the science and natural history categories, winning most creative channel, production company, and the natural history series *British Isles* receiving the number one programme award. With regard to reality entertainment, the commercial channels fared better, with ITV winning most creative channel and production company, and *The X Factor* taking the top slot.

British factual television is significant both in terms of broadcast hours, revenue and quality production, and these skills help with large export sales. In the independent production sector, export sales came to £79 million in 2005, with the majority of revenue from US sales: 'factual and factual entertainment genres generated the largest sales abroad, accounting for 45 per cent (£36 million) and 40 per cent (£32 million) of the total reported turnover respectively' (Ofcom 2006a: 66). The kinds of British factual programming that do well abroad, either acquired or co-produced, also include historical or science documentaries that contain a high concentration of dramatic structure and storytelling. According to the head of documentaries for ProSieben Television in Germany, 'the UK is certainly the most important exporter of high quality factual programming. It's also where many ground breaking programmes and new factual trends are created' (Bulkley 2006: 27). ProSeiben is a commercial channel which shows many American drama imports, and also British documentaries, such as the BBC's *Walking with Monsters*, or *Supervolcano*. The channel is 'not looking for lifestyle or biography documentaries, nor for factual entertainment' but 'partially or fully drama-tised programmes' (ibid.). The head of documentaries for France 2 is looking for 'big primetime documentaries on history and science that make a buzz and appeal to a wide audience with dramatic storylines' (ibid.). France 2 produced the *Odyssey of Life*, a nine-month documentary using CGI that charted the growth of a baby. France 3 co-produced the BBC's *Walking with . . .* series. The head of documentaries for France 2 explains, 'we are always interested in new ways of telling stories and the UK market is always at the cutting edge of innovation . . . and combines strong dramatic structure with knowledge' (ibid.).

The Vice President of UK production and development for Discovery US comments: 'the key thing is finding innovative and surprising shows and the UK is where most of these types of shows come from. It's always been much more of a factual market' (Bulkley 2006: 28). Discovery co-produced *Going Tribal* with the BBC, and also *I Shouldn't be Alive* with Channel 4. Discovery 'don't want shows that are pure entertainment without any knowledge angle. . . . We want our shows to be immersive, adrenalised, and intelligent' (ibid.). The public service broadcaster SBS in Australia has acquired documentaries such as ITV's *The Second World War in Colour* or BBC's current affairs programme *The Power of Nightmares*. They co-produced the reality relationship format *Desperately Seeking Sheila* with Carlton, as well as producing *Mythbusters*, their own popular documentary series which has sold well abroad. According to the acquisitions and development buyer for SBS, the channel likes 'stuff that gets people talking' and looks to the UK for ideas.

Television news provision is also significant in terms of 'stuff that gets people talking'. An opinion poll conducted for BBC, Reuters and American thinktank The Media Centre reported that television news is the most important source of information about the world (Globescan 2006). Ten thousand people were surveyed in ten countries, including the UK, USA, Brazil, Egypt, Germany, India, Indonesia, Nigeria, Russia and South Korea. Seventy-two per cent of the sample said they followed news closely every day. Seventy-seven per cent claimed to use several news sources, with television news the most trusted source (82 per cent), followed by national and regional newspapers (75 per cent). People placed great trust in national news providers, followed by internationally known news brands such as the BBC and CNN. More people trusted the media than the government, although there were variations across countries. For example, in the USA 67 per cent trusted the government compared to 59 per cent the media, in the UK 51 per cent trusted the government compared to 47 per cent the media, whereas in India 82 per cent trusted the media compared to 66 per cent the government, and in Nigeria 88 per cent trusted the media, and only 34 per cent the government. Trust was very important to respondents; over a quarter claimed to stop using a news source because they had lost trust in it. In terms of new media, a small proportion of respondents claimed the internet was the most important news source, for example 8 per cent in the UK, 11 per cent in Germany, 10 per cent in Brazil and 14 per cent in the USA. However, younger people were more likely to use net sources, with one in five aged 18–24 using online news. An Ofcom report (2006a) also indicates television is the main source of news in Britain in 2005. Seventy-two per cent claimed their source of world news was from television. People's reliance on television news has increased over the past ten years by 15 per cent, compared to newspapers which have decreased by the same amount. The importance of news as a trusted source was emphasized by respondents, as 94 per cent claimed television news should be impartial. The share in television news on broadcast channels has reduced due to multichannel options, but the opportunities for trusted news sources such as the BBC to continue to provide quality news provision are there, especially given the low trust levels in online news sources.

A related trend is the international reach of reality TV formats made by production and format houses and sold to countries worldwide for local production. Reality entertainment formats have been described by Moran as examples of 'New Television' (2005). He claims that 'a unique intersection of new technologies of transmission and reception, new forms of financing, and new forms of content' has led to a global type of television programme, 'drawing upon but transforming older practices of transnational adaptation, the format is simultaneously international in its dispersal and local and concrete in its manifestation' (ibid.: 291, 305). Reality event formats such as *Idol* have been phenomenally successful worldwide. FremantleMedia (with 19TV) own the *Idols* brand and the details on their official website promote it as an international bestseller. They sold the format to over 30 territories, including amongst others the UK, the USA, Australia, France, Germany, Sweden, Poland, Iceland, Kazakhstan, Russia, the Pan-Arabic regions, South Africa, India and Singapore. The original series shown in the UK in 2001 aired for 16 weeks, with the finale attracting 14 million viewers, and a 57 per cent share (72 per cent amongst 16 to 34 year olds). There were almost nine million votes cast in the finale, which saw the winner and runner up begin a nationwide tour and produce albums and top ten selling singles in the same year. The American version of *Idol* has been very successful, with the fourth series on Fox averaging 26 million viewers, a 23 per cent share, and 500,000,000 cumulative votes. In Singapore, *Idol* had a market share of 60 per cent in 2004. Network 10 showed *Idol* in Australia in 2004 and the series ranked as its highest since 2000. Ten million people voted for *Idol* in South Africa (third series in 2005), and the winner and runner up got to meet Nelson Mandela. The format has won awards in Australia, America and Britain, for example in 2002 it won the Rose d'Or (Golden Rose of Montreux) for best entertainment programme or series. There was even a *World Idol*, with series one winners from 11 different countries taking part during a Christmas special in 2003. FremantleMedia also own other successful reality formats such as *The Apprentice*, first shown in America on NBC, and sold to 16 countries to date, including the UK and Sweden. They have licensed the British documentary series *Jamie's School Dinners* to over ten countries to date. They also sell *X Factor*, a similar talent format to *Idols*, which has been shown in the UK, Australia, Belgium, Russia and Colombia.

Endemol own the rights to *Big Brother*, described by Peter Bazalgette as 'the most perfectly converged piece of entertainment ever conceived' (2005:

284). The format has been shown all over the world, since its original transmission in Holland in 1999. Series seven in Britain managed to attract between 5 and 7 million viewers and around a 30 per cent share, with a 40 per cent share of 16–34-year-old viewers. Its two spin off shows *Big Brother's Little Brother*, and *Big Brother's Big Mouth* also did well during the summer run in 2006. In 2005, CBS showed series six in America, RTL2 aired series six in Germany, Channel 10 showed series five in Australia, Globo TV series five in Brazil, TV Norge series four in Norway, and Televisa Canal series three in Mexico (Bazalgette 2005). Other countries airing a fifth or sixth series included Italy (Canale 5), Spain (Tele 5) and Sweden (Kanal 5). *Big Brother* has also been locally produced in South Africa, Pan Africa, Argentina, Ecuador, Columbia, Croatia, Poland, Serbia, Thailand and the Middle East, amongst others. According to Bazalgette, Chief Creative Officer of Endemol International, 'viewers have switched *Big Brother* on eighteen billion times. More than a billion votes have been cast via telephones and interactive TV. Six and a half billion page views have been recorded at *Big Brother* web sites' (2005: 284).

Mark Burnett, the reality TV super producer, is responsible for some of the most successful reality formats since 2000. An extreme sports producer, he took the adrenalin of competitive sports and transformed it into reality-based entertainment. According to Burnett, reality TV deals with 'contrived situations creating genuine emotions' (Littleton 2004). His production company made the American version of *Survivor*, which won an Emmy award for outstanding non-fiction programming in 2001, and won the People's Choice Award four years running (2001–2004). Mark Burnett Productions also make *The Apprentice*, a business reality competition format, *The Contender*, a boxing reality competition format, and *Rockstar: INXS*, a music reality competition format, all of which have proved very successful in their first run on American network television and also in export revenue. Burnett feels part of the success of these formats is connected to feelings of inclusion and exclusion: 'both *The Apprentice* and *Survivor* have something in common, which is dealing with the emotional pull that all humans feel from being excluded from something' (Littleton 2004). His formats include audiences not only through the emotional drama, but also by other forms of participation in the competition, such as voting, and online interactive elements. *Rock Star: INXS* has a live studio audience, voting options, and also an interactive website that allows users to vote, download video and music, and join in regular web logs. His company has a business relationship with Yahoo, which provides an online portal to series such as *The Contender*. The portal helps to drive users to online advertising, and also specially produced content for the official site, including boxing matches, and games where users can box with one another.

How news and current affairs, documentary and popular factual television intersect with each other is part of the story of the restyling of factuality. The provision of quality news content has been criticized for being heavily commercialized, for crossing over into entertainment news, and adopting what are perceived as tabloid, or infotainment news values (Calabrese 2005). The success of 'mega documentaries' such as *Supervolcano* is linked to their dramatic storytelling, and computer-generated special effects, and these documentaries seem far removed from the documentary modes commonly identified with the genre. Reality formats contain contrived situations, and are examples of convergent entertainment, both of which take them to the limits of factual television. The cross-pollination of factual genres will be addressed in the next section.

The restyling of factuality

In *Media and the Restyling of Politics* Corner and Pels (2003) outline their argument for connecting political communication to a broader understanding of political culture. In referring to political processes and behaviours they address 'elements of political culture that, amongst other things, interconnect the "official" world of professional politics with the world of everyday experience and with the modes of "the popular" variously to be found within work and leisure' (ibid.: 3). Corner and Pels reject two dominant arguments within political communication concerning the causal relationship between media and politics. One argument is based on the assumption 'that the media are necessary agents in the practice of modern popular democracy'; the other argument views the media as undermining democracy (ibid.: 3). They reject these two models, 'refusing any suggestion of separate realms involved in some kind of play-off of convergence or super-imposition' in favour of 'a commitment to seeing the complex mutuality of contemporary political and media systems' (ibid.: 5).

There is a rejection of traditional divisions between politics and culture, 'breaking down some of the fences that separate politics from entertainment and political leadership from media celebrity' (ibid.: 2). Boundaries between political and media institutions are blurred, and people 'travel more freely across these institutional and classificatory boundaries' (ibid.: 7). There is a 'new aesthetics of the political self' where performance, public relations and spin are paramount (ibid.: 6). Political style becomes a major part of people's understanding of politicians, where voters identify with individuals rather than parties, where 'audiences "read" political characters and "taste" their style, enabling them to judge their claims of authenticity and competence' (ibid.: 7). The focus on spectacle, emotion and personality leads to a sense of a performative politics which 'foregrounds the politician as actor, whose performance on the public stage is continuously judged in terms of authenticity, honesty and "character"' (ibid.: 10). The presentation of the political self draws on the work of Erving Goffman (1959) and his idea of the presentation of the self in everyday life. Professional politicians manage various roles, 'many of them performed in a cultural context where the relationship and interplay between the "public" and "private" realms is indeterminate and changing' (ibid.: 10). One response to performative politics is for people to be cynical of style, the political 'spin' many associate with contemporary political parties. Another response is for people to renew their interest in the authenticity of politicians that appear to have escaped the system, who can be trusted in a world of spin doctors. The emphasis placed on trust and truth draws attention to 'the changing conditions of political trust' and how this relates to media and reception practices (ibid.: 11).

All of the above points can also be found in the restyling of factuality. The two dominant arguments in factual television concern the role of factual content in furthering or undermining modern democratic practices. Traditional factual genres, in particular news and current affairs, have been the subject of academic research that is connected to the 'public knowledge project' (Corner 1998). This project is concerned with the power of public service factual genres to inform and potentially influence the viewer. Traditional factual genres can inform viewers about political, economic and social issues, and can help in their development as citizens who take part in democratic processes. The counter-argument is to see factual content as undermining democracy through an overemphasis on entertainment. Commercial factual genres are thought to be infotainment, providing poor quality, overly stylized, ratings-driven programmes that work against the knowledge project. The increased commercialization of factual content has also infected public service factual genres, subverting the goal of those genres to inform citizens, treating them instead as consumers of 'tabloid' TV. The play off between public service and popular factual genres, and the citizen and consumer, fails to address the complex mutuality between public service and commercial production and reception practices. This doesn't mean to say that there are no tensions, contradictions or concerns about the interplay between information and entertainment genres in relation to factual television, but it is to say that there are other models for critically examining factuality.

In *Entertaining the Citizen*, van Zoonen (2005) rejects the distinctions between politics and entertainment in favour of hybridity, where traditional dichotomies become blurred and lose their stable meanings. She points out that popular culture, with all its flaws, 'needs to be acknowledged as a relevant resource for political citizenship; a resource that produces comprehension and respect for popular political voices and that allows for more people to perform as citizens' (ibid.: 151). The notion of cultural citizenship encapsulates the hybridity of politics and entertainment and allows for convergence across popular and political culture (see Hartley 1999; Hermes 2005). One example of cultural citizenship is evident in the way public service broadcasters have looked to balance their information and educational programming with more entertainment-led output. Ellis characterizes this as 'popular public service' (2000: 32). The term usefully sums up a move within public service broadcasting to appeal to popular audiences. This kind of industry response to commercial imperatives shows how research into popular factual genres is connected to the transformation of the public knowledge project. When traditional dichotomies become blurred there is an opportunity for debate about the meaning of public service factual genres. Corner (2002a) has shown how the success of reality programming generated debate in documentary values. Couldry (2002) also highlights how reality programmes have become part of public debate about the cultural value of factual television. It is also possible to see how the public knowledge project has influenced debate about popular factual genres. Bolin (2007) points out that journalistic production practices have been incorporated into televised popular entertainment. For example, the style of local news production in on-scene footage of events as they happened became part of early reality programming based on crime and emergency services (Hill 2005). News journalists have been used to present *Big Brother* in America, or *Survivor* in Britain and Sweden.

There is much evidence in audience responses to factual television that supports the play off between public service and commercial factual genres. The distinctions made within the evaluation of factual television are common to audiences; they echo the dominant discourses of factual content as part of the knowledge project, but also undermined by commercial concerns, and the influence of hybrid genres on the intrinsic, public service values of news and current affairs, or documentary. The value judgements for public and popular factual genres can be mapped onto prevailing arguments concerning quality, knowledge and entertainment. However, there is just as much evidence to contradict these value judgements, as audiences reflect on the practices of watching various factual and reality programmes. Rather than collapse distinctions between public and popular, audiences draw on these common points of reference at the same time as reflecting on their meaning in everyday life. It is the complex mutuality of values and practices that makes factual television such a good site for analysis of changing attitudes and experiences of the public knowledge project and popular culture.

Another model for considering cultural and political participation is put forward by Peter Dahlgren (2005). Civic cultures are examples of the interaction and engagement on behalf of citizens that are preconditions for the public sphere. The public sphere refers to the work of Habermas (translated in 1989) and the idea that the media can offer 'unconstrained access to information, on a wide range of views' and encourage 'discussion amongst citizens as the foundation for political opinion formation' (Dahlgren 2005: 411–12). The public sphere is a normative concept, and Dahlgren proposes civic cultures as stepping stones towards democratic ideals. Civic cultures include five integrated circuits located around knowledge and competence, values, affinity and trust, practices and identities:

> Such cultures are important in facilitating engagement in the broad domain of what we might term the politically relevant, in creating a

climate that is conducive to citizen participation in the shaping of society's political life, and in fostering fluid communicative borders between politics and non-politics.

(Dahlgren 2005: 413)

The characteristics of civic cultures are evident in issues concerning factuality. Dahlgren refers to debate on reality TV as an example of how contemporary television is moving away from 'the traditions that strive for "objective" rendering of the world toward approaches that underscore the personal, sensational, the subjective, the confessional, the intimate' (2005: 416). Although reality TV may represent the opposite of rationality, it also allows engagement with a more emotional public sphere. Various kinds of popular factual content can offer diverse groups of people both rational and affective experiences, opening up notions of a singular public sphere to multiple public spheres. Lunt and Stenner (2005) examine how talk shows such as *Jerry Springer* can provide examples of an emotional public sphere. Johansson's research on tabloid readers suggests objective and subjective approaches to news can provide opportunities for political and cultural citizenship (2006). Indeed, Seaton (2005) shows how the historical tradition of news, and in particular news about violence, has always drawn upon emotions and the body in order to communicate to the public. As Dahlgren points out, our experience of the world involves thinking with our head and our heart, and our experience of all different kinds of factual content will be no different.

The various forms of factual content available to the public open up possibilities for greater diversity and creativity within civic cultures. Thus, it is important to consider the existing knowledge and expectations of audiences for news and current affairs, documentary and popular factual genres. Their generic knowledge will highlight disengagement, or help to further engagement, in issues addressed within factual programming about the world we live in, and our connections to it. The personal, social and cultural values that are associated with factual genres are also significant in contributing to citizen participation, and a sense of public and private judgements about what is important in the provision of factual content. The trust people place in factual content is enormously significant to their evaluation of representations of reality. This is also related to what people feel they can learn from factual content, how news or documentary can enlighten them, or how popular factual can be used as a resource for knowledge and awareness of the self and identity formation. In short, the reception practices of factual television are evidence of civic cultures in the making.

The emphasis on performance that Corner and Pels highlight as so significant to the transformation of political communication is also apparent in factual television. So much of factual content is concerned with spectacle, style, emotion and personality. Goffman's notion of the presentation of the self in everyday life is particularly apt when considering the abundance of what Dovey describes as 'first person media' (2000), where ordinary people perform themselves, provide confessions to camera, allow us to see into their private lives as seen on television. A reality series such as *Survivor* is more about the spectacle of staging a gameshow on a remote island than people's real experiences. The documentary series *Planet Earth* offers the ultimate spectacle of the natural world for television viewers at home. The terrifying footage of the collapse of the twin towers of the World Trade Center during 9/11 have become symbolic of the spectacle of violence, repeated over and over on TV around the world.

The focus on emotions has become a trademark for many factual programmes, where the premise is to observe or put people in emotionally difficult situations. *Children's Hospital* is about the heartbreaking and also uplifting stories of how families cope with illness. *The Boy Whose Skin Fell Off* is a moving observation of one man's struggle with a disease that will ultimately kill him. Many reality formats particularly focus on negative emotions, where feelings of humiliation, anger, superiority, jealousy become part of our expectations for the genre. Palmer (2003) has pointed out how crime reality programming shames and humiliates criminals. The participants in *Big Brother* are deliberately picked so that different and larger than life personalities clash, where there is so little to do that arguments abound and negative emotions run riot. This is not an example of the managed heart (Hochschild 1983), where feelings are subject to mutually agreed rules of engagement, but rather an alternative reality where people run riot with their emotions. Watching series seven of *Big Brother* UK can feel like being part of a secure mental health unit, only no one is taking their medication.

Much emphasis is placed on personalities in factual programming. News presenters and journalists become national stars, appearing in other non-fiction programming. Calabrese shows how the cult of personality and personal image dominates American news, where consulting firms advise news anchors on 'talent performance tips', or 'hot tease tips' in order to maximize ratings (2005: 277). News presenter Michael Buerk was deliberately chosen by the BBC producers of the emergency services reconstruction series *999* because he lent the series an air of gravity, and helped to distinguish it from its commercial cousin *Rescue 911*, which was presented by William Shatner from *Star Trek* (Hill 2005). Sometimes people appearing in a documentary series can become media personalities, such as Pat Loud from *The American Family* in the 1970s, or Mr and Mrs Armstrong from *The Armstrongs*. Winners of reality gameshows can find fame, although it is often short lived. Talent show formats promise to find the next rockstar, model, band, actor, film maker out of hundreds of thousands of open auditions, looking for ordinary people they can transform into a star. People who choose to take part in popular factual formats know programme makers are looking for personalities in the making, and they become reality performers, with agents waiting in the wings. The 2006 series of *Celebrity Big Brother* UK contained an unusual twist – one of the so-called celebrities was a fake. Chantelle was quickly revealed to be an ordinary girl from Essex and went on to win the show. However, before participating in *Celebrity Big Brother* she worked as a celebrity look-a-like, appeared in the *Sun* tabloid paper as a topless page three model, and had signed with notorious 'agent to the tabloid stars' Max Clifford. This is an example of the reality performer, someone who uses the production of personalities in reality programming as an opportunity for a media career.

Factual television is performative and reflexive. In this performative environment, audiences judge the claims of authenticity within various factual programmes. One response to the focus on style is to become cynical of the authenticity of factual content, questioning the truth claims made within programmes and the honesty of people participating in them. The cynicism of people towards politicians is partly to do with their performance in the media. News journalists who aggressively question politicians are popular with audiences because they are perceived to get behind the perform-ance in order to inform the public about what is really going on. The use of dramatic structures and computer-generated effects in documentaries such as *Walking with Dinosaurs* means audiences question the veracity of the content and its historical and scientific facts. When there is a fakery scandal this has great impact on audiences, who become distrustful of documentary truth claims (Ellis 2005). Most audiences regard reality TV as entertainment and expect people to perform in front of the cameras. They find little that is truthful about these performances, or the settings within which reality is staged. The cynical factual viewer has a high degree of critical engagement with the authenticity of factual television. Perhaps because of this engagement audiences place great value on trust and truth in factual content. The more emphasis is placed on spectacle and style, the more audiences look for authenticity in people's behaviour, emotions and the settings for representa-tions of reality. They draw on complex strategies for evaluating what is natural or artificial in factual television.

The restyling of factuality has become so extreme that programmes can become bloated and overly complicated. *Space Cadets* is a good example of an extreme trend in the reality genre. The idea behind the £4 million Endemol produced show is that a group of people are tricked into thinking they are at a Russian astronaut training base. Four of them are selected to go into space, but really they will be in a fake shuttle, made originally for a Hollywood film, with special sound effects and a custom-built screen portraying images of planet Earth. The premise is reliant on the winners not realizing the joke. Channel 4's factual entertainment commissioning editor said, 'we've taken a big risk with *Space Cadets*, and we don't know who will have the last laugh' (BBC News 2005). Some actors were also part of the hoax, including a comedy writer and friend of the producer. In case the joke was rumbled early on, Channel 4 lined up an alternate schedule during the two-week run in December 2005. *Space Cadets* ran every night, with an hour-long live show presented by entertainer Johnny Vaughan, and round-the-clock live streaming on the digital channel E4, a spin-off show, and accompanying website and mobile downloads. The series started with 2.6 million viewers, the average ratings for that slot in the Channel 4 schedule, and was beaten by other programmes on other channels every night, with the lowest ratings dropping to 1.2 million. *Space Cadets* was universally panned. The *Guardian* critic wrote:

> There are elements of *Changing Rooms* to this; *Big Brother* too, and a bit of *Candid Camera*. But it's also like *The Truman Show* for real, though it's hard to know what's real now that reality certainly isn't. If all goes to plan, a lucky few will actually board a shuttle replica and think they've blasted off into orbit. It is a funny idea, but it's also mean as hell. . . . I don't think many people will, in 35 years' time, be asking where you were when they didn't send nine gullible young people into space.
>
> (Wollaston 2005)

Many critics pointed out that the show was based on one joke. The 'remote controller' for *Private Eye* (2005) explained:

> The joke on day one – that they all think they're going up in a rocket – remains exactly the same gag on day ten. Reality television often claims to have learned from drama; but no fiction series would ever expect a single plot-line to sustain across ten episodes . . . the number one view out in the telly blogosphere is that the whole thing's a joke and all the contestants are played by actors; but that would make it even more of a waste of time. . . . Ground control to major network: there's definitely something wrong.

Even the Director of Programming for Channel 4 admitted afterwards that the show was a mistake – 'it was grim' (interview at the Edinburgh International Television Festival 2006).

One of the outcomes of the restyling of factual content is a move back to reality, away from the spectacle of reality entertainment. One of the most successful series on BBC2 in 2006 was *Who Do You Think You Are?* (5 million viewers), based on the premise that celebrities look into their family tree. Another popular series for BBC2 was *Springwatch*, which was number seven in the most creative popular factual series of 2006 (*Broadcast* 2006). This series is a wonderfully simple observation, with live footage and commentary on birds and animals and plant life emerging out of winter into springtime in Britain. The series picks up on the success of wildlife watching holiday packages where you can watch bears in the woods, wildlife cameras installed in official nature reserves so that you can see chicks in a nest without disturbing the birds, and wildlife webcams where you can see streaming video or updated stills of wildlife around the world. For example, the webcam for a pair of bald eagles and their two eggs in Hornby Island, Canada, attracted ten million people every day. The McNeil river bears at wildcamgrizzlies made news headlines in August 2006 because so many millions of users were tuning in to watch bears be bears. As Wollaston (2006) explains:

> Oh my God, it's wonderful, by far the best. In the top-left corner of my screen, the McNeil river thunders past. It's 3pm in London, early morning in Alaska, and the sun is just peeping over the horizon. There are about eight grizzlies, sitting on rocks in the river, or in the river itself, looking down. It looks cold in the water. A salmon jumps, a bear takes a swipe, misses, licks his lips. And I'm watching this live in London. How excellent is that? And it's so nice not to have any commentary, just the rush of the water, and the occasional screech of a gull. Forget *Big Brother* and *Love Island*. Turn on your computer instead and watch I'm An Alaskan Bear, Leave Me Alone.

The simplicity of *Springwatch* or wildcamgrizzlies is partly a response to overly complex, highly stylized reality entertainment formats. As the reality genre has become so bloated, viewers are looking for alternative representations of reality that are what they claim to be. In fact, the birds or bears in Britain or Alaska are also performing, but it is a different notion of performance that occurs in nature, where animals are engaged in the dynamic process of life itself. The sense of nature as performed gets at the heart of the way audiences respond to the restyling of factual content. There is factual content that is real and at the same time performed, that is to say it has referential integrity and also aesthetic value. And there is factual content that is artificial, and performed in such a way it loses its hold on reality. In the next section, the reception practices for factual television highlight how viewers evaluate different factual genres and the restyling of factuality.

Viewing practices

The approach used in this book is one which understands audiences as engaged in dynamic and creative practices. It is an approach taken up within contemporary studies in the environment and society (see, for example, Franklin 2002; Franklin *et al.* 2000; Macnaughton and Urry 2001). Nature and culture are involved in 'a co-performance of a number of different, interactive and evolving individuals, species and processes' (Szerszynski *et al.* 2003: 3). Nature is understood to mean both materiality (an organism, or landscape) and a process (evolution, life itself). Nature is also 'a world of meanings and significance' with various associations for individuals and societies, and an abstract concept we use to connote the 'real' (ibid.: 2). Performance is understood as several distinct yet related processes. It is an activity, or practice. The act of performance can sometimes be associated with giving life to something through performance, that a person, object or experience wouldn't exist outside the performative act. Performance also means repetitive practices, something we do on a daily basis, and yet something that slightly varies each time we perform so 'variation and difference emerge in the spontaneous creative moments between iterations' (ibid.: 2–3). Performance in its theatrical context is concerned with creative acts, and with codes and conventions within the arts. In this sense, performance, including improvisation, is produced with an audience in mind, although this is not always the case. As mentioned in the previous section, Goffman's work (1959) on the performance of the self in everyday life adds a sociological dimension, where he suggests that our front and back stage 'selves' are part of how we communicate with people, sometimes performing a certain role (mother, daughter, friend, worker) necessary for day-to-day interaction, and sometimes revealing more intimate aspects of ourselves. Goffman says that we are all performing, and judging the performance of others, all the time, and we use props (people, objects, animals, nature and the media) to help us in the performance of the self, and our ongoing identity work.

Szerszynski *et al.* point out that there is nothing new in connecting nature with performance: 'the idea . . . was most dramatically asserted and sustained through biological perspectives that have built on Charles Darwin's evolutionary theory . . . that the nature we see (nature as *materiality*) is the ongoing product of a performance (by nature the *process*)' (2003: 3). Szerszynski *et al.* are not suggesting nature is only a matter of performance, but they are showing an historical understanding of nature as having multiple meanings and experiences. Nature interacts with other individuals and processes; it is a mutual performance where practices are co-produced in an ever-changing, evolving environment. In discussing mutual improvisation in the natural world, Szerszynski *et al.* point out that 'one loses a sense of nature as pre-figured and merely "played out"; instead the performance of nature appears as a process open to improvisation, creativity and emergence' (ibid.: 4). Importantly, this way of treating nature as performance 'necessitates a different way of thinking about knowledge – not as static or passive, but as active, distinctly relational, forming distinctive events and experiences by which it is possible to know more' (ibid.: 4).

This connection between nature and performance can help to further understanding of the dynamic processes of factuality. Factual content is something we see, both in the real world and as representations, and an ongoing process of production and reception practices. Factual broadcasting involves co-performances in the production and reception of factuality. The knowledge produced within factual broadcasting is active and relational, and as Nichols (2001) suggests, it encourages us to want to know more, to further our understanding of nature, science, history, politics, people, and hopefully ourselves. Nature as a metaphor for the 'real' is a powerful concept for factual genres. We understand and make judgements all the time about actuality as true to life. News presents itself as a witness to events, natural or man-made. Undercover journalism promises to go beneath the surface to get at what is really going on. Natural history documentaries claim to document the real world. Observational documentary claims to be a fly on the wall. Aesthetic judgements are made all the time about footage, editing, presenting, and the performances of professional and non-professional actors. The binaries of nature/artifice, real/staged, genuine/fake, all help to construct cultural discourses of factual genres. Factuality as a process opens up value judgements, allowing abstract ideas to be experienced in a creative, evolving production and reception environment.

In media reception studies, Abercrombie and Longhurst identified 'the spectacle/performance paradigm' as a network of assumptions and research ideas that responded to 'the changing nature of the place of the media in the social life of the contemporary advanced Western world' (1998: 160). This paradigm is characterized by the notion of a diffused audience consuming different kinds of media. It is a paradigm where the media is constitutive of everyday life, and research methods pertaining to studies of everyday life are most appropriate for audience studies. It is also a paradigm where contemporary society is performative, spectacular, and focused on the self and individual identities (1998: 175). Aspects of this paradigm relate to the approach taken here regarding viewing practices, in particular the sense of the viewer as performing their role as an audience, as reflecting on social interaction with the media and everyday life. Silverstone's research on *Television and Everyday Life* (1994) is particularly helpful in this respect as he points out the central role of television in trust and identity formation. He highlights how news is the most important genre in maintaining trust, and how programme makers and audiences work on trust relations on a day-to-day basis. The research in this book is less associated with a particular paradigm, and more with exploratory work occurring in audience studies regarding dynamic practices. Such work is not located around any one particular method but is rather multimethod in its approach. Nor does it focus on the idea of performance as spectacle, but also as a practice that is as much to do with repetition as variation or creativity. The focus on the self and individual responses is one aspect of this research, but there is also an emphasis on the audience as a public, as having shared values and practices. Hermes, whose early work on women's magazines is cited as an example of the performance/spectacle paradigm, has also noted in recent research how popular culture is about bonding, about forming, maintaining and reflecting on alliances and affinities. This understanding of the shared values of factual television is the most dominant one to emerge in the audience research here. Thus, the approach used in this book uses viewing practices as a means to understand the restyling of factuality, to compare audience responses to different factual genres in order to highlight the role of the audience in the transformation of factual television.

Other recent reception studies also adopt a similar position. For example, Livingstone's work on young people and new media (2002, 2005b) focuses on the changing practices of online users, and how through their experiences of new media in the home they are formulating their own understanding of public and private space from a young adult's perspective. She argues that through looking at new media processes, notions of public and private are 'unpacked into a series of distinct but intersecting questions of meaning, value, agency and responsibility' (2005b: 180). Hermes (2005) calls for a new understanding of popular culture 'in terms of practices (of inclusion and exclusion and of meaning-making) rather than in terms of identities, for example, to allow for as wide a variety of possible experiential knowledges and styles of reasoning' (ibid.: 151). Gauntlett's exploration of creativity and play in audience research opens up alternative meanings of the relationship between media and identity work (2007). Through looking at practices we can understand the various strategies audiences use to engage with and reflect on the changing nature of contemporary media.

Research methods

The initial idea for this project came from one of the key findings of previous research on reality TV, which was that viewers used a fact/fiction continuum to evaluate the various programmes that were part of a wide ranging mix of popular factual output (Hill 2005; see also Roscoe and Hight 2001). Therefore viewers did not see reality TV in isolation but as part of the production and reception of fact/fiction genres. The seed was planted for a larger audience study of different kinds of factual programmes. It was also the case that in the reality TV research viewers were aware of its evolution, so that at the time of the study when *Big Brother* first arrived in Britain (2000) they were evaluating the impact of this new format on the reality genre as a whole. The central question therefore became one concerned with audience responses to a wide range of factual genres.

The project first began in Britain in 2003, with funding from the former regulatory bodies the Broadcasting Standards Commission and Independent Television Commission; during the data collection period of 2004–5 the project opened up to become a comparative one between Britain and Sweden, thanks to the funding and support of Jonköping International Business School, and the Society, Opinion and Media Institute, Goteberg University. In 2005, a smaller collaboration was also possible with Helsinki University in Finland (see Appendix), and in 2006 further comparative research with the University of Lisbon in Portugal (ongoing at time of writing). Chapter 2 contains more detailed discussion of how the project was designed to address culturally specific factual television production and reception practices, but at the same time be able to explore similar themes.

The main point of comparison in this book is audience responses to the differences and similarities of various factual and reality genres. The driving force of the research is to examine how audiences are critically engaged with the restyling of factuality, and that their experiences of different kinds of factual and reality genres means they are evaluating what is factual about contemporary factual television. The experiences of British and Swedish viewers are remarkably similar in their engagement with the restyling of factuality. Therefore, the comparisons between Britain and Sweden are secondary to the comparative analysis of different factual genres. The differences between countries are mainly concerned with specific differences in the scale of television production in the two countries. These are two countries with similar broadcasting structures, but with quite different size populations and media industries. The point of comparison in the book between Britain and Sweden is used strategically to highlight specific production contexts which allow for minor variations in audience responses to various factual genres.

Some brief facts and figures for Britain and Sweden show they are two northern European countries with different size populations, but similar social and cultural trends. Britain has a population of about 60 million (with 50 million living in England), and Sweden a population of about nine million. There is an even spread of men and women in the general populations. Both countries also have an aging population (OECD 2006). Life expectancy has increased in Britain and Sweden, and there is a decrease in time spent in paid work, with younger people spending more time in education and older people more time in semi- and full retirement (see Social Trends 2005; Swedish Statistics 2006). The proportion of the British population from a non-white ethnic minority is 8 per cent, although ethnic diversity is much higher in cities, and amongst younger people (41 per cent of those aged under 15) (Social Trends 2005). The number of people born outside of Sweden is 1.1 million, however the majority of immigrants are from Finland (Swedish Statistics 2006). Similar to Britain, there is a concentration of non-white ethnic minorities living in the main cities (ibid.). The number of foreign-born persons with tertiary education (as a percentage of all people with tertiary education) is similar in Britain and Sweden (around 10 per cent) (OECD 2006). The growth rate for the gross domestic product in Britain and Sweden for 2004 was 3.2 per cent and 3.7 per cent (ibid.). The numbers of long-term unemployed are very similar in both countries, with around 20 per cent of the total unemployed (ibid.). Britain has one of the highest rates of employment in the European Union, following Denmark and Sweden (Social Trends 2003). A visitor to Britain would find only two other European countries as expensive, Sweden and Denmark (ibid.).

Both countries adopted social policies during the post-war period contributing to a strong sense of a welfare state, where the state assumes primary responsibility for its citizens. The dominance of the Social Democratic Party in Swedish politics since the 1940s has ensured fairly consistent emphasis on universal welfare policies funded through taxes. Britain has seen both Labour and also Conservative party rule since the post-war period, significantly a long right-wing party period from 1979 to 1997, which worked to overturn welfare policies. The impact of the political situation in Britain and Sweden can be seen in some of the social differences in both countries. Income tax (and employee and employer contributions) is significantly higher in Sweden, at almost 50 per cent, than Britain, at 30 per cent (OECD 2006). Educational levels are higher in Sweden than Britain, for example the percentage of people with tertiary education aged 25–34 is 10 per cent higher in Sweden (40 per cent) (ibid.). In terms of public social expenditure, Sweden spends significantly more of its GDP than Britain, with 30 per cent compared to 22 per cent, respectively (ibid.). There was an 80 per cent turn out for the last Swedish general election in 2002, compared to 61 per cent in Britain in 2005. The 2006 Swedish general election also had a similar voting turnout, although the key difference was the election of the Conservative Alliance over the Social Democrats. Obesity levels are much higher in Britain, almost a quarter of the population, compared to Sweden (10 per cent) (ibid.). This may have something to do with the three main activities carried out by people in Britain – sleeping, working, and watching TV and videos/DVDs or listening to music (National Statistics 2005). The average household spending on recreation and culture as a percentage of the gross domestic product was 7.9 per cent in Britain and 5.73 per cent in Sweden in 2006 (Maley 2006).

In terms of broadcasting, both countries have dominant public service broadcasters, BBC and SVT. The British Broadcasting Corporation was founded in 1922 with a mandate to inform, educate and entertain, and started airing television alongside radio in 1932. Commercial television broke its monopoly in 1955 with the start of ITV. Now there are five main channels, including the public service commercial Channel 4 and commercial Channel Five. Sveriges Televison was modelled after the BBC, and had a monopoly until 1987 when the satellite commercial channel TV3 was launched, followed by the public service commercial channel TV4 in 1992. Like Britain, there are now five main channels, including the commercial Kanal 5. Both the BBC and SVT also have digital channels, concentrating on news, children's programming and factual content, as well as radio, mobile and online services. Swedish broadcasting law restricts advertising, and so many commercial satellite channels are broadcast from other countries (for example, TV3 and Kanal 5 from Britain). The historical context to broadcasting in both countries is significant, as the late arrival of commercial television in Sweden has ensured different public attitudes towards the main channels and their provision of factual content. For example, in 2006 Channel 4, Sky and ITV all won the top awards for the most creative production of news (*Broadcast* 2006). News is therefore a genre which has public service credentials and quality provision on all the main channels, regardless of their public service or commercial makeup. In Sweden, SVT dominates news provision, followed by TV4, but TV3 only provides around one hour of news per week, and Kanal 5 none at all (see Chapter 2 for more details). Therefore although there are similarities in broadcasting structures in both countries, there are also minor differences in the production and reception of factual content. A point of comparison for later discussion focuses on how the relatively small scale television production in Sweden means that the media industry struggles to support itself and has to restrict the amount of domestic content in favour of foreign imports and formats.

The main research questions focused on basic issues to do with genre and factuality, such as viewing preferences, genre evaluation, social and personal value judgements, trust, truth claims, knowledge and learning, ethics and fair treatment of participants in factual programming. In the British survey there were also questions on interactive and online elements related to factual content. The majority of the sample did not use interactive services or websites related to factual television programmes. For example, 73 per cent of respondents never used digital interactive features or websites linked to news, documentary and reality programmes. Younger adults were more likely to have used interactive and web features in factual programmes than older adults. For example, 20 per cent of young adults (16–24) used interactive and web features, compared to less than 10 per cent of older adults (55–64). As so few people in the survey accessed factual content outside of television this was dropped from the Swedish survey, although it was open to discussion in the qualitative research. It is a topic that will feature more prominently in forthcoming research (see Hill and Kondo 2006).

The project became a comparative study of a wide variety of different factual categories, but the breadth in factual genres was counterbalanced by a focus on television. The trends outlined briefly in this chapter show how television is the main source for factual and reality genres. Other multiplatform factual content has not been ignored, and further publications will be forthcoming on interactive media and factual content (Hill and Kondo 2006). However, the story of factual television is the focus for this book, as it has been the focus of audience responses in the quantitative and qualitative research.

There were four themes addressed in the design of the survey and focus groups:

1   How do adult viewers understand and evaluate the changing generic environment of British factual programming? How do viewers define factual or non-fictional programming? What value judgements are used

for factual and reality programmes? To what extent do viewers categorize different factual programmes as informative, entertaining, or both?

2   How do adult viewers evaluate the truth claims of different types of factual programming? What are viewers' attitudes towards accuracy of information in factual programming? What are viewers' opinions of the truth claims of different factual programmes? What are viewers' attitudes towards performance in factual programmes?

3   What do adult viewers consider they learn from different types of factual programming? Do viewers use factual programmes to help them form opinions about things?

4   What attitudes do adult viewers have towards fair treatment of different social groups within news and current affairs, documentary and popular factual programmes? Is it important to viewers that particular social groups are treated fairly?

A number of methods were used in the project in both countries to explore these themes and research questions. The research methods included an analysis of media content of a range of factual and reality programmes over a six-month period, and a scheduling and ratings analysis of a range of programmes during the same timeframe. A series of interviews were also conducted with a range of media professionals working within the television industry in Britain and Sweden. This background analysis formed the basis for qualitative and quantitative audience research.

In Britain, a quantitative survey was conducted with a representative sample of 4,516 people. The sample included people aged 16–65+ living in Britain. In Sweden, a quantitative survey was conducted with a representative sample of 944 people aged 16–80 living in Sweden. The distribution amongst responses compared with the British and Swedish population as a whole. A series of semi-structured focus groups were conducted in Sweden and Britain. There were 24 groups, 12 in each country, with a total of 129 respondents aged 18–60. The recruitment method used was quota sampling and snowball sampling. The sample was based on the criteria of age (roughly split into two groups of 20–30 year olds, and 40–60 year olds), gender (even mix of male and female), socio-economic status (working and middle class, and educational levels from school to university). Occupations ranged from unemployed, students, administrators, teachers, sales assistants, technicians, office workers, carers, artists and retired people. There were people from Swedish, British, British Asian, black and European (German, Greek, Norwegian, Polish) ethnic groups, which was not by design but reflects the diversity of the population where recruitment took place. The focus group questions provided valuable insight into general attitudes of the survey. A series of open questions were asked regarding the four key questions of genre, actuality, learning and fairness. A game was used, whereby participants were asked to group a range of programme titles into categories and to discuss their reasons for the clusters of titles (see Appendix for further details).

The use of the data in the book highlights the strengths and weaknesses of multimethod research and comparative research. A pattern established in Chapter 3 is to use the quantitative data to paint a general picture, and draw on broad trends, followed by the use of the qualitative data to support these trends and, just as importantly, to show contradictions, variation and complexity in responses. A serious lack of space means that each chapter only touches the surface of the data and is reliant on the main findings. The more detailed analysis and inclusion of minor findings will be published in other places, although wherever possible there is an attempt to flag up these issues. Inevitably, there is not space to do justice to the richness of the data sets, to analyse specific factual genres, to isolate particular social groups, or to provide accompanying textual analysis alongside the scheduling, ratings and reception analysis. The pattern for the analysis has been to generally highlight similarities, as these were the most striking results of the research. The most obvious differences for British and Swedish programmes and responses are addressed wherever possible, and feature in more focused comparative analysis in other publications (Hill *et al.* 2005, 2007).

Age was also the most significant factor in research on opinions of news in ten different countries, using a sample of 10,000 people (Globescan 2006). Gender and educational levels were comparatively similar across these countries, but age differences showed younger people with different news preferences. Similarly, analysis of the data in this study highlighted different viewing preferences according to age, with minor differences for other variables. A detailed analysis of age, gender and education is conducted in Chapter 3 in order to show this point, and also to highlight the similarity in the evaluation of factual genres across these variables. In other chapters, reference is made to gender and socio-economic status where possible, but mainly issues related to this are set aside in favour of the broad picture. Ethnicity was also something that had little impact on the evaluation of factual genres, although there were minor differences in viewing preferences. More focused analysis of specific groups of people for specific categories may very well highlight greater diversity in the results. There are, for example, different attitudes to the fair treatment of ethnic minorities in Britain and Sweden (see Chapter 7) and further analysis would be useful to learn why this is the case. In short, the main findings of the research have been used in the book as the basis for the argument about the restyling of factual television and the strategies viewers use to make sense of this.

Book outline

The book begins with an examination of the various genres that are part of factuality. Chapter 2, 'Mapping factual TV', concerns the large terrain of non-fictional programming. The changing generic environment of factual television is constructed within culturally specific broadcasting environments and commonly understood genre categories. The chapter maps factual genres according to pre-existing categories, using prototypes and typical examples to help illuminate differences and similarities within factual content over a period of time. The analysis of various factual and reality genres within British and Swedish television schedules highlights how viewers experience these genres as part of a broad understanding of factuality. The next two chapters in the book examine viewing strategies for dealing with genres on the move.

Chapter 3, 'Public and popular', considers the importance of classificatory practices for factual television audiences. In particular, it shows the use of pre-existing value judgements regarding public service and popular factual genres as a framing device for genre evaluation. It outlines viewing preferences for different types of programmes. It explores audience definitions of factual television which are connected to normative ideals and viewing experiences. Audiences use classificatory practices to make factual genres knowable and manageable. Viewers who are watching a wide range of programmes, in particular reality TV, are also re-evaluating and re-classifying factual genres and therefore deeply involved with the restyling of factuality.

Chapter 4, 'Genre work', highlights another significant viewing strategy. Genre work is the work of being both immersed in watching a genre, and reflecting on the experience of a genre. Genre work allows viewers to draw on their knowledge of genres to personally respond to various programmes, highlighting the often contradictory and confusing responses that are part of dealing with the changing nature of factuality. There are distinct but related modes of engagement with news and current affairs, documentary and reality TV. Audiences are especially critical of reality TV and the strange dreamlike experience that is associated with watching this genre. Thus the restyling of factuality raises problems in that some genres have gone beyond the limits of factuality, occupying a troubling intermediate space between fact and fiction that is unsettling to audiences.

The rest of the book examines classification and genre work in more detail, connecting these strategies to the ongoing process of factuality. Three chapters address the core issues of truth claims, knowledge and fair treatment. Each chapter looks at these issues in relation to news and current affairs, documentary and reality TV, examining similarities and differences in viewing responses. Each chapter highlights how the restyling of factuality has had a disruptive influence on these core issues, challenging viewers to make sense of the changes taking place and to re-evaluate their own knowledge and experiences along the way. Each chapter shows how viewers constantly work to resolve the inherent contradictions between their ideal values for factuality, generic developments in television production, and their viewing experiences.

Chapter 5, 'Truth claims', addresses the importance of a criterion of truth when responding to factual genres. Audiences apply a 'truth/performance rating' to factuality. This is a simple tool for evaluating a range of genres. This classificatory practice shows that the binaries of nature/artifice are part of how audiences make sense of actuality. The social and cultural ordering of news at the top of a truth scale and reality TV at the top of a performance scale effectively relocates reality TV into entertainment. This genre evaluation foregrounds the referential integrity of factuality. Another, more reflexive mode of engagement foregrounds the aesthetic value of factuality. There are different modes of engagement for news and current affairs, documentary and reality TV, but what is similar is that viewers are aware of changes within these genres and the impact this has on the social and personal evaluation of truth claims in factuality.

Chapter 6, 'Knowledge and learning', examines the rich and complex knowledge profile of factual television, with news and current affairs, documentary and reality genres bringing different kinds of knowledge to viewers. In order to make sense of this knowledge profile, viewers make distinctions between knowledge about the world, knowledge about the media and self-knowledge. They also make a distinction between knowledge as facts and learning as experience. The understanding of knowledge as objective facts ensures news is at the top of the scale and reality TV at the bottom. However, audiences also reflect on traditional notions of public knowledge alongside more personal notions of learning. Learning as getting something from a programme, something for yourself, is most commonly associated by audiences with some types of documentary and popular factual. This 'environment of information' shows that the knowledge profile for television is contextual to viewers' understanding of factuality.

Chapter 7, 'Participation', is focused on audience attitudes towards fair treatment of people who participate in the media, specifically non-professionals, public figures and celebrities. There is a moral and social ordering to attitudes to fair treatment. There is also a context specific position that draws heavily on people's motivations, and professional practices, within different genres. Viewers make a distinction between ordinary people in news, or documentary, and reality performers who are thought to be 'media hot', motivated by fame. The perceived shameless behaviour of many reality performers is a reason viewers are interested in watching the genre. Viewers also feel ashamed at their interest in watching 'humiliation TV'. Audience attitudes towards the fair treatment of social groups in various genres highlights different ethical positions, from shallow to deep ethics.

The concluding Chapter 8, 'Containing factuality', synthesizes the key findings and presents an overview of the main argument in the book. The restyling of factuality is challenging for audiences. On the one hand, change is exciting and can provide new opportunities for representing different kinds of reality to popular audiences. On the other hand, the pace of change is unsettling and can threaten the integrity of existing factual genres. The more extreme reality TV becomes, the more audiences become concerned about the intrinsic value of factuality as truthful and informative. One means of containing factuality is for viewers to re-locate reality TV into entertainment. The movement of reality TV to entertainment opens up opportunities for a re-evaluation of factuality. Reflecting on the research findings, a picture emerges of a viewer navigating their way through a busy, noisy and constantly changing factual television environment.

Chapter 2

Mapping factual TV

'Factual TV is fact not fiction.'

Factual television constitutes a large and varied terrain of non-fictional programming. The production of factual takes place in departments such as news, documentary, features, light entertainment and new media. The content of factual includes communicative forms such as direct reportage, studio debates, observational documentary, presenter-led formats and drama-tized reconstructions. The people who take part in factual programmes include presenters, journalists, experts, politicians, celebrities, members of the public and actors. One of the ways to make sense of the wide-ranging programmes that are part of this area of television is to organize them into production contexts and categories. Mapping factual TV is a process that turns a chaotic world into a territory that is recognizable according to common values and criteria. This chapter explains how the changing generic environment of factual television is constructed within culturally specific broadcasting contexts and commonly understood genre categories.

Economic, policy and production changes in broadcasting influence the content and reception of contemporary factual television. In many ways, the restyling of factual television is driven by changes in broadcasting, and in turn by changes in viewing strategies. Mittell (2004) argues that television genres are social and cultural constructions. Factual genres are constructed within specific production contexts, often responding to public service or commercial imperatives, and developing alongside existing practices and popular formats. Factual genres are also constructed within specific reception contexts, taking into account audience responses and viewing habits, and developing alongside genre expectations. Reality gameshows such as *Big Brother* are a good example of the relationship between the production and reception of factual genres. Reality gameshows are a hybrid genre that fill a gap in the market for format-driven popular factual television, and this hybrid genre continues to change each year to accommodate audience expectations. Two countries are used in this chapter to illustrate the construction of factual genres within specific social, economic and cultural contexts. One of the key points to be made is that in countries with similar broadcasting structures such as Britain and Sweden there are similarities and differences within production and reception contexts, creating common generic categories and also nationally specific content and value judgements.

The latter half of the chapter maps factual genres according to pre-existing categories – news, current affairs, documentary and popular factual. In each category, further genres are identified in order to show the development of factual television within these distinct areas. Illustrative case studies are used in order to provide detailed examples of the kinds of communicative form and programme design viewers can expect when watching these programmes. These examples are by no means exhaustive, but cover a range of programmes available. The categories and examples should be broad enough for them to be applicable in many countries, but of course their dominance or absence in some countries more than others will indicate cultural differences in broadcasting factual television.

Broadcasting structures

There is a common assumption that factual television is the domain of public service broadcasters (PSBs). PSBs operate on a business model whereby they receive a sum of money paid for by members of the public, usually in the form of an annual licence fee. In return for this reliable source of revenue, these broadcasters are charged with 'informing, educating and entertaining' the public. They are a natural home for traditional factual such as news or documentary and PSBs from the beginning have made a commitment to a consistently high level of factual output. Many genres such as natural history documentaries, or political debate programmes, are most often located within PSB schedules. As PSBs have changed to respond to more commercial television markets, they have looked to balance their information and educational programming with more entertainment-led output. Ellis characterizes PSBs as 'popular public service' (2000: 32). The term usefully sums up a move within a PSB such as the BBC to optimize its audience. The rise of popular factual programming in the BBC during the 1990s is indicative of its popular public service agenda. It is therefore more appropriate to think of PSBs as vehicles for traditional and popular factual programmes. Indeed, historical research on the origins of reality TV suggests PSBs have always made popular factual radio and television programmes (Holmes and Jermyn 2004).

As a result of the common association of factual output with PSBs, commercial channels are often assumed to produce primarily entertainment-based content. Commercial broadcasters operate on a business model whereby money is generated by advertising, and in some cases also a monthly fee paid by subscribers. This model means commercial broadcasters must optimize their audiences to receive the most amount of revenue. Entertainment is therefore a dominant genre in the commercial portfolio. However, it would be wrong to assume that commercial broadcasters eschew factual output. Well-established commercial channels can have a strong commitment to news and current affairs, such as ITV in Britain, or CBS in America. Dedicated news channels, such as CNN, Fox News, or Sky News, are all commercially-owned channels. In recent years, commercial channels have produced much popular factual output, creatively responding to market pressures by generating non-fiction programmes that will appeal to popular audiences. The rise of reality TV in America is a good example of how commercial channels, such as Fox, can be a home for popular factual programming. Nevertheless, the relatively small market share for PBS, the public service channel in America, has meant that traditional factual has struggled to make an impact during primetime schedules on the main network channels (Murray and Ouellette 2004). Therefore whilst factual output is not the domain of PSB, it tends to flourish in countries with strong PSB channels. The following section presents a broad overview of two Northern European countries, Britain and Sweden, and the broadcasting structures for factual programming.

British broadcasting

The British broadcasting landscape was dominated by a dual system of public service (without advertising) and commercial broadcasting for 30 years from the 1950s to the 1980s. The BBC and ITV offered a combination of information and entertainment-based programming, with an emphasis at the BBC on public service genres, and at ITV on more popular genres. Both channels were associated with strong news provision, and had flagship current affairs and documentary series. The arrival of Channel 4, a public service commercial channel, in the 1980s opened up the broadcasting environment, and in the 1990s the introduction of satellite/cable television, and a fifth commercial channel, Five, established multichannel television in Britain. In 2006, 70 per cent of the British population had access to multi-channel television, and during a weekday profile of 23 million viewers the market share for multichannel television rivalled that of the main five channels (Ofcom 2006a).

The 1992 Broadcasting Act was crucial to changes in British broadcasting. The Act opened up competition from independent producers, and placed pressure on the BBC to deliver cheaper programming. It also encouraged a more competitive environment all round. It is no coincidence that the BBC was the major developer of popular factual programming during the 1990s, and paved the way for the dominance of the reality genre in peaktime schedules in the 1990s. Hybrid genres began to attract high ratings, and particular genres emerged which could hold their own in peaktime schedules, with 30 per cent shares and above. The outcome of increased commercialization in British factual production has been that news has remained consistent in the schedules, but there has been a growth in other kinds of factual, in particular popular factual. A survey by Dover and Barnett (2004) showed a consistently strong news output for the main channels, with the number of hours of news maintained across a 50-year period (approx 15 per cent in peaktime). The same survey indicated there was an increase in documentaries and popular factual, and a decrease in current affairs on the main channels over the past decade. Research on factual international programming in particular shows how there has been a growth in the number of hours on terrestrial channels (around 1,000 hours), but the proportion of political or environmental factual international programming is far lower than popular factual travel programmes about the 'Brits abroad', for example in 2005 23 per cent of the total hours for factual international programming was for popular factual compared to 10 per cent for 'harder programmes' (Seymour and Barnett 2005).

The reference to the growth genre of general factual in the Ofcom Report of 2006 (see Chapter 1) also supports this trend. If we take the case of ITV, the total number of hours of news content (including weather) remained the same from 1998 to 2002 (570 hours) (Independent Television Commission 2003). In fact, ITV increased the number of hours of news during peaktime (from 128 to 183 hours). The total number of hours of current affairs increased from 80 to 123 hours during the same timeframe, but much of this was shown out of peaktime, indicating a lack of commitment to current affairs in the evening schedule. ITV responded to this trend in 2002 with the scheduling of the current affairs series *Tonight with Trevor McDonald* twice a week during peaktime. Similarly, documentary series increased from 61 hours (1998) to 148 hours (2002), but as with current affairs much of this was shown out of peaktime. The biggest difference can be found in the production of popular factual, which increased from 720 to 1,203 hours. ITV's factual output shows the use of news and popular factual as part of peaktime schedules. In the next section, the schedules and ratings are analysed in more detail in order to highlight the significant role factual plays in peaktime programming for popular audiences.

British schedules and ratings

Peaktime schedules are packed with factual and reality programming. The BBC and Channel 4 dominate the schedules with a range of news and current affairs, popular documentary, lifestyle, life experiment and reality gameshows and talentshows. However, other commercial channels offer factual and reality programming during peaktime, and recently ITV has had significant success with reality gameshows such as *I'm a Celebrity, Get Me Out of Here . . .* or *Celebrity Love Island*, the latter counter-scheduled against *Big Brother* on Channel 4. On average, 30 factual programmes are shown during peaktime every night of the week on terrestrial and digital terrestrial channels. This great appetite for factual programming shows a major shift in the commissioning and scheduling of a range of genres (Ofcom 2006a).

Ellis (2000) has discussed how scheduling is significant to our understanding of the 'power of television'. Figure 2.1 illustrates the number of factual and reality programmes on the main channels from 6.30pm to 11pm during May 2003. There were three key points in the timeframe: 6–7pm when the main news bulletins were shown, 8–9pm when the focus was on documentary and popular factual, and 10–11pm when there was the evening news bulletin. The BBC led the peaktime schedule, and ITV favoured fiction from 7–10pm. Channels 4 and Five adopted similar scheduling strategies until 9pm, when Five dropped factual for drama. BBC1 often showed fiction from 8–10pm, shifting factual to BBC2.

Table 2.1 charts factual programming during one evening in May 2003. The schedule clearly showed news was stripped across weeknights, leaving room for other factual to perform well from 7–10pm; 7–8pm was a slot dominated by soaps on BBC1 and ITV1, and lifestyle was used as a buffer after news, and before or after the main soaps. Lifestyle also heavily featured in the 8–9pm slot. Brunsdon *et al.*'s observation of the prominence of lifestyle during this timeframe in the 1990s is relevant, and we can see how lifestyle works so well it now features prominently in the 7–8pm slot as well (2001). Documentary was prominent on all the channels, from 8–11pm, with different types of documentary, from natural history to crime, holding their own during peaktime. This heavy use of documentary in the schedule is a new development, partly resulting from the success of reality TV during the 1990s (Hill 2005), and partly from the production of 'popular documentary' for precisely this slot. The use of documentary from 10–11pm shows its connection with news in the schedules. The emergence of life experiment

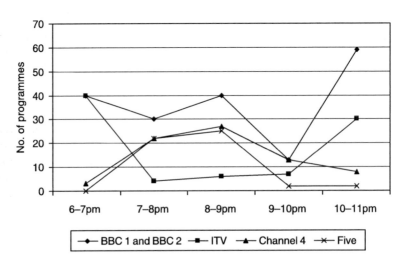

Figure 2.1 British factual TV schedules.*

* All factual and reality programmes during weeknights in May 2003, source BARB.

Table 2.1 British factual TV schedules

Time	BBC1	BBC2	ITV1	Channel 4	Channel Five
6.00pm	News		Local news		
6.30pm	Local News		News		
7.00pm	Bargain Hunt Live Lifestyle			News	News
7.30pm		Your Money Or Your Life Lifestyle	Carol Vorderman's Better Homes Lifestyle	News	
8.00pm		Wild . . . with Bill Oddie Natural history	Holiday Airline Observational documentary	Selling Homes Lifestyle	The Hindenburg Mystery History documentary
8.30pm		Bill Oddie's Best of British Documentary	Home on their Own Observational documentary	The City Gardener Lifestyle	
9.00pm		The Race for Everest Documentary		Trust Me I'm a Teenager Life experiment	
10.00pm	News		News	Big Brother Reality gameshow	
10.30pm	Tabloid Tales Documentary	Newsnight	London's Richest Documentary		Iceman: Confessions of a Mafia Hitman Documentary

Source: *Radio Times*, 27 May 2003.

programmes, a variation on makeover and social experiment documentaries, marks a new development in factual in the early 2000s, and the battle over the 9–10pm slot for BBC2 and Channel 4. The counter-scheduling of news and *Big Brother* at 10pm highlights Channel 4's targeting of younger audiences (aged 16–34), and a general lack of interest in news for this age group. The audience reach amongst 16–24 year olds during evenings is only 28 per cent compared to 60 per cent for the over 60s, and even this figure is falling (Ofcom 2006a). Channel 4 use scheduling to attract what younger audiences there are to their programming.

The ratings for the top factual programmes during the same timeframe indicate the attraction of popular factual with viewers. Table 2.2 shows that

Table 2.2 British factual TV top ten

Programme	Day	Time	Channel	Rating (mill)	Share (%)	Share MCH (%)
I'm a Celebrity . . .	2	20:30	ITV1	7,304	33	28
Big Brother	23	20:30	C4	6,145	28	34
Baliffs	1	20:00	BBC1	5,378	27	26
Tonight with Trevor McDonald Special	9	20:30	ITV1	5,287	25	19
Changing Rooms	1	20:30	BBC1	4,751	22	21
Big Brother	23	22.45	C4	4,717	37	41
Holiday	1	19:00	BBC1	4,427	25	19
News	1	22:00	BBC1	4,288	22	13
News	1	18:30	BBC1	4,261	30	21
How Clean is Your House	21	20:30	C4	4,256	18	16

Source: BARB, May 2003.

reality gameshows dominated the market share for factual programmes during this period, followed by observational documentary series, and long-running makeover series. BBC news was ranked in the lower half of the table, and although the BBC had the greatest number of programmes in the table, reality gameshows on ITV and Channel 4 outperformed the BBC. These results suggest that younger audiences represent a promising group of viewers for factual, and as we shall see in the next chapter do indeed watch a wide range of factual and reality programmes, although they are not regular viewers of news. In an effort to retain audience interest in a specific channel's factual output, many programmes contain crossovers. For example, during May 2003 there was an ITV1 news story about the celebrity Daniella Westbrook, and her appearance in a *Tonight with Trevor Mc Donald Special* 'The Daniella Westbrook Story', a current affairs report on her struggle with drug addiction. Daniella Westbrook was also a contestant in *I'm a Celebrity . . .* showing on ITV1. Channels will also schedule programmes one after the other, creating a wall of factual during peaktime. For example, Channel 4 schedules back to back lifestyle, or reality gameshows, to build brand loyalty and attract audiences with similar interests.

Swedish broadcasting

The Swedish broadcasting landscape for many decades was dominated by public service broadcasting without advertising. In the mid-1980s it was permitted to receive satellite channels and in 1987 the first Swedish satellite channel, TV3, began commercial broadcasting (Hadenius and Weibull 2003: 183). In the following years, TV4 and Kanal 5 started as satellite channels. In 1991, it was decided on a Swedish terrestrial TV channel financed by advertising. After a tender the concession was given to TV4, owned by a Swedish consortium of publishers and organizations, which formally started its terrestrial transmission in 1992. However, both TV3, owned by the media conglomerate MTG, and Kanal 5, owned by the American broadcasting company SBS, developed their satellite channels by increasing the share of Swedish programmes (Gustafsson and Weibull 1995).

Swedish viewers spend on average two hours per day watching television, primarily in the evening, from 7.30–9.30pm. According to Wadbring and Grahm (2001), most people regard themselves as watching TV in a planned manner, especially viewers of PSB. The amount of time Swedish viewers spend watching television has altered little over the past 30 years, despite the increase in channels (Hadenius and Weibull 2003: 420–1). However, the amount of time Swedish viewers spend watching particular channels has changed significantly since the 1970s, and an average of 40 per cent of the viewing time in households is spent watching satellite channels, which has led to an overall reduction in the viewing for SVT. This figure increases to 50 per cent when considering younger viewers (ibid.: 423).

The Swedish media analyst Bengt Nordstrom points out that SVT has a strong position when it comes to audience attitudes to traditional cultural and factual genres, but has a weaker position when it comes to younger viewers' attitudes towards entertainment-based genres (2001: 241–3). He argues that 'for the Swedish TV market and viewer one could say that the altogether strongest side of public service television is to act as a guarantor and as a stimulator for a strong and qualitative TV programming range as a whole' (2000: 254). It is the case that public service organizations have a higher trust rating than commercial channels, and this is both as a consequence of trust in the quality of PSB programmes, and also the association of factual genres such as news or documentary with PSBs. However, Hadenius and Weibull suggest 'one risk lies in that we in Sweden will get a sharper divide between "elite media" and "popular media" in the same way as in many other countries. The former turns to a knowledgeable few, while the latter turns to the broad audience with content where the emphasis is on entertainment' (2003: 350).

In a report from the Broadcasting Commission (2004), 'Swedish TV programming 2003', the relationship between Swedish and foreign programming and factual genres was highlighted. Seventy-five per cent of the programming of SVT and almost half of TV4's programmes are produced in Sweden. In comparison, about two-thirds of TV3 and Kanal 5's programming consists of American programmes. Factual and entertainment programmes are mainly Swedish, with reality TV gameshows the largest growth genre for Swedish production (2004: 86). The Broadcasting Commission report detailed the number of hours allocated to particular genres during 2003. Selecting the factual and reality genres reveals a sharp divide between news and documentary on SVT, and reality programming on commercial channels, with TV4 in between those positions (Table 2.3).

Hadenius and Weibull point out changes in channel identity and viewing preferences, with a much older profile of viewers for SVT compared with the commercial channels (2003: 430). They also note that in 2000:

> the position of traditional soaps was weakened among audiences. In that situation the channels started to try so called reality close fiction or 'reality TV'. . . . *Expedition Robinson* (1997) was one of the first attempts in Sweden. The success of the series contributed to a literal explosion of the genre, which meant that every channel had to profile themselves with a docusoap.
>
> (Hadenius and Weibull 2003: 430).

This comment is also echoed by the Broadcasting Commission: 'in only one aspect is there a homogenous trend for the commercial channels: a heavily increased offering of Swedish reality entertainment. In their programme schedules the introduction of the docusoaps has meant the departure of the soaps' (2004: 87). As one industry professional explained, the success of docusoaps has led to a broader trend in reality entertainment: 'the major reality show within entertainment was *Expedition Robinson* . . . reality is a very good way of telling a story, and ever since it has been the dominating TV entertainment trend if we now can use a very wide concept like entertainment' (interview with Skalse for this project 2004).

The growth genre of docusoaps, or reality entertainment, is also connected to the tabloid newspaper coverage of the participants and events, in particular reality series, such as *Robinson, Big Brother* or *Farmen*. One newspaper headline in the broadsheet paper *Dagens Nyheter* claimed: 'The tabloids have their own soap' (14 February 2004). An industry professional commented: 'it means that you can live in symbiosis, the tabloids can sell their papers on these TV

Table 2.3 Swedish factual and reality programming, 2003 (hours per week)

	News	Factual	Reality entertainment
SVT1	15.16	22.33	1.23
SVT2	9.18	26.39	2.42
TV3	1.00	3.20	10.30
TV4	15.25	8.36	4.17
Kanal 5	0.00	11.09	20.30

Source: The Broadcasting Commission, Sweden.

series . . . I think the tabloids are more in a relationship of dependence on the TV channels and their products, especially the dailies, as an effect of the development of reality TV rather than the other way round' (interview with Skalse for this project 2004). One of the problems with the heavy emphasis on daily docusoaps is that the commercial channels can become known solely for these populist genres. TV4 has shifted its branding from a public service commercial to quality commercial channel (Bolin 2004). However, it has been criticized for becoming too commercial. This former television journalist of TV4 explained, on quitting the channel: 'For me and many others who have worked for TV4 during a long time it is obvious the channel is about to lose its soul. . . . The result is content-free docu-soaps at the expense of news and sport reporting' (*SVD*, 12 March 2004).

The wider trend in reality entertainment has also influenced other forms of factual programming. For example, a move towards popular documentary has been criticized in the press for devaluing the public service credentials of the genre, and pushing it out of peaktime schedules. One newspaper journalist called these popular documentaries freakshows: ' *"The Perfect Vagina"*, *"Tall People"* and *"Diet or Die"*. One has been able to see it all on Swedish TV channels during the past few years, and all of it has come under the definition "documentary". What do the TV channels' freakshow documentaries mean for the future of the genre?' (Kalmteg, *SVD*, 9 December 2003). However, another view of popular documentaries is that they can appeal to broader audiences on commercial channels, as this industry professional explained: 'our entertainment channel sees the possibilities of making profit from documentary films or documentary series today . . . there are enormous commercial interests in it, and a really good documentary is entertaining and commercial' (interview with Skalse for this project 2004).

Swedish schedules and ratings

Like Britain, Swedish schedules are packed with factual and reality pro-grammes. SVT and TV4 dominate the schedules with news and current affairs, lifestyle and reality gameshows and talentshows. Less documentary and life experiment programmes are shown during peaktime schedules than in Britain. Other commercial channels offer mainly reality programming during peaktime, aggressively scheduling reality gameshows such as the Swedish made *Farmen*, or imported series such as *High School Reunion*, against news on SVT. Swedish television mainly has a narrow primetime schedule, where news is stripped on SVT at the same time as reality gameshows are stripped on commercial channels.

Figure 2.2 illustrates the number of factual and reality programmes on the main channels from 6.30pm to 11pm during September 2004. There were three key points in the timeframe: 7–8pm when the main news bulletin was shown on SVT and reality gameshows were shown on the other channels,

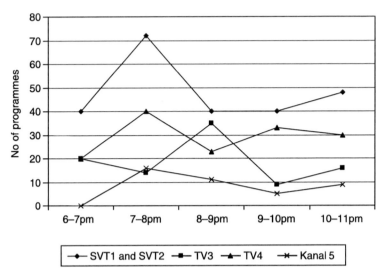

Figure 2.2 Swedish factual TV schedules.*

* All factual and reality programmes during weeknights 13 September to 8 October 2004, sources www.svt.se; www.tv3.se; www.tv4.se; www.kanal5.se; *Expressen TV*.

8–9pm when popular factual programmes were shown, and 10–11pm when there was the evening news bulletin on SVT and TV4. SVT led the peaktime schedule, and TV4 matched the scheduling, especially from 6.30–8pm, but showed different genres during the 7–8pm slot. The absence of soaps in the schedule can be seen most clearly in the use of news and reality gameshows during this time period. TV3 scheduled reality TV during the 8–9pm slot, choosing to offer viewers this type of programming when SVT and TV4 were offering more fiction and light entertainment. TV5 mainly offered imported drama and films, with reality genres shown between 7–8pm in an attempt to garner those younger audiences who were not watching news, or other reality, on the rest of the channels. The impact of counter-scheduling, and close analysis of the competition on other channels, is evident in the narrow scheduling of factual genres.

Table 2.4 shows in more detail the types of programmes shown during a typical weeknight in September 2004. The differences between the British and Swedish schedules become even more apparent as the Swedish schedule is broken up with the use of short news bulletins of between five and 30 minutes on many channels and the heavy competition for the 7.30–9pm slot. Table 2.4 indicates how this slot was dominated by *Rapport* on SVT, stripped every weeknight at 7.30pm. SVT1 and 2 mainly showed news and current affairs, with some lifestyle and documentary on SVT2. TV4 did not compete with news during the 7.30–9pm slot, offering popular

Table 2.4 Swedish factual TV schedules*

Time	SVT I	SVT 2	TV3	TV4	Kanal 5
6.55pm			TV3 Nyheter News		
7.00pm		Kulturnyheterna News, cultural issues		Nyheterna News	High School Reunion Reality
7.10pm		Regionala nyheter Regional news			
7.30pm	Rapport News		Robinson Reality	Farmen Reality	
8.00pm	Uppdrag granskning Current affairs	Naturfilm Wildlife	Fab 5 Lifestyle	Äntligen hemma Lifestyle	Tjockholmen Reality
8.55pm			TV3 Nyheter News		
9.00pm		Aktuellt News			Extreme Makeover Lifestyle
9.30pm		Toppform Lifestyle			
9.55pm				Local nyheter Local news	
10.00pm	Debatt Current affairs	Nyhetssammanfattning News		Nyheterna News	The Apprentice Reality
10.15pm		Regionala nyheter Regional news			

* Tuesday 21 September 2004.

Sources: www.svt.se; www.tv3.se; www.tv4.se; www.kanal5.se; *Aftonbladet TV* 16–22 September.

factual instead, but did compete with their flagship news bulletin at 10pm, shown at the same time as both SVT1 and 2 offered news. This late evening news stand-off allowed the commercial channels TV3 and Kanal 5 to offer fiction and reality genres. The schedules appear to be targeting two different groups of viewers, those who watch PSB and those who don't (see Chapter 3).

The ratings for the top factual programmes during the same timeframe indicate the attraction of news for viewers, the opposite for British viewers, who preferred reality gameshows. Table 2.5 demonstrates that news dominated the market share for factual programmes during this period,

Table 2.5 Swedish factual TV top ten*

Programme	Day	Time	Channel	Rating (%)	Reach (%)	Share (%)
Rapport	26	19:30	SVT1	18	23	50
Otroligt Antikt	26	20:00	SVT1	17	21	41
Rapport	24	19:30	SVT1	15	20	47
Rapport	20	21:00	SVT2	14	18	41
Rapport	21	19:30	SVT1	13	17	40
Rapport	25	19:30	SVT1	13	15	44
Farmen Skärgården	24	21:20	TV4	13	16	33
Rapport	22	19:30	SVT1	13	17	38
Idol	24	22:20	TV4	13	15	41
Äntligen hemma	21	20:00	TV4	13	19	33

* 20–26 September 2004.

Source: www.mms.se; HotTop.

followed by lifestyle and a long-running Swedish-made reality gameshow. SVT dominated the top ten. These results suggest that older audiences represent a leading group of viewers for factual. As we shall see in the next chapter, this older group watch a narrow range of factual programmes and are not regular viewers of reality gameshows.

One of the reasons for a narrow primetime schedule when it comes to factual and reality genres is that small budgets for Swedish-made programmes mean resources and slots are condensed into a few flagship factual and reality series. The pressure for these programmes to perform means there is a risk that channels over rely on more of the same. One industry professional commented: 'Swedish schedules are condensed versions of the UK schedules. All the money from the broadcasters tends to go in the slots from 7.30–10.30' (interview with author 2004). Another explained: 'For Kanal 5 there might be a maximum of four to six new [locally produced] programmes in a year. . . . We don't want to invest millions into something which doesn't work for more than one season' (interview with Skalse for this project 2004). For SVT, the success of the news show *Rapport* is both positive and negative, as it is a strong format up against the wall of reality of the other channels, but it is also a show that attracts older viewers. To come up with an alternative would be a huge drain on resources, and also would take long term commitment to establish a different genre in that slot. Another media professional explained:

The difference between the UK and Sweden is partly to do with tradition, and culture, and very much to do with money. Money plays such a major part in condensing the schedule, squeezing out part of the spectrum of programming. SVT is moving to create a middle ground. We tend to be top heavy, with high brow programming, and that is a problem because we are supposed to be there for everyone. We need an understanding of how popular culture works and how that is reflected in our programming.

(Interview with author 2004)

Smaller budgets and less willingness to produce a range of programmes for peaktime schedules mean Swedish viewers have a more limited choice of factual programmes in comparison with Britain.

Factual categories

In this section, the term factual is broken down according to common characteristics. There are four core genres addressed here: news, current affairs and investigations, documentary, and popular factual. News has long-standing traditions and dominant practices that can be traced across other factual genres. Current affairs and investigations are closely related to news and journalistic traditions. Documentary is made of various modes, sustaining many factual genres under one roof. And popular factual is a result of marriage between factual and other genres, such as drama or light entertainment. In each category, further genres are identified in order to show the development of factual television within these distinct areas. Illustrative case studies are used in order to provide detailed examples of the kinds of communicative form and programme design viewers can expect when watching these programmes. The analysis of programmes in this section benefited from the research of Caroline Dover.

Nichols points out in his discussion of documentary that rather than fix one definition of the genre, it is necessary to 'look at examples and prototypes, test cases and innovations as evidence of the broad arena within which documentary operates and evolves' (2001: 21). Coming up with one definition for news, current affairs and investigations, documentary and popular factual is similarly fraught with difficulty as definitions change over time, and no one definition covers all programmes. Suffice to say that the following examples and prototypes are used as guides for typical qualities and not every example will display all the qualities that are the hallmarks of specific factual genres. As all of the examples are taken from Britain, it is necessary to frame them within a dominant public service environment, and see their development as part of this particular production ecology. As we shall see in the next chapter, genre expectations are dependent on production contexts, and what is commonly understood to be reality TV in one country will not necessarily be the same in another.

News

News is a category that encompasses regional, national and rolling news programmes. News programmes are often flagship productions, providing the main source of public information. Corner defines news as 'regularly updated information about, and depictions of, significant recent events within a particular geographical area or sphere of activity' (1995: 55). There are differences in form and content between news produced for different channels, and news transmitted at different times on the same channel; for example, there are differences between the 6 o'clock and 10 o'clock BBC News, and between Channel 4 and Five News. There can also be different kinds of news content, for example news about the weather, sports news and entertainment news. For the most part a distinction is made in this project between news about world or national events, and sports/entertainment news. This distinction is based on audience distinctions between news journalism, sports journalism and entertainment news. Work by Schudson (1995), Corner (1995) and Philo and Berry (2004), amongst others, offers detailed analysis of news in different countries and journalistic traditions. In particular, Jensen connects the polysemic texts of news with multiple interpretations from audiences around the world (1986, 1998).

News programmes usually combine stories with a special report. There will be a news presenter, often in the studio, but sometimes presenting live from the site of a major event. The news presenter will sometimes interview people at a news desk, or via a telephone or film link up from another location. There will also be reports on location by other journalists speaking to camera, specially prepared reports with the journalist on camera, and/or providing voice-over, interviews with other people involved in the news story, or commentating on it, and/or footage of the interviewee(s). For example, the *BBC 6 O'Clock News* (BBC1) is broken into segments – an introduction, a summary of brief overseas stories, a special report, a preview of regional stories to come in the regional news, a re-cap of the main headlines, the final story. These segments are signaled by graphics, a shift from one presenter to another and/or the presenter's position within the studio (from behind the desk, in news presenting mode, to standing in front of a blue screen for an introduction to a special report). The special reports tend to focus on consumer and domestic issues surrounding news stories. When appropriate, the viewer is encouraged to take part in an online discussion relating to one of the news stories/reports (bbc.co.uk/sixforum). Other news and current affairs programmes are trailed in this programme, for example a *Panorama* investigation will be presented as a BBC exclusive.

Current affairs and investigation

This is a broad category that encompasses both long form journalism, political debate, consumer-based stories and investigative journalism. Ofcom refers to current affairs as a key purpose of PSB, 'to inform ourselves and others and to increase our understanding of the world through news, information and analysis of current events and ideas' (Ofcom 2006b). Current affairs is defined as 'a programme which contains explanation and analysis of current events and ideas, including material dealing with political or industrial controversy or with public policy' (Ofcom 2006b). 'Current affairs . . . draws on the production values and skills both of news programming, with which it has often been institutionally paired, and a range of forms of documentary' (Corner and Hill 2006). In some cases, certain styles of reporting topical news stories have been further developed within their own sub-categories, for example consumer programmes. See Corner (1995), de Burgh (2000), Corner *et al.* (2007) and Turner (2006), amongst others, for detailed analysis of current affairs and investigative journalism.

There are magazine, presenter-led programmes (for example, *Tonight with Trevor McDonald*) and also single programmes that may be broadcast as part of a strand (for example, *Panorama*). Both current affairs and investigative documentaries involve investigative journalism, and undercover filming is often used. These programmes tend to have domestic topics, often emanating from news stories. In some cases, a topic may be based on a celebrity story that can then become a news item, for example the *Tonight Special: Living with Michael Jackson* was also a news item on ITV News. An important feature of all current affairs and investigative programmes is 'the exclusive', and wherever possible producers present new evidence and original investigation that has been conducted by the programmes' own researchers and/or reporters. For example, *Tonight with Trevor McDonald* (ITV1) will typically contain a variety of news stories and approaches to topical events. Topics range from consumer-based reports, to political issues, to state of the nation debates. A report may be a celebrity story, and can be extended to a 'special'. One such celebrity special was *The Daniella Westbrooke Story* (9 May 2003). This was presented by Martin Bashir in the studio, using a tone implying an exclusive: 'her story in her words of her journey back from the brink.' Most of the material presented was archive footage, including an old interview Bashir conducted with Westbrooke. The only new material was a short interview with Westbrooke (on the set of ITV's *I'm A Celebrity . . .*). The second part of the programme consisted of a further update on the *Who Wants to be a Millionaire* scandal – again, an example of a story directly related to another ITV programme. This second report also re-hashed earlier reports and archive footage.

There are relatively few politics programmes. Significant strands, such as *Breakfast with Frost* (ITV1), *The Politics Show* (BBC1) and *Jonathon Dimbleby* (ITV1) are often scheduled on Sunday mornings. Examples vary from *Question*

Time (BBC1), to documentary profiles of political figures and one-off debates and interviews, such as *What the World Thinks of America* (BBC2, 17 June 2003). In *Question Time*, there is a presenter who moderates a panel of politicians, experts and social commentators. Typically, the programme takes a hot topic in the news, and invites questions from the studio audience for the consideration of the panel. Heated debate usually follows. A satire of *Question Time* in the comedy series *The Day Today* (BBC2) depicted the politics programme coming from Wembley Stadium, with thousands of people jeering and clapping the panelists. The sketch cleverly mocks the performative aspects of the programme, and its public profile, which is that it is more talked about than watched.

Consumer reports are often magazine strands or series that are presenter-led and involve original investigations by the programme makers into everyday products and services. Prime examples are the BBC's *Watchdog* and *Health-check*. These programmes are distinct from consumer/lifestyle programmes such as *Holiday* because they present investigations of problems conducted by the programmes' researchers. They are also distinct from reconstruction programmes because they involve journalistic investigation. Current affairs programmes have increasingly come to investigate consumer topics but consumer reports are distinguished by a much greater degree of audience participation, with opportunities for viewers to 'tell their own stories' via emails and letters. For example, *Watchdog* (BBC1, 7pm, half hour) uses a variety of techniques, such as anchors in a studio, researchers and phone operators visible in the studio background, and reporters for location films. The show presents itself as a tireless crusader for the viewer/consumer, involving original investigative work. The opening introduction: 'Watchdog: your money, your show' emphasizes the audience participation, and the presenter Nicky Campbell makes further reference to the viewer/consumer with introductory comments such as 'three big stories you put us on to'. In one example (6 May 2003), the first story covered technical problems with PlayStation2; the second focused on service problems with a stair-lift company; and the third looked at Caribbean holidays gone wrong. Reconstructions and undercover filming are also used in some reports. Wherever possible, wrong-doers are confronted, and a resolution to the problems sought. If there is no resolution in a particular programme, the presenters say 'we'll keep an eye on [the story]', letting the audience know their views are important to them.

Undercover investigations are a staple of current affairs strands, but they can also stand alone as single programmes or series. For example, *The Secret Policeman* (BBC1, 2005) was an award-winning undercover investigation into racism within the British police force that was a one-off investigative documentary. *McIntyre Undercover* (Five) is a series based on a well-known investigative journalist who goes undercover to expose various activities, from football hooliganism, to gambling scams in dog racing. Some series, such as

House of Horrors (ITV1), are a hybrid of consumer and undercover, or hidden camera, investigations where crooked plumbers or electricians are secretly filmed working on repairs in a specially built house for the series. These series also share similarities with the hoax, and also consumer programming.

Documentary

This is a difficult category of factual programming. Nichols (2001: 21) claims that documentary cannot be reduced to a dictionary definition because 'documentaries adopt no fixed inventory of techniques, address no one set of issues, display no single set of forms or styles'. In the broadest sense, documentary 'stands for a particular view of the world, one which we may never have encountered before even if the aspects of the world that is represented are familiar to us' (ibid.: 20). One way to categorize documentary is to consider the institutional settings within which documentary practices exist. In relation to British documentary television, broadly speaking there are specialist documentaries in history or science, religion or arts, and natural history. There are observational documentaries, either as singles, or as series, some of which are sometimes called docusoaps. General documentaries can either be a strand, or stand-alone documentaries on any number of topics. There are investigative documentaries, discussed briefly in the previous section, which share common ground with current affairs. Another area of documentary includes international or authored documentary films that are often directed by international film makers. Experimental documentaries, documentary shorts, video diaries and slots for first-time directors should be considered under this broad category. There are also some more recent developments in popular factual that may be part of documentary, for example a trend for contemporary, or popular documentaries that contain an experiment, or celebrity presenter. Work by Nichols (1994, 2001), Winston (1995, 2000), Corner (1996), Bruzzi (2000), Ward (2005) and Austen (2007), amongst others, offers detailed analysis of the documentary genre.

Specialist documentary can be organized into sub-groups by topic — nature, arts, religion, science, history, culture and, of course, these topics can overlap considerably. Single programmes are often broadcast as part of established strands such as the BBC's *Timewatch, Horizon* and *Wildlife on One*, ITV's *The South Bank Show* and Channel 4's *Secret History* or *Equinox*. Examples of specialist series include *The Human Body* (science), *The Life of Mammals* (natural history), *Simon Schama's History of Britain* or *Tate Modern* (arts and culture). Programmes may have presenters, or else may rely on a narrator to explain the audio-visual information presented. By far the most recognizable specialist documentary is natural history, and in particular the documentaries presented by David Attenborough. His long-standing commitment to natural history series and the public's long-standing love affair with his body of work make natural history documentaries synonymous with series such as

Blue Planet. Typically, these natural history documentaries contain footage of animals and their natural environment around the world. Early Attenborough documentaries such as *Zoo Quest* in the 1960s were very different to series like *Blue Planet*, with the early documentaries influenced by zoology and later ones more influenced by environmentalism.

Most general documentaries include traditional documentary characteristics (a narrative, interviews and/or observational footage of non-actors and explanatory voice-over), but do not fall into the categories above. Neither do they seem to qualify as popular factual, although the dividing line is blurred. Many general documentaries are concerned with domestic topics that range from 'heritage' programmes on BBC4 (*The British Seaside*), through character-based stories for ITV1's *Real Life* strand, to Sky One's *UFO Secrets*. It is a catch-all category for documentaries that are not specialist or observational documentaries. Commissioning and production departments also call these contemporary or popular documentaries. For example, the documentary *Are Your Kids on Drugs?* (Five), presented by the news reader Kirsty Young, is a guide to different drugs and their effects for parents. The general message is that we need to deal with the issue of drugs and young people in a measured, informed and realistic way. The documentary presents information in an accessible manner, with fast-paced editing, graphic presentation of facts, dramatic reconstructions, vox pops, pop music and interviews (with children, parents and experts).

Observational documentaries tend to follow a group of characters over a series. They are sometimes called fly on the wall documentaries because of the observational techniques used to record people and their experiences over a period of time. They are generally based in an institution/workplace and show 'everyday life', with an emphasis on slightly unusual and dramatic people and events. For example *Life of Grime* (BBC1) is a long-running returning series that follows the day-to-day experiences of a local council and its environmental health workers. The documentary observes workers clearing rubbish and ensuring health and safety in homes and local businesses. The people they meet along the way become regular characters. There is observational footage, combined with participants' direct communications to camera, and a guiding voice-over that links the stories into an overarching narrative. The general tone of the series is one of curiosity about people's extreme domestic circumstances, sympathy for the council workers and some of the 'clients', livened by occasional pathos and disbelief at the state of environmental health in Britain.

Popular factual

Another type of factual programming that defies categorization is that of popular factual, also called factual entertainment, reality entertainment and reality TV. This is a broad category for a variety of one-off programmes, series and formats that follow real people and their everyday or out of the ordinary experiences. As these programmes have developed into distinct sub-genres, celebrities have also begun to feature prominently in popular factual programmes. Whether this type of content should be labelled as factual is hotly debated and will be addressed in later chapters. There are sub-genres within the 'so-called reality genre': infotainment, often about crime or emergency services; docusoaps, often about institutions or groups of people; lifestyle, often about making over someone's home or personal appearance; life experiment programmes, usually about a social experiment where people swap lifestyles or jobs; reality gameshows, often about an experiment with a group of people or situation; and reality talentshows that showcase members of the public and celebrities and their entertainment skills. The reality hoax is another format that includes an elaborately staged scam, where ordinary people or celebrities are mocked. There has also been a rise in list, or compilation, programmes, such as *50 Greatest Reality TV Moments* (Five), that fit into the popular factual category. These programmes combine interviews with television archives to countdown 'the best' in relation to the programmes' particular topic (typically a popular culture or consumer subject). The celebrity profile, closely associated with entertainment news, is also a style of popular documentary that would work better in this category than the previous one. Work by Biressi and Nunn (2005), Holmes and Jermyn (2003), Andrejevic (2004) and Murray and Ouellette (2004) offers more detailed accounts of the reality genre.

There are two broad distinctions within popular factual – programmes that film situations already taking place, and those that create the situation for the purposes of the programme. One type of popular factual is more observational in nature, the other is more constructed. Sometimes production and commissioning departments separate the two into formatted and non-formatted, implying there is a distinction between formatted constructed popular factual, and more non-formatted observational programmes. The boundaries are not clearly marked, and the nature of popular factual is to continuously blur boundaries and rely on hybrid genres. But it is useful to bear in mind that a distinctive feature of observational popular factual programmes is that they rely on filming people in their normal environment, and any changes that occur would mainly have happened if the cameras were not there. The distinctive feature of constructed popular factual programmes is that someone is removed from their normal environment and placed in a new one, and any change that takes place would not have occurred without the proactive and deliberate intervention of the production company. All documentary filming alters 'real life' situations but that alteration is the raison d'être of these programmes, rather than something that producers seek to minimize. We might call these programmes made-for-TV factual, and it places them close to other non-fiction genres such as sports or light entertainment, and other fictional genres, such as soap opera or melodrama.

Reconstruction programmes involve the use of close circuit television or home-video footage and/or the dramatic reconstruction of recent events – typically accidents and crime-related incidents 'caught on camera'. The programmes may be studio-based with presenters introducing stories, or there may be a series of stories or clips explained through a voice-over. A number of incidents and stories will be covered in any one programme. Examples range from entertainment-led shows such as *The Planet's Funniest Animals* (ITV2), through *Police, Stop!* (Sky One) and *Neighbours From Hell* (ITV1) to 'citizen-advice' programmes such as 999 (BBC1). The latter differ from consumer programmes in that they involve the retelling of stories, rather than any further investigation. *Honeymoons from Hell* is a good example of this kind of category, taken from the long-running '. . . from Hell' series. The programme uses an eclectic range of styles, including interviews with victims, mixed with dramatic reconstructions and CCTV/camcorder footage. There are dramatic stories (for example a couple who nearly got shot in the middle of a military coup) and more mundane ones. The voice-over antici-pates some of the drama, and often has to provide it when there is a lack of dramatic visual material. The dramatic reconstructions tend to be quite simple, with blurred close-ups that are evocative rather than literally illustrative.

Life experiment programmes involve participants who are followed over a pre-determined period of time (typically, a few weeks) experimenting with an alteration to their lives: living with someone else's family; masquerading in an alternative, unfamiliar profession; living without an 'essential' utility/service/object; living by the domestic rules imposed by strangers, and so forth. The tensions, triumphs and failures of participants' experiences are then filmed in an observational manner. The end of filming signals the end of the experiment and a return to 'normal' for the participants. Typical examples include *Wife Swap* or *Faking It* (Channel 4). *Faking It* involves someone given the challenge of training in a new career in only one month and then fooling a panel of judges into believing they are a true professional. Observational filming is used, incorporating straight-to-camera conversations between dir-ector and subject combined with 'confessional' camcorder pieces recorded by the main participant. A voice-over provides explanation. Participants are selected because of their potential but also unlikeliness for success; for example, a punk band musician is trained as a classical conductor, or an emergency services operator is trained as a TV studio director. The career training not only requires new skills but also experience of a very different social world (and the etiquette that accompanies it). The faker is put together with one or two mentors and the relationships that develop between them (antagonistic and/or nurturing) are central to the programme. The trials and triumphs of the transformation are followed, with the climax being 'will they or won't they' pull off the final challenge in front of the expert panel? Participants often succeed, at least partially, in making a convincing trans-formation. At the end of the programme, the faker returns to his or her normal life, although their experiences may well have consequences for their life after the programme.

Lifestyle programmes address topics such as homes and gardens, buying/ selling properties, food and drink, domestic budget management, clothes and dating. Advice and ideas about products are offered and most programmes are underpinned by the theme of 'self-improvement', generally achieved through changing your domestic environment or your appearance, but also through adjusting your 'inner self'. An important element of all lifestyle is a combination of the presenter(s) and/or expert(s) and ordinary people. Broadly speaking, there are two types of lifestyle: instructional and makeover programmes. Instructional programmes offer straightforward advice and are close to consumer programmes. Makeover programmes focus on the transformation of something, and are closer to constructed popular factual. Traditional lifestyle programmes include *Gardeners' World* (BBC2). This is a short programme, led by presenters who offer advice and/or review products. The presenters talk to other participants and straight to camera. Specific information and advice is offered about particular plants, with some demonstrations. The tone is completely un-ironic (compared with some 'newer' lifestyle formats). The presenters are friendly, reliable, 'safe hands'. In makeover programmes, one individual or a group of people are assisted in a lifestyle project by the presenters/ experts, and their progress forms the narrative of each new programme. For example, the process followed may be the search for a house to buy, or the programme may be structured around a makeover (in clothes, home or garden). Programmes in this category include *Changing Rooms* (BBC1), *What Not to Wear* (BBC2), *Life Laundry* (Channel 4) and *House Doctor* (Five). For example, *What Not to Wear* has regular experts/ presenters who makeover a new person in each programme. Much the same sort of advice is offered each week – the variations are derived mostly from the participants. The experts are predictably prescriptive in their advice and their definition of what is 'right', in behaviour, clothes and matters of taste in general.

Entertainment-based popular factual programmes are similar to the compilation shows cited above (utilizing interviews and clips), but do not involve voted-for lists and are presented, instead, as historical overviews. Other programmes within this category are celebrity profiles (*Heather Mills: the Real Mrs McCartney*, Channel 4), and behind-the-scenes programmes (*Cold Feet: the Final Call*, ITV1). Entertainment news may be considered within popular factual rather than news. For example, the celebrity news show *Liquid News* (BBC3) is a live studio-based show with alternating presenters and outside reporters, who interview studio guests. Reports are about gossip, the latest film openings, and so forth. Limited research is necessary, as few if any of the stories are exclusives. The appeal of the programme would seem to lie not so much in actually hearing anything new, but in the light-hearted, fun approach that gently mocks celebrities whilst also celebrating them.

In reality gameshows, participants (be they celebrities or members of the public) are placed, temporarily, in new, often self-enclosed, environments created for the purpose of the television programme. A crucial element of this format is competition between the participants to win a prize or be voted the most popular and/or talented. Votes are cast by the participants themselves and/or a panel of experts and/or the viewers. Examples include *Fame Academy* (BBC1), *I'm A Celebrity, Get Me Out of Here . . .* (ITV1), *Pop Idol* (ITV1) and *Big Brother* (Channel 4). A new development in the reality gameshow is the reality hoax, where contestants are tricked into taking part in a programme, but are unaware of a vital piece of information. For example *Joe Millionaire* (Fox) is a reality dating gameshow where the hoax is that 'Joe' is not a millionaire, and the female contestants are unaware of this until the final stage of the game where the truth is revealed. Another example is *There's Something About Miriam* (Sky One), a reality dating gameshow where male contestants compete for the attention of Miriam, who is really a pre-op transsexual. *Space Cadets* (Channel 4) took the reality hoax to an extreme level when it pretended contestants were in space when in fact they were in a simulated space shuttle in a film studio.

The celebrity reality gameshow is a popular format, and sits in border territory between popular factual and light entertainment. For example, in *I'm a Celebrity, Get Me Out Of Here . . .* celebrities live together in the Australian jungle, and are voted for by the public to face gruesome challenges and eviction. The presenters are central to the entertainment value of the series. Although the participants appear to be filmed extensively, a minimal amount of observational footage is actually shown. Emphasis is placed on the challenges, the evictions and the presenters' comic analysis of the proceedings. Very short excerpts are cut together, with some footage shown more than once. Additional focus is placed on apparent disagreements and flirtations between contestants. Print media coverage is an inherent element of a series such as this, providing additional gossip about the participants. Everything about the set-up is entirely artificial, even the jungle is treated as merely the set's back-drop and no attempt is made to disguise the presence of many cameras and a large crew. However, the premise is that contestants will show their real selves. Those who are considered to be 'acting' and/or manipulative are commented on and castigated; it is those who are considered to be 'most genuine' who tend to do best in terms of the public's votes. Performances are judged in tandem with personalities. The programme's graphic titles hint at a lighthearted take on the 'celebs' – a lizard wearing jewels. They illustrate how the jungle setting takes the celebrities 'back to basics' and also potentially humiliates them (not only do they become hungry and irritable, they lack their usual costume and make-up). However, there are voting rewards for those who overcome these obstacles. It is ultimately a popularity test, largely for celebrities with flagging careers.

Other non-fiction genres

There are so many popular factual programmes, and so many of them are closely connected to other non-fiction genres, that it is difficult to cover all the main areas in one large generic category. There are well-established genres such as talkshows which may well fit within popular factual. Talkshows are certainly influential in relation to popular factual formats, and theories about reality TV draw on much of the research on talkshows conducted during the 1990s. They involve ordinary people, or celebrities, in studio debates on personal stories and experiences. This genre is not included here because they stand apart from popular factual, with their own production practices and history within broadcasting (see Gamson 1998; Livingstone and Lunt 1994). Similarly, pop music shows are related to popular factual programes, indeed *Pop Idol* is based on popular music performances. Once again, series such as *Top of the Pops* (BBC1) have their own distinctive production histories that make them part of light entertainment. Sport is part of non-fiction television, and yet it is a separate category of programming, influential within popular factual – see for example *The Games* (Channel 4) – but nevertheless not popular factual as such. The same can be said of gameshows, a major genre for the development of reality gameshows such as *Big Brother*, but with a long production history that sets it apart from popular factual. In the next chapter, audiences discuss what they think should be included in their definition of factual television.

Programme categories

The audience research in this book is based on surveys and focus groups. The survey required that programme categories were used in order to gather information on viewing preferences and attitudes. As a result of selective genre, scheduling and ratings analysis for news and current affairs, documentary and popular factual programmes, categories were chosen to represent the broadest range of programmes available to viewers during peaktime, weekday television schedules for the main public service and commercial channels. In Britain, 14 categories were used, and in Sweden 11. The list of factual categories and typical programme examples were not exhaustive. These categories were used in order to signal to respondents that when answering questions they should consider a representative range of programmes. The categories shown in this section indicate those which were comparable in both countries.

- News (*Nyheter*), e.g.:
  - *BBC News* or ITV's *News at Ten*
  - *Rapport, Nyheterna, TV3 Nyheter*
- Current affairs/documentaries (*Samhällsprogram/dokumentärer*), e.g.:

- *Tonight With Trevor McDonald* or *Panorama*
- *Dokument utifrån, enskilda dokumentärer*
- Investigative journalism (*Undersökande journalistik*), e.g.:
  - *Kenyon Confronts* or *House of Horrors*
  - *Uppdrag granskning, Kalla fakta, Insider*
- Political programmes (*Politiska debattprogram*), e.g.:
  - *Question Time* or *Jonathan Dimbleby*
  - *Agenda, Debatt, Ekdal mot makten*
- Consumer programmes (*Konsumentprogram*), e.g.:
  - as *Watchdog* or *Rogue Traders*
  - *Plus, Kontroll, Motorjournalen*
- Nature programmes (*Naturprogram*), e.g.:
  - *Life of Mammals* or *Survival*
  - *Mitt i naturen, Farligt möte*
- Documentary series (*Dokumentära serier*), e.g.:
  - *Real Lives* or *Cutting Edge*
  - *Djurpensionatet, Barnsjukhuset, Veterinärerna*
- Reconstructions (*Rekonstruktioner*), e.g.:
  - *999* or *Police, Camera, Action!*
  - *Efterlyst, På liv och död*
- Lifestyle experiment programmes (*Livsstilsexperiment*), e.g.:
  - *Faking It* or *Wife Swap*
  - *Par på prov, Switched, Blind Date*
- Lifestyle programmes (*Livsstilsprogram*), e.g.:
  - *Changing Rooms* or *House Doctor*
  - *Äntligen hemma, Solens mat, Roomservice, Fab 5, Gröna rum*
- Reality gameshows (*Dokusåpor*), e.g.:
  - *Big Brother* or *Pop Idol*
  - *Big Brother, Farmen, Riket*

There were three categories that were used in Britain only: undercover investigative programmes (e.g. *Kenyon Confronts* or *House of Horrors*), history or science documentaries (e.g. *History of Britain* or *Timeteam*) and observational documentaries (e.g. *Airline* or *Vets in Practice*). One extra category was used in Sweden: talkshows (e.g. *Sen kväll med Luuk, TV-huset, David Letterman Show*).

The use of these categories highlights the mixture of traditional and popular factual genres in both countries. The categories that did not work in both countries reveal interesting differences in production contexts. For example, talkshows were not included in the British sample because they were shown in the daytime, and therefore outside the remit of the survey. In Sweden talkshows are a staple of peaktime television. In the British survey more documentary categories were used, for example specialist documentaries such as history or observational documentary, which reflects the tradition of documentary television and its place in peaktime schedules, whereas in Sweden documentary series was the only category that was used, reflecting the absence of different kinds of documentary in peaktime schedules.

Differences within sub-genres further highlight culturally specific examples of programmes. For example, current affairs in Britain is associated with a combination of topical documentary style reportage and investigative journalism. In Sweden, the two styles are associated with two sub-genres, topical documentaries and investigative journalism. Thus whilst the communicative styles may be similar, the categorization of current affairs means subtly different things to British and Swedish viewers. In Britain, natural history means programmes about wildlife around the world, for example *Blue Planet*. In Sweden, there are foreign wildlife documentaries, but homegrown programmes are more often about the Swedish natural environment.

Reconstruction programmes show the impact of public service versus commercial broadcasting in both countries. In Sweden, the main reconstruction programme is shown on the commercial channel, TV3, a channel popular with younger audiences. In Britain, there is a long tradition of reconstruction programmes on the BBC and also ITV, two public service and commercial channels with an older age profile. Lifestyle programmes highlight the dominance of a particular sub-genre of lifestyle, the makeover, in Britain, whereas in Sweden lifestyle refers to a range of instructional and makeover series. In each category there are subtle genre variations, and these variations impact on genre expectations amongst viewers in both countries. A final point relates to homegrown versus acquired programmes. The programme examples were specifically chosen to represent British and Swedish content. However, in Sweden the common use of foreign programming, in particular from America and Britain, impacts on the programme categories, especially documentary and reality gameshows.

Conclusion

Factual television resists categorization. It is an umbrella category for a wide range of non-fiction programmes, from news to natural history, investigative journalism to reality gameshows. These programmes are constantly changing, borrowing ideas from existing genres, mixing one factual genre with other television genres, from gameshows to soap opera. One way to make sense of this chaotic world is to categorize factual television according to broadcasting categories. The changing generic environment of factual television is constructed within culturally specific broadcasting environments, and commonly understood genre categories. These production and generic contexts will change, but we can look for prototypes and typical examples to help us see differences and similarities within factual content.

In terms of broadcasting, public service and commercial imperatives impact on the commissioning, production, scheduling and ratings of factual programmes. It is an over-generalization to say that news and current affairs, and documentary, are the domain of public service channels and popular factual is the domain of commercial channels. Commercial channels can be just as committed to serious news programmes in peaktime as public service channels. However, it is the case that most countries with strong public service broadcasters tend to have more factual content in peaktime, and a greater range of factual genres, than those with weak or non-existent public service channels. The basic commitment of public service broadcasting to inform, educate and entertain ensures factual content is a staple of the schedules.

A comparative analysis of Britain and Sweden suggests, on the one hand, a similar public service and commercial system and, on the other hand, a different history for both types of broadcasting. In Britain, the long-standing tradition of commercial television, with some commitment to public service genres, shows an overall wide range of news and current affairs, documentary and popular factual programmes on PSB and commercial channels. It is also the case that larger budgets, and a greater willingness to produce a variety of factual and reality programmes scheduled during peaktime, means viewers have a wide choice of programmes on offer. In Sweden, the relatively recent arrival of commercial television, and its lack of commitment to public service genres, shows an overall narrow range of news and current affairs on PSB channels, and a large amount of popular factual programmes on commercial channels. Smaller budgets, and less willingness to produce a range of programmes for peaktime schedules means viewers have a comparatively limited choice of programmes.

There are difficulties in defining news, current affairs and investigations, documentary and popular factual because these definitions change over time. Nevertheless, it is worthwhile coming up with examples and prototypes that can be used as guides for typical qualities within factual genres. News, and current affairs and investigations, are two broad categories, and include sub-genres such as politics programmes, consumer programmes and investigative journalism. Documentary is another broad category, and includes a range of sub-genres such as natural history, or history/science documentaries, general or popular documentaries, observational documentaries, and authored documentary films, amongst others. Popular factual is the broadest category, with a wide range of content that can be summarized into programmes that film situations already taking place, and those that create the situation for the purposes of the programme. One type of popular factual is more observational in nature, the other is more constructed. Examples include reconstruction programmes, life experiment programmes, lifestyle, entertainment-based programmes and reality gameshows or talent-shows. Whether popular factual is part of a family of factual genres is open to debate. The analysis of various factual and reality genres within British and Swedish television highlights how viewers experience these genres as part of a broad understanding of factuality. In the next chapters, audiences talk about what they consider to be factual television, and the ways they map factual programmes according to common categories and value judgements.

Chapter 3

Public and popular

'It's something else which decides whether they're good or bad.'

Genre evaluation is a powerful framing device for factual television. It is a means of understanding the changing world of factual television by defining, categorizing, and differentiating one type of programme or genre from another. We evaluate genres by using a variety of criteria, from practical, to personal, to commonly agreed value judgements. For example, production techniques can be used as a criterion for evaluating factual genres, from live or pre-recorded filming, to camera styles, or picture quality, to the use of presenters or ordinary people. Personal value judgements are often used as a criterion for evaluating if a factual programme is 'good' or 'bad', or if it relates to personal interests. This connects with commonly agreed quality criterion for informative and/or entertaining programmes, and other wider social values often concerned with abstract concepts such as knowledge, truth and morality. Other common social value judgements are framed according to a number of axes: public service versus commercial channels; home versus foreign programmes; public versus popular genres. These ways of categorizing and valuing factual programmes highlights the complex processes at work in understanding genre. The evaluation of factual genres underscores the importance of broadcasting conventions, private preferences and pre-existing public attitudes towards television production, content and reception.

This chapter examines the power of genre evaluation. It focuses on classificatory practices that are based on repetition and variation. In this sense, there is an inherent performativity to classification that makes it both repetitive, but also adaptable and reflexive. Viewers use social, cultural and moral orderings to classify factual genres. They used traditional categories for public and popular genres to re-enforce a perceived natural order between public service and commercial broadcasting, including some genres in the scheme and excluding others, notably reality TV. However, in the act of classification viewers also flexibly responded to developments within factual broadcasting and their construction of factual genres.

Definitions of factuality are closely connected to value judgements, and in particular commonly held opinions on the quality of television and its role as a knowledge provider or entertainer. The main argument is that viewers classify and evaluate factuality according to public versus popular genres. Viewers value traditional factual genres associated with investigations of reality more than popular genres associated with constructions of reality. These value judgements influence the reporting of viewing preferences, as there is low reporting for watching popular genres which is not matched by the ratings profiles for these genres. The reliance on the traditional framing device of public and popular shows how audiences have turned to familiar values in order to make sense of the restyling of factuality. However, normative ideals for factual content are rarely matched by personal experience of watching television, and this creates a contradictory viewing mode whereby public genres such as current affairs are highly valued but not watched, and popular genres such as reality gameshows are watched but not valued. Age is the most significant difference in viewing preferences, with clear groups of older traditional factual viewers, and younger, contemporary factual viewers. It is these younger viewers who are most engaged with a re-evaluation of factual genres, and therefore involved in the restyling of factuality.

Public and popular genres

The relationship between the public and the popular is partly based on generic discourses. Jason Mittell (2004), in *Genre and Television*, argues for an examination of television genres as 'cultural categories'. He explains that genres matter to people, institutions and scholars precisely because they are not bound only to their textual properties, but also to the cultural processes of media experiences. He says:

> Television genre is best understood as a process of categorization that is not found within media texts, but operates across the cultural realms of media industries, audiences, policy, critics and historical contexts . . . genres can be seen as key ways that our media experiences are classified and organized into categories that have specific links to particular concepts like cultural value, assumed audience, and social function.
>
> (Mittell 2004: xii)

Thus, factual genres matter to audiences as a means to work out what is fact and fiction, what is informative and entertaining, and whether it is important to show specific types of genres on television or not. Mittell points out that 'the prevalence of generic mixing and niche segmentation' means genres may be 'even more important today than in previous television eras' (ibid.: xiii).

Mittell suggests that the broadcasting environment significantly shapes generic discourses. In this project, audiences in two public service dominated

Northern European countries draw on commonly held views about factual television as public service content. Thus factual genres are linked to policy debates and initiatives about television as a form of popular culture that should inform, educate and entertain. Factual genres are most associated with the idea of television as a knowledge provider, connecting with 'the knowledge project' (Corner 1998). Viewers rely on traditional ways of classifying and evaluating genres according to a public/popular axis. Audience definitions of factual TV as truthful and informative highlight the core principles that lie behind the provision of public service broadcasting. They also point to broad generic discourses concerning journalistic practices and popular factual practices. Viewers cluster those genres which use an investigative approach to social issues and real life, with news as the most distinctive genre. They also cluster those genres which take a more constructed approach to people and their everyday lives, with reality gameshows as the most distinctive genre. As one female participant explained: 'docusoap [reality TV] is when you gather a bunch of people and let them live in a room or you follow them or something, the other is that you look at a phenomenon and investigate it, or interview people on something specific.'

Many of the ideals associated with factual television are also connected to the concept of the public sphere. The public sphere is a normative concept suggested by the German scholar Jurgen Habermas (1989); it is an ideal space where citizens can engage in rational and political debate. Researchers have argued that public service broadcasting (PSB) is the institutional embodiment of a modern public sphere (see Collins 2003 for an overview). It is a space that operates outside of pure market considerations, a broadcasting space for citizens rather than consumers. One of the criticisms of PSB, and the public sphere, is that it fails to address the various publics that live in contemporary society. Thus, the public sphere, and PSB, can be accused of being elitist and exclusive. Collins argues that PSBs' commitment to informing and educating audiences was restricted to 'an audience of their imagination'. It was the arrival of commercial broadcasting that changed this approach:

> Bottom up public services, which gave voice to a real public, and represented a demotic and genuinely democratic public sphere were conspicuous by their absence until competition with commercial services compelled public broadcasters to address a real public rather than that of a broadcaster's imagination.
>
> (Collins 2003: 43–4)

Some critics argue that the impact of market forces on PSBs has ensured they address a wider range of audiences on topics that appeal to the different publics that make up society. Others argue that the shifts in PSBs to attract popular audiences have weakened their public service credentials, making them little different from commercial organizations. The normative idea of

PSB as a modern public sphere is therefore one that changes in relation to media policies and production contexts.

Murray comments on the categorization of reality formats, suggesting 'the distinctions we make between forms of nonfictional television are not based on empirical evidence but largely contained in the evaluative connotations that insist on separating information from entertainment, liberalism from sensationalism, and public service from commercialism' (2004: 54). The fact that these evaluations are part of historical and culturally specific media experiences shows how significant social and political structures are to generic discourses. Murray's comment relates to her analysis of shifting definitions of two factual series, categorized as documentary and reality on different American public service and commercial channels. Her findings emphasize the persistence of the public/popular frame for factual genres.

Mittell argues genre discourses shape power relations. These discourses are part of a larger debate about high culture and popular culture. For example, Bilteryest (2004) has shown how intense criticism of reality TV formats like *Big Brother* can be seen as 'media panics', an historical phenomenon whereby the introduction of a new mass media, or genre, can cause intense public reactions. He demonstrated how public debate in many European countries mirrored a media panic, with social commentators denouncing the arrival of *Big Brother* as lowest common denominator TV, and as morally wrong. Mathjis (2002), in a detailed analysis of Belgian press debate about *Big Brother*, also charted the initial outrage at this format, and how this outrage reduced and changed over a period of time, leading to general (though not always uncritical) acceptance of the format in later series. According to Drotner (1992: 60), media panics address cultural quality in times of social change, and media panic discourses contain 'various strategies of using "quality" culture as a means of a moral, and by implication, social elevation'. Media panics are often located around concerns to do with young people and new media, or new genres, and this highlights the influence of media panic discourses on attitudes towards popular culture for younger audiences. Media panic discourses contributed to debates about factual TV in Britain and Sweden, as reality TV was seen to pose a threat to the core ideals of factuality, quality culture and perceived moral standards.

There is an argument that generic discourses of factual television are framed by an elitist view of culture. So influential is this discourse that even those viewers who watch popular factual genres categorize and evaluate them as popular, entertaining and of low social value (Hill 2005). However, factual TV is a good space for audiences to openly debate issues concerned with quality, information, entertainment, and public service and commercial content (Winston 2000). Genre evaluation is about ideals and practices to do with the public and the popular. Livingstone (2005b) has argued that notions of the public and popular are bound to specific contexts and mean different things to different people. She shows how young adults see the private as a positive, creative space for new media practices in the home. The research in this book also highlights how notions of public and popular genres are connected to the contexts of factual television in Britain and Sweden. Rather than resist or subvert the distinctions between public and popular factual genres, audiences turn to these pre-existing categories as a starting point for understanding change. This means public/popular discourses are important to audiences because they offer strategies for dealing with genres on the move. These strategies necessitate looking beyond generic discourses to also consider classificatory practices.

Waterton analyses classificatory practices in environmental studies. She uses an experiment in the field, classifying plant life in agricultural grassland, as an opportunity to think about the central role of classification in 'making sense of complex phenomena of the world' (2003: 113). When we classify things we often apply our own value judgements. Our categories are used as 'a critique or re-enforcement of the human order, justifying some particular social or political arrangement on the grounds that it is somehow more "natural" than any alternative' (Thomas 1984: 61, cited in Waterton 2003: 113). Classifications are performative of 'natural, social and moral orderings', and the 'construction sites' for classification can reveal 'tacit understandings, conceptual frameworks, and inclusions and exclusions that underpin a classificatory scheme' (2003: 113–14). Through her observations of classifying plant life, Waterton comments that classificatory practices are based on repetition and variation, and that there is an inherent performativity to classification that makes it flexible, adaptable and reflexive (2003: 126).

In the quantitative and qualitative research in this chapter, viewers use social, cultural and moral orderings to classify factual genres. They use traditional categories for public and popular genres to re-enforce a perceived natural order between public service and commercial broadcasting, including some genres in the scheme, and excluding others, notably reality TV. In the act of classification viewers flexibly respond to developments within factual broadcasting, and are adaptive and reflexive in their construction of factual genres. The public and popular signify audience understanding of the policy environment within which public service and commercial broadcasting operates, and the cultural environment within which factual genres are produced. These pre-existing categories provide a conceptual framework for debates about quality standards and the core ideals of factuality. They also allow for movement between the public and the popular, and for reflections on the impact of popular factual on public service factual content.

Viewing preferences

In this section the discourses surrounding public service broadcasting and popular culture impact on the reporting of viewing preferences for factual and reality genres. Some clear trends emerge in the responses of viewers to dominant cultural discourses for news, and other public service factual content, and popular factual genres. Viewers over-report watching factual genres they classify as public service and socially important in the public knowledge project. Viewers under-report watching popular factual genres they classify as popular and not socially important to the public knowledge project. The classification of factuality according to a public/popular axis has an influence on the self-reporting of viewing preferences, and highlights how viewers wish to be perceived as knowledgeable viewers, connected to wider social and cultural debates about factuality. In the previous chapter, ratings data showed a high proportion of British viewers watching popular factual programmes and Swedish viewers watching news. Ratings give a picture of what popular audiences prefer at particular times in the schedule. The data in this section goes further in showing cultural trends for types of factual programmes across gender, age, socio-economic status and country. The data was analysed in collaboration with Lennart Weibull and Åsa Nilsson (see Hill et al. 2005, 2007). Personal preferences for a wide range of factual programmes match the common ways television programmes are watched in relation to each other and not in isolation. The quantitative data in this section connects with value judgements about the restyling of factuality, and these judgements influence the reporting of viewing preferences.

News is the most regularly watched factual genre in Britain and Sweden. In both countries there is a sharp distinction between news and every other kind of factual genre, with very high levels of viewing for news and low viewing for all other programmes, especially reality TV. Figure 3.1 details the

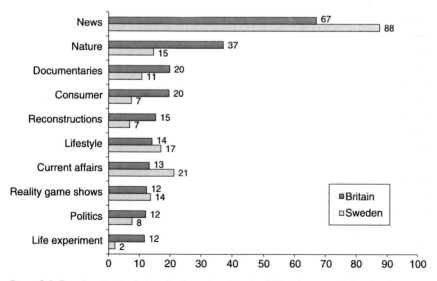

Figure 3.1 Regular viewing habits for factual and reality TV in Britain and Sweden.*

* British survey unweighted sample 4,516, Swedish survey unweighted sample 944.

regular viewing habits of British and Swedish respondents (watching a few times per week). There was a high percentage for people, on a regular basis, watching the news (67 per cent in Britain, 88 per cent in Sweden), and a low percentage for reality gameshows (12 per cent in Britain, 14 per cent in Sweden). The power of scheduling is apparent as viewing trends map scheduling trends for most genres, with news stripped daily and other genres usually shown once per week. If we compare the figures for news in relation to daily rather than regular viewers, there is a marked cultural distinction. Swedish viewers were twice as likely to watch the news on a daily basis as British viewers (66 per cent and 33 per cent, respectively). Swedish viewers seem to be far more committed to daily news bulletins than British viewers, despite the fact that in Britain there are more frequent and lengthier bulletins in peaktime on PSB and commercial channels. We shall see in the next section how the reporting of viewing habits in Sweden matches a high social value accorded news.

Figure 3.2 shows occasional viewers in both countries (watching at least once per week). There is a wider spread of viewing habits across a broader range of genres. The dominance of news becomes less distinct when occasional viewers are taken into account. However, there is still a preference for news, current affairs and documentary over more popular factual genres. For example, both countries showed a high preference for news (91 per cent Britain, 95 per cent Sweden) and current affairs (58 per cent Britain, 61 per cent Sweden), and a low preference for reality gameshows (27 per cent Britain,

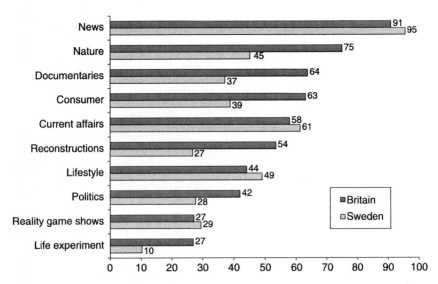

Figure 3.2 Occasional viewing habits for factual and reality TV in Britain and Sweden.*

* British survey unweighted sample 4,516, Swedish survey unweighted sample 944.

29 per cent Sweden). The reporting of viewing habits for popular genres, in particular reality gameshows, is low compared to high ratings in both countries. This is partly explained by the percentage of older viewers who do not watch these programmes. It is also the case that respondents under-reported their viewing habits due to the lack of value they attach to these populist reality series (see next section). Given the intense scheduling of some reality formats in Britain (e.g. *Big Brother*), and many formats in Sweden which are stripped during weeknights, there is certainly a discrepancy between the scheduling and ratings performance of reality TV and the reporting of viewing habits in both countries.

There are differences across the two countries in terms of occasional viewing preferences for genres. Overall, these differences show British viewers like a wide range of factual genres, whereas Swedish viewers prefer a more narrow range. These genre preferences are as much to do with the production con-texts and scheduling of factual as taste in particular genres. For example, there was a marked preference for natural history programmes in Britain (75 per cent), which showed the tradition and long-term popularity of wild-life documentaries, such as *Blue Planet* (BBC), whereas there was less pre-ference for nature and environment programmes in Sweden (45 per cent). Twice as many British viewers watched politics programmes, documentary series, consumer programmes and reconstructions than Swedes. Why this is the case is partly related to the predominance of these genres over the past decade in British schedules. We should note that there was a minor difference in the way British and Swedish respondents were asked about frequency of viewing, with the category of 'most of the time' for Britain and 'several times a week' for regular viewers, 'sometimes' and 'at least once a week' for Sweden. Although some minor variations in responses may be connected to the use of different terms, the patterns in response established in these tables are patterns that recur elsewhere in the data.

Age, gender and education

The relationship between the reporting of viewing preferences and dominant cultural discourses for public and popular genres is made more complicated by a breakdown in viewing preferences according to key variables. Differences emerge within social groups if general viewing patterns are broken down according to age, gender and socio-economic status (Tables 3.1a–c). In terms of age, reality gameshows, lifestyle programmes and life experiments attract a younger profile than news and current affairs. For example, news was regu-larly watched by 48 per cent of younger adults and 81 per cent of older adults in Britain. The corresponding figures for Sweden were 58 and 96 per cent. With regard to reality gameshows, there is a similar pattern. In Britain, this genre was regularly watched by 37 per cent of younger adults, and only 2 per cent of older adults; in Sweden by 37 and 4 per cent, respectively. This

Table 3.1a Regular viewing habits for factual and reality TV by age (Britain and Sweden, %)

	Britain		Sweden	
	16–24	65+	16–24	65+
News	48	81	58	96
Nature	22	44	7	33
Documentaries	20	21	10	15
Consumer	20	27	6	12
Reconstructions	22	19	10	6
Lifestyle	23	6	21	9
Current affairs	7	18	12	30
Reality game shows	37	2	37	4
Politics	4	23	4	16
Life experiment	29	3	6	0
Total respondents	241	778	109	156

Table 3.1b Regular viewing habits for factual and reality TV by gender (Britain and Sweden, %)

	Britain		Sweden	
	Men	Women	Men	Women
News	71	60	88	88
Nature	39	34	16	13
Documentaries	16	22	9	12
Consumer	19	19	9	6
Reconstructions	13	17	7	7
Lifestyle	8	19	11	22
Current affairs	12	13	20	22
Reality game shows	6	17	10	17
Politics	14	10	9	7
Life experiment	6	16	2	2
Total respondents	1,991	2,327	436	497

pattern is repeated for most categories. What is striking is that the age profiles for reality TV indicate groups of non-viewers and viewers, with older viewers likely to be what we might call 'reality refusniks' (see later section).

The age factor can be further highlighted by comparing the most and least watched programmes across two age groups in Britain (using a mean from a five-point scale for high to low frequency of viewing). The top five most watched programmes amongst young adults (aged 16–24) were news (69%), undercover investigations (50%), observational documentaries (48%), natural history (46%) and reality TV (45%). The least watched programme was politics (18%). Older adults (aged 55–64) most watched news (76%), natural

Table 3.1c Regular viewing habits for factual and reality TV by education (Britain and Sweden, %)

	Britain				Sweden			
	Low	Med. low	Med. high	High	Low	Med. low	Med. high	High
News	69	64	66	68	92	81	93	90
Nature	37	37	37	37	24	12	18	7
Documentaries	22	21	21	17	10	14	12	8
Consumer	26	20	15	16	10	7	10	3
Reconstructions	20	16	14	10	6	9	9	3
Lifestyle	17	12	15	14	15	21	16	15
Current affairs	15	12	14	12	18	19	30	21
Reality game shows	14	12	12	11	12	19	11	8
Politics	12	9	12	14	10	6	10	6
Life experiment	12	13	13	10	12	11	13	10
Total respondents	357	890	813	987	196	324	183	215

history (58%), history/science (56%), observational documentaries (50%) and consumer programmes (45%). They least watched reality TV (14%). There is a group of traditional genres which all ages watch to varying degrees, but a clear division for reality TV, which many older viewers simply refuse to watch. We can read these results alongside the classification of public/popular factual genres as representative of changes within the quality standards of factuality. The reality refusniks are part of a group of older viewers who are aware of and buy into the media panic discourses discussed in the previous section. Reality TV represents all that is 'bad' about the restyling of factuality and therefore something to be avoided. This evaluation of reality TV by older viewers is strongly supported by the open question in the surveys, discussed in the second half of this chapter.

Gender differences are less significant than age. In terms of common trends across both countries, women were more likely to watch reality gameshows and lifestyle programmes than men (see Table 3.1b). In Britain, there is a gender divide with regard to the popularity of life experiment programmes, popular since the early 2000s, and often scheduled alongside lifestyle or reality genres. There isn't such a gender divide in Sweden, where this format has only recently been introduced. The most striking difference across both countries concerns news; Swedish women and men watch news to the same extent, whereas in Britain there is a clear gender difference. Looking more closely into this result by controlling for age, this is partly explained by the fact that older women watch less news in Britain compared to older women in Sweden. Although there are some interesting comparisons according to gender in viewing preferences, we shall see in the next section and later chapters that men and women tend to share similar value judgements about factuality, even if they are watching different programmes. There is awareness amongst male and female viewers of cultural discourses concerning public service factual content and commercial factual content, and an evaluation of factual genres that draws heavily on pre-existing categories.

In this section education has been used as an indicator of socio-economic status, as other indicators are not applicable in both countries. The general observation is that there are relatively few clear-cut differences between individuals with low (secondary school), medium (further education) and high (higher education) levels of education (Table 3.1c). Any existing patterns should be interpreted with caution since education is highly correlated with age, especially in Sweden. If programmes on nature or politics at first sight seem to be more popular amongst people with a lower education level in Sweden, this is not the case in the older population, which is more interested in these programmes in general. Controlling for the age factor, the only genre which seems to be related to education in a substantial way in Sweden is reality gameshows, which are less popular among people with higher educational levels than others. In the UK, the level of education seems most decisive when it comes to watching politics programmes, a more popular genre among people with higher levels of education, regardless of age.

Overall, age is by far the dominant differential in viewing preferences. The data highlights how assumptions about audiences, and their taste in television genres, are often based on readings of the programmes and ideological matters concerned with the construction of distorted representations of ordinary people (or the working class), and gender and identity (see, for example, Bell and Hollows 2005: 6–9). Whilst this is valuable analysis, it needs to be set against the viewing preferences for these programmes and the demographic makeup of the audience. Already we can see that an assumption that lower-educated groups watch more reality TV than others is too simplistic, and doesn't acknowledge the way reality TV addresses younger viewers and appeals to younger viewers with different educational backgrounds.

Public value

The association between public service broadcasting and the concept of the public sphere highlights the importance of PSB as a service for the public good. As we saw in the early part of this chapter, the evaluative connotations between public and popular are connected to public service and commercial factual content. The public value of factual genres is closely associated with the value of public service television, which has a formal duty to inform and educate viewers. One of the ways genres such as news or documentary can be judged by viewers is linked to their perceived importance on television. If a genre is considered to have public or social value, then it is important that it is shown on television, providing the audience with reliable information and knowledge. The public value test also works as a quality criterion, and viewers tend to associate news or documentary as quality genres and popular factual as lower quality genres. Research has shown the more entertaining a factual programme is, the less important it appears to viewers (Hill 2005). Swedish studies also show a strong positive correlation between trust in a medium and its perceived content of news and public affairs (Weibull 2004b; Westlund 2006). As there are other ways of assessing the value of factual genres, for example the 'watchability' of a genre, the emphasis on the public value, or the social importance, of various factual genres highlights the connections between factuality and public service broadcasting.

Respondents were asked how important they perceived it that various factual genres were shown on British/Swedish television. Figure 3.3 summarizes the value of factual and reality genres (the indicators of 'fairly' and 'very' important have been combined together). Two clear generic groups emerge. The first consists of news, current affairs, investigative journalism, political and consumer programmes, nature and documentary series, which between 63 and 99 per cent of respondents regard as important. The second group, which only one-third or less regard as important, consists of reconstructions, lifestyle programmes, reality gameshows and life experiments. The clustering of traditional factual genres as important and popular factual genres as not very important reveals a clear division between public and popular genres in both countries.

The difference between public and popular genres is even more striking if the indicator of 'very important' is isolated. The examples of two extreme

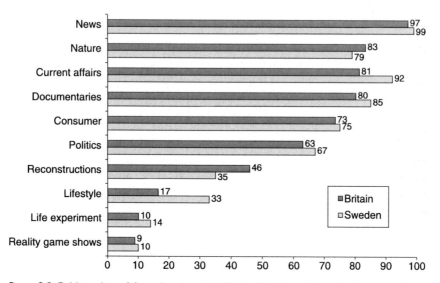

Figure 3.3 Public value of factual and reality TV in Britain and Sweden (per cent 'very important' and 'fairly important').

* British survey unweighted sample 4,516, Swedish survey unweighted sample 944.

responses for news and reality TV illustrate the high value accorded to a traditional public genre (over 80 per cent), and the low value accorded to a contemporary popular genre (less than 5 per cent). In both countries, there were views on the public value of news, which reflected the high status of the news genre in countries with strong public service broadcasters. It is notable that traditional factual genres, such as current affairs or political programmes, have a relatively average value when the statistics for 'very important' are isolated. Documentary also has a low value rating when 'very important' is isolated. Given that these genres are most associated with public service channels, it raises issues regarding the public value of these genres. News is the one genre which stands apart as publicly important to almost all viewers.

The dominance of the public/popular axis influences audience attitudes to programmes. Even when programmes cut across boundaries, such as lifestyle, they tend to be categorized as popular, and therefore less valued than other traditional genres. Some of the differences between Britain and Sweden are around popular factual genres, such as lifestyle and reconstructions. The differences are connected to specific production contexts in both countries (see Chapter 2). Overall, the evaluation of various factual genres as 'important' serves to underscore the dominance of pre-existing cultural discourses on public service broadcasting. It also highlights how audiences are aware of the restyling of factuality, and quality debates about the impact of reality TV on the standards of public service factual content.

The comparison between public value and frequency of viewing reveals interesting cultural trends. With the exception of news, regular viewing of all other programme categories remains fairly low in comparison with the perceived high value of these programmes. Current affairs, investigative journalism, political debates and consumer programmes are important genres that are associated with prestige, but this does not mean that they are regularly watched. The observation has been made for the same type of genres in the daily press, for example editorials and political comments (Nilsson and Weibull 2005). Lifestyle and reality gameshows function the other way round: they are watched more than they are regarded as important. In research on young adults and news in Holland, Costera Meijer (2006) observed a similar pattern in the high social value but low personal interest in news, and a high personal interest but low social value for reality TV. She calls this a 'double viewing paradox'. She argues that although television news has a high social status in Holland, and young adults expect news to address important issues, to be an important public service for knowledge provision, news is also something to be accessed from other sources, including peers or family members, as well as other media sources. Thus the importance of news is relative to its everyday presence in people's lives, and there is a sense amongst these young adults that if something important happens they will find out about it one way or another.

Comparative analysis between British and Swedish viewers shows common reference points, with only minor variations. The national differences once again indicate the high value of news and current affairs in Sweden. These genres are closely associated with public service channels, and perceived as threatened by commercial channels and counter-scheduling during peak-time (see Chapter 2). It may be the case that Swedish viewers feel it is more necessary to defend the public value of these genres in the face of commercial imperatives. In Britain, traditional factual is not immune from commercial pressures, but it is regularly scheduled on both public service and commercial channels, and in the case of documentary has attracted strong ratings. This production context is reflected in the broader range of factual genres valued and watched.

Age, gender and education

In terms of age, gender and socio-economic status, there are some differences in attitudes to public value, but these are not as pronounced as the age factor for viewing habits (Tables 3.2a–c). This shows common value judgements in Britain and Sweden. There are some variations across both countries. An important reason for these variations is age. Elderly people in Sweden rate most genres higher than the elderly in Britain. Current affairs stands out as one genre rated more highly by young and old in Sweden, and this relates to nationally specific debates about current affairs. In terms of gender, the connection between age and gender is also apparent; older women in Sweden generally rate news and current affairs higher than older women in Britain.

In terms of education, there are differences in attitudes towards the public value of traditional factual genres. Individuals with high levels of education,

Table 3.2a Public value of factual and reality TV by age (Britain and Sweden, %)

	Britain		Sweden	
	16–24	65+	16–24	65+
News	82	83	89	96
Nature	22	30	18	31
Current affairs	25	24	45	44
Consumer	27	24	20	32
Politics	17	21	25	26
Documentaries	10	10	15	10
Reconstructions	9	11	14	2
Reality game shows	6	1	10	1
Lifestyle	2	1	9	2
Life experiment	3	1	4	0
Total respondents	241	778	108	155

Table 3.2b Public value of factual and reality TV by gender (Britain and Sweden, %)

	Britain		Sweden	
	Men	Women	Men	Women
News	82	83	94	96
Nature	33	31	22	32
Current affairs	25	26	52	61
Consumer	23	26	26	36
Politics	24	20	27	37
Documentaries	9	13	12	22
Reconstructions	7	9	5	8
Reality game shows	1	2	3	4
Lifestyle	1	2	4	7
Life experiment	1	2	1	2
Total respondents	1,991	2,327	434	488

Table 3.2c Public value of factual and reality TV by education (Britain and Sweden, %)

	Britain				Sweden			
	Low	Med. low	Med. high	High	Low	Med. low	Med. high	High
News	77	80	87	88	92	94	98	97
Nature	26	29	36	36	29	24	30	30
Current affairs	21	23	27	33	43	50	69	71
Consumer	28	24	23	21	30	29	36	34
Politics	17	18	22	30	24	23	39	50
Documentaries	11	10	11	11	17	18	16	19
Reconstructions	12	7	6	6	6	8	5	5
Reality game shows	2	1	1	2	3	5	3	2
Lifestyle	2	1	1	2	3	7	6	6
Life experiment	2	1	1	1	1	3	1	2
Total respondents	345	883	813	985	195	319	182	212

in particular university degrees, rate traditional genres such as politics programmes and current affairs as more important than those with lower levels of education (Table 3.2c). The pattern is the same in both countries, the correlation between education and evaluation being slightly higher in Sweden. These two correlation patterns also remain if age is taken into account. Other patterns found in Table 3.2c are weakened or broken when the age factor is brought into the analysis. What the results indicate is that education and age play a part in attitudes towards traditional factual genres, such as politics, but not when it comes to popular factual genres, where opinions remain similar no matter what the educational background of the respondents.

Finland

For comparison, another country with a similar broadcasting structure to that of Britain and Sweden is Finland. In an online survey similar results were found for the social value of news, documentary and reality TV, highlighting the dominance of cultural discourses regarding public service broadcasting and commercial television. This survey was part of a national study of the production and reception of *Big Brother* (Aslama forthcoming). The survey was placed on the website for TV3, the most popular website in Finland and also the channel that shows *Big Brother*. A total of 1,745 people responded to the self-completion questionnaire (see Appendix). The sample was not representative of the Finnish population as there was a high proportion of female respondents (1,419 females, compared to 312 males). Nevertheless, it provides a useful comparison with Britain and Sweden regarding general attitudes. The same questions were used in this survey as those in the British and Swedish surveys. However, rather than a full range of programme categories, only three genres were identified with the questions: news (*uutiset*), documentary (*dokumentit*) and reality TV (*tosi-TV-ohjelmat*).

The results are very similar to those of the British and Swedish survey, with a public/popular scale applied to factual and reality genres. An overwhelming majority of the sample regarded news as very important (92 per cent). The figure rises to 99 per cent if we combine the categories of 'very' and 'quite important'. Finnish respondents had very strong feelings regarding the social value of news, similar to Swedish respondents. Documentary was placed in the middle of the scale, with 56 per cent claiming it was very important. A further 38 per cent thought documentary was quite important, making a much higher rating overall (94 per cent). This suggests that although documentary does not incite such strong feelings as news, it is still socially valued by Finnish respondents. As expected, reality TV was at the bottom of the scale, with 7 per cent claiming it was very important. A further 20 per cent claimed it was quite important, suggesting a slightly higher social value accorded to reality TV than in Britain and Sweden. However, the high proportion of female respondents, who are also those viewers most likely to watch reality TV, would be a major factor accounting for such a difference. To re-enforce the low social value of reality TV, 73 per cent of the sample claimed it was not important whether it was shown on television.

There were few differences according to gender or age, despite the high proportion of female respondents. For example, 97 per cent of males and females thought news was very important. The same number of men and women aged under 25 (99 per cent), 25–44 (99 per cent) and over 45 (100 per cent) agreed on the social value of news. With regard to documentary, the only difference was that women were more positive towards this genre than men, with 62 per cent of women compared to 46 per cent of men claiming documentary was very important. In terms of age, this was most apparent in women aged 25–44 (58 per cent of females, 46 per cent of males). Attitudes towards the social value of reality TV were similar across gender and age, with some slight variations. For example, 24 per cent of males and 19 per cent of females thought reality TV was very important.

Information/entertainment

Another way viewers categorize factual genres is according to axes of information and entertainment. The categorization of factual genres maps onto the value accorded to these genres. Thus, news is categorized as important and informative, and reality gameshows are categorized as not important and entertaining. Some genres, such as nature series or lifestyle, are located somewhere in between both value and categorization.

Figure 3.4 outlines the common patterns, with news categorized by almost all respondents as informative and reality gameshows as entertaining. The results highlight extreme ends of a fact/fiction scale used by viewers (Roscoe and Hight 2001; Hill 2005). The results are very much in line with respondents' rating of importance: information = important, entertainment = not important. There were a number of respondents who categorized traditional public service genres such as current affairs or political debate programmes as both informative and entertaining, which may reflect the use of different stylistic techniques in current affairs, and the performance of politicians in

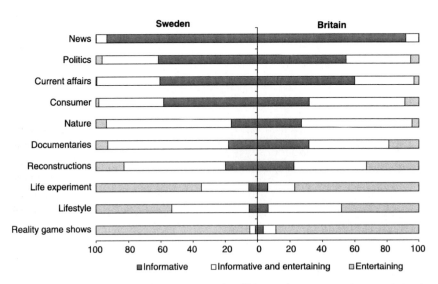

Figure 3.4 Categorization of factual and reality TV as informative and entertaining in Britain and Sweden (per cent 'informative', 'informative and entertaining' and 'entertaining').*

* British survey unweighted sample 4,516, Swedish survey unweighted sample 944.

debate programmes (see later chapters). Documentary and reconstruction programmes were primarily categorized as a mixture of information and entertainment, which given the content of these programmes is not surprising. Lifestyle programmes were a genre which respondents could not agree on, with the same numbers categorizing it as informative and entertaining, and purely entertaining. This is related to the popular makeover formats of many lifestyle programmes (see Dover and Hill 2007).

There is a connection between particular genres and communicative forms, in particular investigative approaches to society, more observational approaches to everyday life, and constructed or staged approaches to real people and their experiences. Thus, connections between genre, communicative form and categorization are consistent across public and popular value factors and genre evaluation. The almost identical responses for both countries signal how powerful the traditional axes of public and popular, information and entertainment are as framing devices. The historical context to broadcasting in both countries does mean there are differences in the production histories for factual programmes and in the development of specific genres, such as documentary. These differences in production contexts impact on the genres available and viewing profiles for specific genres. However, there is little difference in the categorization of a range of genres as informative or entertaining, or both. British and Swedish audiences are confident in using traditional categories for evaluating genres. The classificatory practices of viewers indicate a high degree of repetition, and also shared understanding of pre-existing categories and value judgements. In the next section, public/popular values also feature as a means to classify factuality. The qualitative data shows some variation within classificatory practices, picking up on the variations according to age and viewing preferences in the survey results.

Defining factual TV

To highlight the connections between classificatory practices and the evaluation of factuality, this section of the chapter analyses audience definitions of factual television. As Waterton suggests, the 'construction sites' for classification can reveal 'tacit understandings, conceptual frameworks, and inclusions and exclusions that underpin a classificatory scheme' (2003: 113–14). Definitions of factual TV underscore audience understanding of this kind of content as public service broadcasting. The conceptual framework outlined in this chapter for public service and commercial broadcasting underpins the classificatory schemes for factuality. Significantly, the inclusion and exclusion of certain factual and reality programmes shows how viewers are dealing with the restyling of factuality, and attempting to map factuality as they understand it and also as they would like it to be understood by other viewers and programme makers. The age factor that was so prominent in viewing preferences also features as a marker in different classifications of factual TV by younger and older viewers. There emerge two kinds of viewers, reality refusniks, who feel reality TV is a no-go area, and contemporary viewers, who are living in a cosmopolitan factual television environment. This suggests different degrees of engagement with the restyling of factuality, and viewing experiences for news, and other traditional factual genres, and more popular factual ones.

The question 'what is factual TV?' is not an easy one to answer. Some people rely on programme titles, listing one or many as representative of what factual TV literally is to them as viewers. Others offer abstract, often philosophical discussion of what factual means in terms of truth, facts and objectivity. Programme examples can be used as evidence for or against the abstract notion of factual TV. Indeed, when factual TV is an ideal form of audio-visual documentation it can be difficult to find concrete examples that meet this ideal. Viewers provided articulate, detailed, sophisticated, passionate responses, as well as the exact opposite. In the questionnaire, respondents were given an open question, asking 'what do you personally consider to be a factual television programme?' The majority of respondents gave detailed answers, offering examples of factual programmes to help explain their personal definitions. Most respondents approached the question with an abstract concept of factual television as a public service genre. Therefore the common way of defining factual television was to consider what factual ought to be, and reflect on particular programmes that met personal criteria. Although the criterion of public and popular features largely in the classification of factual TV, other concepts emerge, such as truth or knowledge. These defining characteristics for factual television are very powerful in shaping audience understanding of factuality, and will feature in discussions in later chapters.

Idealists

One pattern to emerge was the idealist, or traditional factual viewer. This type of respondent is typified by this quote: 'If it's not true it's not factual' (male, aged 65+, Socio Economic Status (SES) C2). The apparent simplicity of the statement barely masks a complex set of philosophical questions – factual is categorically truthful, but what is truth and what is fact? And yet, there is something powerful and attractive to viewers in this kind of simple statement, where the ideal concept of truth is used to answer the question. Many respondents in the surveys defined factual television as truthful *and* informative, for example: 'factual means that the programme will contain facts and no fiction. Programmes that are true and about real issues' (female, aged 35–44, SES C1). This coupling of two abstract concepts together makes a strong union of ideals. Truth and information matter to viewers and factual TV is one form of culture that promises to exemplify these ideals. Information is closely connected to objectivity, another core ideal for factual content.

For example, factual TV is 'any programme that deals with verifiable facts or opinions backed with evidence' (male, aged 25–34, SES C1). Reality is another ideal ingredient for factual content. As this respondent explained, factual TV is 'a programme based on real people, real events, real places' (female, aged 35–44, SES C1). Or as this respondent put it, 'my definition would be not made up, but something based on things which have happened or are happening' (male, aged 25–34, SES C1).

Traditionalists

Another type of viewer is the traditionalist. A traditionalist would typically respond with the answer 'News'. Older respondents were most likely to use traditional factual genres as examples for what factual TV meant to them. For example:

> News and current affairs, history (non-dramatized), science, natural history (male, aged 55–64, SES DE).

> (1) News, (2) Investigations of *real* events (no added features) (female, aged 65+, SES AB).

> News and documentaries are factual to my way of thinking (male, aged 65+, SES AB).

All three examples explain factual as traditional public service content. This content is commonly associated with the BBC, but viewers also mean public service content on any channel, for example Channel 4 news.

In Sweden, traditional viewers are also closely connected with the PSB. Whilst in Britain, older viewers commonly watch the BBC, and the channel profiles show an average age of 45–55, the commercial channel ITV, and to a lesser extent Channels 4 and Five, attracts older viewers as well. However, in Sweden older viewers tend to watch SVT (with a profile of 50+), a mixed age range watch TV4 and a mainly younger age group watch all other commercial channels. Channel evaluation is therefore also linked with genre evaluation, and age is a key factor in different attitudes to both. The kinds of programmes used as examples of factual TV in the Swedish survey are news (*Rapport, Aktuellt*), investigative documentaries (*Kalla fakta, Uppdrag Granskning*), social debate programmes (*Debatt*), all of which are PSB programmes.

Reality refusniks

There is a connection between the traditionalist and another type of viewer, the reality refusnik. News, current affairs and documentary (all with some exceptions) are concrete examples of 'quality' factual content, which viewers will also characterize as truthful and informative, objective and real. But, this content is becoming increasingly vulnerable to other kinds of popular factual, or non-fiction, content. For idealists and traditionalists, news and current affairs and documentary are threatened species of factual television, and need to be protected at all costs. The reality refusnik is the conservationist of the factual broadcasting environment.

Respondents who could be categorized as reality refusniks gave passionate responses to the question of defining factual TV. These illustrative examples highlight the way many respondents drew a line between traditional and more popular content:

> One which gives straightforward facts and information to the viewer. News and current affairs are obvious examples. I would also include natural history, science and history programmes. I would not include programmes such as *Wife Swap, Pop Idol, Big Brother* (female, aged 55–64, SES AB).

> News, documentaries and educational programmes. Such things as game-shows, so-called reality programmes, docusoaps, chat shows and most audience participation programmes which are clearly not fiction I would put in a third category: entertainment (male, aged 35–44, SES DE).

> Factual TV is the opposite of fictional TV. Examples include news programmes, discussion, scientific and real life stories. I suppose that dreadful genre of reality TV falls into this category but I instinctively resent that (male, aged 35–44, SES AB).

The final quote contains a note of anger towards popular factual programmes. Many older viewers were angry towards reality TV and its unwelcome intrusion in the broadcasting environment. These examples illustrate the intense feelings of reality refusniks:

> Thousands of so-called reality programmes. These are devastating television programmes to the detriment of viewing. It is a descent into the pit (male, aged 65+, SES AB).

> (1) Programmes made cheaply involving members of the public, mirroring Andy Warhol's 15 minutes of fame. I would not consider watching such drivel. (2) Programmes presented and compiled about events in history or immediate interest. (1) is rubbish, (2) is often very worthwhile (male, aged 45–54, SES C1).

> Factual programmes are those which convey factual explanations, historical facts, current events, discussion of subject matter. Note I do not count reality programmes as factual. They are unscripted fiction, carefully chosen individuals are put into false situations and fed stimuli and change whilst watched (male, aged 45–54, SES C2).

Repetitive use of negatives such as 'drivel' and 'rubbish', and the emphasis on traditional factual as the opposite of reality TV, makes the reality refusnik's position loud and clear. It is perhaps the most common position the public take towards reality TV, and in this project, as in previous research, even reality TV viewers tend to agree with this description of it as rubbish (Hill 2005).

The position of the reality refusnik is also the most common public position adopted in the press, and in televised and/or public debates. For example, at the Edinburgh Television festival (2005), the news presenter John Humphreys criticized reality TV and its detrimental effect on news and society in general in much the same way as these viewers. This defensive position is one that dominates debate on factuality, and is vocalized by many social and public commentators. Many older viewers also take a defensive position and, along with idealists and traditionalists, represent a highly influential group whose opinions are well known to other viewers. Those viewers who evaluate factual television as truthful and informative, and not popular, who count news and documentary but not reality TV as factual, are those who most influence others in their evaluation of factual, and who are most clear in the division between the public and popular. In the section on viewing trends, the people who watch and value news, current affairs and politics programmes are likely to be older, and more highly educated, than other viewers. They therefore represent an influential group of factual viewers who help to shape generic discourses and socio-cultural values.

Contemporaries

Those viewers who watch a range of factual genres, including popular factual, can be characterized as contemporary viewers, in the sense that they have knowledge of a fairly wide variety of news, current affairs, documentary and popular factual genres. These viewers tend to be younger, aged 16–45, and more likely to be female, which matches the viewing trends for these genres. Some contemporary factual viewers will rely on a hierarchy of genres, as also used by traditionalists. So, they will define factual as news, but also refer to some popular factual programmes. These quotes illustrate the range of genres included in contemporary factual viewers' definitions:

> Anything that is about things or events that have actually happened or about real people, so everything from the news and *Panorama* through sport, wildlife programmes to the docusoaps and reality TV (male, aged 16–24, SES AB).

> Whatever the subject it is true not false – news, documentary, fly on the wall, educational, reality, makeover, current affairs, political, consumer (female, aged 45–54, SES DE).

> Documentary, the news, arts programmes, current affairs (as long as opinion is kept out), historical documentary, docusoaps, consumer programmes, reality programmes – mostly factual! (*Big Brother, Wife Swap*, not *Pop Idol*) (female, aged 25–34, SES C1).

Most of these examples echo points made by traditional factual viewers, including ideal concepts of factual as 'true not false', programme examples that begin with traditional factual genres, and a discerning eye regarding different kinds of popular factual that can be included in the category. What makes them different is the reference to popular factual genres as well. The range is therefore one that embraces the whole factual family (with some exceptions).

There are other groups of viewers who include seemingly everything they have watched on TV. Some examples show just how wide the definition of factual can become:

> Documentaries – *The Abyss, Life of Mammals*, fly on the wall – *The Salon*, police programmes – *Crimewatch*, reality – *Big Brother, I'm a Celebrity, Get Me Out of Here* . . ., makeovers/home programmes – *Changing Rooms/Property Ladder*, news and features – *Sky News/Countryfile* (female, aged 16–24, SES AB).

> Reality TV – *Big Brother, Wife Swap, Salon*, documentaries and news – *Panorama, News*, factual/real lives – *Life of Grime*, crime documentaries, factual entertainment – *Ready Steady Cook, Flog It*, quizzes – *Countdown, University Challenge* (female, aged 35–44, SES C1).

This can also work in reverse. A minority of viewers, especially younger in age, referred to a narrow range of programme titles, for example: 'I think the following are factual programmes, *Big Brother, Wife Swap, Airline* – all news programmes' (male, aged 25–34, SES C2), or '*Big Brother*, any news programme' (female, aged 25–34, SES C2). Some just referred to popular factual only – 'Programmes like *Big Brother, Pop Idol, I'm a Celebrity* . . ., *Fame Academy* (female, aged 25–34, SES DE).

In Sweden, a similar pattern emerged. Many younger respondents in the survey were often eclectic in their examples, covering programmes within the reality TV genres (e.g. *Nanny-akuten, Robinson, Top Model*). The listings likewise appeared less hierarchical for many of the younger respondents, with programmes and genres often appearing in no discernable order, whereas for example news programmes appeared to be top of the hierarchy for older respondents and were often listed first. Reality gameshows such as *Robinson* and *Big Brother* were commonly listed among the two youngest age groups, and almost absent from the listings of other age groups. This matches the British data, and indicates there are patterns of viewing whereby older groups purposively do not watch popular factual programmes, whereas younger groups are more familiar with a range of genres, although commonly watch popular ones.

Along with familiar categories, respondents also referred to 'reconstruction' programmes, 'discussion' programmes, 'saving buildings' programmes, 'orchestrated factual' programmes, 'proper' documentaries, 'real people' programmes, 'real life TV', 'real time TV', 'how to' programmes, 'airport', 'animal' programmes, etc. Respondents also defined factual television in relation to specific channels, e.g. Discovery, and presenters, e.g. David Attenborough. A minority of respondents also included sports, weather, docudrama, quiz shows and talkshows in their definitions of factual television.

Despite their broad generic knowledge, this group of predominantly younger viewers does not appear to have significantly different value judgements. In previous research, reality TV viewers were acutely aware of the social stigma of watching 'trash TV' (Hill 2005). The common value judgements associated with reality TV as 'just entertainment' have a significant impact on the way viewers evaluate factual genres and report on their viewing habits. They undervalue popular factual despite its presence in their repertoire of factual genres. Why this is the case is partly to do with the dominance of socio-cultural values associated with public service factual genres and their importance in television broadcasting. It is also the case that popular factual viewers are the least vocal about the values of these genres, and also the most vilified in the press and in scholarly research. They are a group which has minimal impact on common value judgements concerning factual television. Their personal preferences for popular factual are rarely taken into account, except in general laments on the seemingly never-ending appetite for formats such as *Big Brother* or *I'm a Celebrity* . . . and yet they are the very people who are watching a range of factual genres. The contemporary factual viewer is engaged in the changes taking place in factual broadcasting, and the generic cross-fertilization that dominates peaktime schedules.

Conclusion

Genre evaluation is a significant strategy in understanding factual television. In an increasingly complex generic environment, viewers turn to the process of categorizing and judging factual genres according to personal preferences, aesthetic issues and socio-cultural values. Factual genres are cultural categories that are mapped by viewers across public and popular axes. The public/popular divide is closely associated with other value judgements, such as public service/commercial, information/entertainment, and is the framing device for understanding factual television. News and reality stand apart from all other genres at extreme ends of a public/popular axis. News is publicly important, reality gameshows are not. News is informative, reality gameshows are not.

The way viewers categorize and value factual and reality programmes highlights the importance of public discourses on television, and pre-existing attitudes towards television contexts and genres.

The concepts of public service broadcasting, and public and popular culture, used to frame general attitudes towards factual television programmes is distinctive in countries that have an historical commitment to strong public service providers. There is an expectation in both Britain and Sweden that to regularly watch news is a good thing and to regularly watch reality TV a bad thing. This is particular to Northern European countries, as similar findings can be found in research in Norway (Hagen 1994), the Netherlands (Costera Meijer 2006) and Finland (see this chapter). Research in other countries suggests there can be quite different evaluations, for example in Estonia, Bengtsson and Lundgren (2005) found that viewers valued commercial programming more than public service broadcasting. Thus, the perception and experience of public service broadcasting is dependent on the political, social and cultural context for public service and commercial content. In Britain and Sweden, audiences are very conscious that they should be watching public service factual content, that such content has been produced for their own good, and that they will be good citizens if they engage with public genres that are part of the knowledge project of television. Thus, tacit understanding of public service factual content as socially acceptable, a healthy aspect of a media diet, is part of the evaluative process for factuality.

Perhaps one of the interesting points to emerge from the research is that despite the social importance of traditional factual programmes, they are not necessarily watched by viewers. Popular factual genres are not regarded as socially important, but they are watched by large numbers of viewers. The discrepancy between the ratings profile for news and reality TV and the self-reported viewing preferences in this chapter indicate that something is amiss in the viewing practices for factuality. This is even more pronounced when comparing age differences in viewing habits and profiles for public service and commercial channels. For example, this viewer explains: 'I have a group of nonsense and nice entertainment, more like brain dead . . . stupid programmes but nice to have on in the background. Well then we have . . . more adult programmes maybe, like well moms and dads watch.' There emerge distinct patterns of viewers, with older viewers likely to favour traditional factual genres, to be reality refusniks, and younger viewers likely to favour a range of genres, in particular popular factual ones.

The rise of reality refusniks is a strong sign of just how far the restyling of factuality has become part of audience understanding of contemporary factual television. These are influential viewers, taking a leading role in cultural discourses for factual genres. They are viewers who reinforce the public service credentials of news and current affairs and documentary at a time when these credentials are being questioned and re-evaluated in the contemporary climate for public service broadcasting. In their definitions of factual TV as truthful, informative, as signifying ideal values, these viewers reinforce a sense of public service broadcasting as enlightenment, and through their definitions of factual TV define public service broadcasting as for the public good (Syversten 2004). The emergence of the contemporary factual viewer is another sign of the restyling of factuality. These younger viewers have a double understanding of public service broadcasting as both for the public good and as a public service. Thus news and current affairs and documentary are socially important, part of the knowledge project, and they are also something to be accessed when viewers feel like it, a service they wouldn't want to be without, but which they can tap into then they need to. Although reality refusniks have taken a position on the restyling of factuality, it is contemporary factual viewers who are the most engaged in the changes taking place. They are caught up in the evaluative process for a mixed range of genres.

Chapter 4

Genre work

'I am not exactly one hundred per cent sure why they are what they are, but they are what they are.'

There are conscious and unconscious ways of responding to factual genres. Viewers carry with them a great deal of prior knowledge, such as past experiences of watching television, reading newspapers and magazines, listening to the radio, accessing websites, or mobile content, chatting with friends and family. At the point of reception, viewers immerse themselves in the experience of watching a specific factual programme, and this prior knowledge mixes with the present experience and transforms into something else. Factual genres are often called 'leaky genres' because they are porous, absorbing other generic conventions, mixing with other kinds of media content, running off in various creative directions. However, it is viewers who are absorbing and flexibly responding to generic material; they are part of the power of factual genres. When viewers watch, talk about and reflect on factual content, they are adapting the basic elements of genres into something far more powerful than their original component parts. Viewers are alchemists, transforming factual genres from audio-visual documentation into cultural and social experiences.

Genre work involves multiple modes of engagement. It is the work of being both immersed in watching a genre, and reflecting on this experience. The term is a play on dream work, a psychodynamic term that describes the processes involved in gathering psychic material, and recounting and interpreting dreams, in order to better understand the relationship between our unconscious and conscious selves. For Bollas (1992), dream work is a never-ending process where we dream work ourselves into becoming who we are, thus connecting psychoanalysis and self-experience. Genre work also refers to the psychoanalytic term 'working through', used by Ellis to explain the way television processes the material world into narrativized forms (2000). The idea of genre work is used to better understand the audience as responding to factual content on conscious and unconscious levels. In this chapter genre work is examined in relation to the mapping of factual television programmes. Viewers position factual programmes in various clusters, associating some programmes with news and information, and others with popular genres and entertainment. However, in the act of mapping factual programmes viewers highlight how they are not always sure why certain programmes go with others, and how they change their minds about the relationship between factual programmes and genres. Thus, the act of classification highlights the conscious and unconscious ways viewers are working through what is factuality. Another aspect of genre work is analysed in the reflections of viewers on themselves. This self-reflexive aspect of audience responses illuminates the relative distinctions between being a news and current affairs viewer, a documentary viewer and a reality TV viewer. The intense self-criticism that is a feature of a reality mode of engagement signals a problem for viewers in working through hybrid genres. When viewers see themselves in the act of watching this is a powerful part of the processes of genre work, where they reflect on their feelings and experiences as an audience.

Between fact and fiction

The rational individual is an important part of thinking behind the 'public knowledge project' and notions of the public sphere. This focus on rationality foregrounds conscious thought processes. A more psychodynamic perspective foregrounds the unconscious aspects of the individual, and the often confusing, repetitive and contradictory ways individuals experience the self. Such a perspective draws on theory and clinical practice in psychoanalysis. The unconscious refers to a space in the human psyche where memories, feelings, fantasies and motivations remain hidden, trapped or repressed inside the self. Being aware of the unconscious dimensions of the self can help in the development of the conscious self: 'the unconscious is formed through social experience and in turn shapes human action' (Lupton 1998: 28). A psycho-dynamic model places emphasis on the irrational self, subjective rather than objective experiences and contradictory responses, all of which are part of viewing practices. This approach is not only connected to individuals, but also groups of people and collective experiences. The psychoanalyst C. G. Jung called the relationship between the individual psyche and a more sociological or cultural unconscious the 'collective un-conscious' (1978).

In his book *Seeing Things* (2000: 75), John Ellis argues that we live in an age of uncertainty where broadcasting 'imbues the present moment with meanings'. In Western societies, the age of uncertainty is characterized by shifting sites of production and consumption, by changing and multiple identities, social inclusion and exclusion, multichannel television and audience fragmentation. In terms of broadcasting, the media has moved from an era of scarcity where public service broadcasters and a handful of commercial channels dominated national broadcasting, to an era of plenty where viewers can choose from multiple channels and platforms. Television's role in the age of uncertainty is to provide 'multiple stories and frameworks of explanation which enable understanding and, in the very multiplicity of those frameworks, it enables viewers to work through the major public and private concerns of their society' (Ellis 2000: 74). Television does not offer certainty, but the means by which viewers can work through the confusion of modern life.

The term 'working through' explains the way television makes and remakes meaning. Ellis takes the term from Freudian psychoanalysis:

> It describes the process whereby material is continually worried over. Freud, in coining the term, describes it as the boring part of the analytic process from the analyst's point of view. The subject of the analysis has undergone a revelation, witnessed something in the psyche that had hitherto remained shrouded. For the analyst, positioned outside the emotional force of the revelation, this is enough. . . . But for the subject, it is another experience entirely. This new revelation lies behind all kinds of resistances, and so has to be integrated with existing understandings and feelings. . . . So, the subject keeps returning again and again to the revelation, turning it over and over. Television finds itself in a similar position. It works over new material for its audiences as a necessary consequence of its position as witness.
>
> (Ellis 2000: 79)

We should not see the process of working through as a simple action whereby television makes meaning out of a confusing situation. Rather, television worries over, repeats, re-interprets and narrativizes people, events and experiences on a daily basis, sometimes offering explanations, but more often not.

It is the repetitiveness of the act of working through which makes it a necessary part of broadcasting in an age of uncertainty. A news programme will use the same structure day after day; it will have a presenter, journalists, headlines, reportage, it will offer information, commentary, speculation, and it will do so on different issues. Thus, news works through material that is similar but not always the same, and allows viewers to witness this on a daily basis. Documentary 'assembles fragments of evidence from the world' and 'attempts to organize a coherent explanation or investigative structure' (2000: 117). The viewer comes to the documentary genre with their own knowledge and experiences, they 'bring their own analytic frameworks to bear' when watching these programmes (ibid.). Ellis points toward open narrative forms, such as soap operas, where characters are involved in ongoing narratives with no clear endings. He reminds us that discontinuity is a common part of broadcasting, where adverts, programme and series breaks segment the schedule on an hourly basis. Television is a form that tends towards 'uncertainty and openness', and it offers a 'relatively safe area in which uncertainty can be entertained, and can even be entertaining' (ibid.: 82).

Although the process of working through can be a positive aspect of television's ability to witness the world, it also highlights several problems within contemporary television. Ellis points out that changes in the provision of public service broadcasting, in particular its ability to speak to and for a wider community, has led to a loss of contact with the public. The community of understanding that Ellis sees as so important to working through becomes at risk to fragmentation, and loses its social role as a witness for the public, or loses its objective status, framing certain events from the point of view of compromised witness with a particular agenda. Thus, working through is not always a benign process. Corner comments on the need to distinguish between different aspects of working through, that witnessing fits into several cognitive frameworks (2001). He argues that the psychosocial profile of television offers various experiences related to the social or political world, and also to more mundane or everyday matters. The quieter moments of television when we 'judge ourselves to be OK' are moments that don't 'cost us much sleep' (ibid.: 559). These different aspects of working through will feature in the rest of this chapter as viewers reflect on the relative differences between working through news, documentary and reality TV, where television news is a particular kind of device for witnessing that seems quite far removed from the highly mediated, witnessing device of reality TV.

Post-Freudian psychoanalysis offers another useful perspective on working through and audiences. In *Being a Character* (1992), Christopher Bollas considers the relationship between psychoanalysis and self-experience. He takes Freud's theory of dream work in *The Interpretation of Dreams* (1909) and relates it to identity work. Dream work is when an individual takes images, ideas, actions, and so forth, as the basis for dreams, transforming everyday experiences into unconscious thoughts. Dreams are how we express ourselves in our unconscious. We collect psychic material throughout our waking experiences and condense it into dreams. Dream work is therefore the process of collecting psychic material for dream experiences and also reflecting on what dreams mean to us in our consciousness. For Freud, dream work describes the work of the analyst and patient, and is a progressive clinical process which can lead to a 'cure' for the patient. For Bollas, dream work is something we are all engaged with, and is a never-ending process where we dream work ourselves into becoming who we are. This kind of thinking on dreams is related to the work of Jung (1978: 3), whereby dream work is an ongoing process where we explore the messages from our unconscious and continually reinterpret and make sense of ourselves: 'dreaming has meaning, like everything else we do.'

Bollas places great importance on the moment between waking and sleeping as a powerful space for dream work. He explains:

> In the dream I am simultaneously an actor inside a drama and an offstage absence directing the logic of events. At the heart of self experiencing is a type of unconscious reflexivity, achieved through the psychic division of labour characterized by the dreamer's two essential positions. . . . Deeply inside the dream, I am . . . absorbed in this hallucination . . . at times, however . . . I very slightly withdraw my fully subjective participation in the dream and glimpse myself as this drama's protagonist. When this occurs I bear witness to myself.
>
> (Bollas 1993: 13–14)

The psychic space we create when dreaming allows us to both experience the dream and at times witness ourselves in the dream. This is a moment when neither fully awake nor in deep sleep we can influence our subjective self. There are two modes of engagement: 'The simple experiencing self and the complex reflecting self enable the person to process life according to different and yet interdependent modes of engagement: one immersive, the other reflective' (ibid.: 15).

Bollas argues that these modes of engagement can also happen outside the dream world. The space between waking and sleeping when we bear witness to ourselves is also a space we occupy on a day-to-day basis when we encounter objects and experiences that become part of our psychic genera. Referring to the psychologist Winnicott, Bollas calls this 'intermediate space': 'the place where subject meets thing, to confer significance in the very moment that being is transformed by the object' (ibid.: 18). For example, when we encounter objects, certain objects mean more to us than others; they might evoke previous experiences, connect with friends or family, or even become part of our dreams, so that the next time we see such an object it carries psychological baggage. The moment of transformation when the object is no longer just another object but is psychically connected to us is a moment when we enter intermediate space, both experiencing the moment and reflecting on what it means to us.

The idea of dream work, as characterized by Bollas, is similar to the notion of working through. However, whereas working through describes the state by which we worry over and return to experiences in order to make sense of them, dream work implies that we are always working on our psyche and that we never fully make sense of our self-experiences. We can apply the idea of dream work to the work of watching factual genres. Prior to the experience of watching factual genres, we have already collected generic material that will become part of how we experience a particular programme. After the viewing experience, we will consciously and unconsciously store generic content and experiences in a holding area, ready to be drawn on at certain moments in our lives. Genre work is therefore the process of collecting generic material for viewing experiences and also reflecting on what genres mean to us. Genre work is an ongoing and fluid process, where we explore the messages from factual content and experiences in order to continually reinterpret and make sense of ourselves. At the heart of genre work is the double role of the audience as viewer and interpreter. We experience watching the news, and at the same time notice ourselves watching the news. We can be deeply immersed, and at times we can also slightly withdraw from full participation as a viewer and glimpse ourselves as the audience. Just as Ellis argues that television witnesses the world, and we witness television's representations, so too do we bear witness to ourselves as viewers. Similar to dream work, genre work is a never-ending process where we genre work ourselves into being viewers.

Factual programmes are particularly rich areas of analysis for genre work because they occupy an intermediate space between fact and fiction. Adding another level of interpretation to genre work, we can experience watching real events in a documentary and at the same time reflect on the authenticity of what we are watching. The experience of watching a factual programme can feel like being in a dream, working through what is real or not, occupying a space between fact and fiction. This is where the viewer participates in the constructed real world of the programme and also reflects on the nature of this real world and how it has been staged for us to watch. Being a factual viewer means taking on multiple roles, as witness and interpreter, and occupying multiple spaces, between fact and fiction. The intermediate space of factual genres is transformative, and at times we will personally connect with something in a programme, reflecting on what that person or real event means to us, creating a powerful self-reflexive space. The intermediate space of factual genres can also be troubling, a negative experience that challenges viewers to address their personal motivations for watching different kinds of factual content.

In the rest of this chapter, empirical evidence is used to explore genre work from the point of view of audiences. The classification and evaluation of different types of factual genres leads to an awareness of different modes of engagement, modes that are both immersive and reflective. Taking Ellis' idea of working through and the confusion of broadcasting in an age of plenty, contemporary viewers of a range of factual genres are confused by the changes taking place within factual programming. Especially in relation to reality TV, viewers describe themselves as watching a bad dream, trying to work out what is real or not in the topsy turvy world of reality entertainment. Many viewers feel uncomfortable when they witness themselves watching reality TV. This is a strong sign that some reality formats occupy a troubling intermediate space between fact and fiction that is unsettling to audiences. Audience research is therefore used as a means of examining how genre work is a challenging experience for viewers who are caught up in the restyling of factuality.

Working through factuality

Genre work takes place in conscious and unconscious moments; viewers know about genres, but don't always know why a genre can be classified or evaluated in a certain way. As one viewer explained: 'I am not exactly one hundred per cent sure why they are what they are, but they are what they are.' Corner argues that documentary aesthetics takes its bearings from 'inside the documentary experience, with its distinctive mix of objective and subjective dynamics' (2005: 56). The value of documentary aesthetics, and analysis of the pictoral, aural and narratological aspects of documentary, lies in a 'reflexive commentary on some of the most important things to be explained' (ibid.). Different factual modes of engagement draw from the distinctive aesthetics of these genres, and also the objective and subjective dynamics of genre work. Thus modes of address connect to modes of engagement. The work of audiences of news and current affairs, documentary and reality TV goes some way towards explaining what is important about these genres.

Birgitta Höijer (1998b: 176) explores how psychodynamic processes are 'embedded in cultural discourses' and 'include a mental room in which the never-ending task to build bridges between our cultural and individual identities takes place'. In her research she shows how viewers identify genres, position themselves as an audience, and at the same time experience conflict or inconsistency in their responses. She argues that viewers live with these contradictions and that they 'are natural parts of our understanding of ourselves and the world' (ibid.: 179). A psychodynamic perspective provides a 'frame of reference for understanding basic dilemmatic aspects of audience reception and for understanding the different functions that different genres have for the audience' (ibid.).

The empirical research referred to in this chapter draws on an open question (hand written) in the surveys, a game using programme titles in focus groups, visual clips from programmes, and probing questions about how to define particular factual categories. Much of the material in this first section is taken from the game, where respondents positioned programme titles into clusters according to their own personal criteria. The game was especially significant to the emergent concept of genre work as it allowed room for the process of mapping factuality, where programmes shift position, moving this way and that depending on a viewer's knowledge of factual television, their personal value judgements, and their awareness of how other people mapped their programmes. Many respondents changed their mind about how to map the various programme titles on the table in front of them, looking to see how their fellow respondents explained their factual maps, and as they talked through their own factual maps, making changes along the way. Thus, the outcome for the game wasn't nearly as important as the process of play-ing the game, and their responses helped to show the conscious and unconscious ways viewers are working through their understanding of factuality.

Most viewers have a genre map in their head. For some, this map is relatively clear and easy to read; it contains familiar areas, no-go areas, as well as territory in between. For others, this map is moving, and shifts positions depending on changes in the generic environment. One response is to locate genres according to pre-existing knowledge and experience, and also respond to changes along the way. Common genre maps created by viewers are often based on generic techniques, such as the way different factual genres report, document and construct real events. Another way of mapping factual genres is to rely on an information/entertainment axis, with adjustments for new developments and alternative modes of address. Yet another is to create new categories that respond to perceived changes in factual programmes. These strategies are part of genre work, where in the act of classification viewers reflect on the meaning of factual genres and try to understand the essentially contradictory aspects of representations of reality.

The following extract is from a discussion by a group of viewers (aged 30–35, SES C1). This example highlights the idea of working through, as discussed by Ellis (2000) in the previous section. It shows how working through is made up of different parts, and that viewers are aware of the relative separation between different ways television is a witnessing device. There are different processes at work in defining news and current affairs, documentary and reality genres:

INTERVIEWER: What is it about a programme that makes it news?
ELEANOR: It's today's events. . . . Informative, hopefully.
IAN: Serious. Genuine.
ELIZABETH: Non-fictional.
SHAUN: Not trying to entertain.
ELIZABETH: But they are.
SHAUN: Well, are they? Well, but they shouldn't be, in a way.
ELIZABETH: It's reporting on certain areas, like, you know, politics.
SHAUN: Well, there is a difference between *BBC News* and something like *Newsnight*. Or *Channel 4 News* is what we have . . . it's almost more like a Sunday newspaper. It has a particular topic, and opinions around that topic, as opposed to a straight news programme, which is just the headlines, followed by sports and weather.
INTERVIEWER: What is it that makes something a documentary?
KARL: It's documenting particular aspects of the world. That's a documentary.
SHAUN: Yeah, in a general sense. Not as something that's particularly exceptional, that's happened.
IAN: A documentary doesn't need to be a current event to qualify.

ELEANOR: And it is all about one subject. For a long time it is reporting on one subject.

INTERVIEWER: What is it that makes a reality TV programme?

ELIZABETH: It is a recreated scenery, and something unfolds in real time, but it's not a real situation.

SHAUN: Yeah, the ones that are on now are formula programmes. But I think when it started, reality TV wasn't like that necessarily. It was more like just a type of documentary making. It was very much based on observation, and now it's much more structured and it's more, like, deliberately made entertaining.

KARL: Humiliating the sort of people in it.

STEPHEN: People trying to act normally, on purpose.

SHAUN: They're acting. It's not actually real.

The description of news as serious, genuine and informative locates it within pre-existing categories and values regarding the news as a public service. As the discussion develops, there is a questioning of the informative function of news, a comparison with different kinds of news bulletins and other news sources. News that is entertaining is criticized for being similar to the Sunday newspapers, something to consume in your spare time. Documentary received little discussion, pointing to its apparently simple function as documenting the world. Yet, when the discussion moved to reality TV, there is a connection with documentary and its part in early reality content. The description of reality TV as 'recreated scenery' encapsulates an awareness of cross-pollination between factual and reality genres, and fact and fiction.

Working through is a process that allows viewers the opportunity to change their minds, or revisit an idea. It is a somewhat messy process, where repetition and variation work together in the viewing experience. Taking Bollas' (1992) concept of dream work as part of self-experience, the processes of collecting generic material and reflecting on them is a never-ending one. When viewers are working through factuality they do not necessarily have an end in sight, a fixed point where the work will be finished. This can be seen most clearly in the way viewers map factual programmes, not always sure why they cluster certain programmes with others, and changing their mind about the positioning of certain factual programmes in the process of mapping. This example is taken from the game used during the focus groups. Participants were asked to take a variety of programme titles which reflected the full range of programmes in each country and cluster them according to how they felt they went together. This 21-year-old male writer grouped his titles into discrete categories that formed a wheel of factual genres. As he put together the wheel on the desk in front of him, other participants kept glancing over at his categories; as he described the reasons for the groups of programmes people started to change their own formations. His explanation is quoted below:

I've noticed now actually that there is a general divide as well which . . . tends to be more of an entertainment one, but this tends to be more information. . . . So, I've started with basically the straightforward live news coverage, just presenting facts as directly as it can. . . . Then, news and current affairs but more opinionated, they're debate programmes, like *Horizon, Panorama*. Then I've got this sort of tight interactive section . . . *X Factor, Big Brother*, they rely basically on viewer participation as much as watching. . . . You've got your more prepared stuff, sort of almost documentary, but they're not as interactive . . . your *Apprentice*, and your *Faking It*, and – actually, no, you've not got your *Apprentice*, that might be a – but never mind . . . your *Airport* and, but there tends to be a lot more, like, human aspects, and, like, watching *Supernanny*, watching people in their life. And then it tends to get a bit more lifestyle-ish, like . . . it's starting to get *What Not to Wear*, and *Jamie's School Dinners* and *Changing Rooms*, and all that stuff. But it's still, like, a prepared thing, and you just watch it, you don't vote or anything like that afterwards. And then, it jumps straight on to the long-term, I guess, documentaries and they're meant to stay. And they're the nature ones . . . *Pet Rescue* and the like I put in its own category. . . . So, it's kind of supposed to be a scale, but there's a bit of a flaw here actually . . . I think this pile [pets], actually [hushed laughter] . . . erm, yeah, it goes there [paper rustling].

The circuitous way he explained the programme clusters illustrated how the wheel created on the table in front of him altered as he talked through the groups. News, current affairs and debate programmes posed little problem for him, but reality gameshows and talentshows became an entirely new category ('interactive') after debate programmes, showing a connection to public participation programmes as well as interactive elements within reality formats, and general social debate on high profile reality shows. 'Prepared programmes' were 'almost documentary', and lifestyle came in between prepared and documentary programmes, which showed the human interest link across all three clusters. Certain kinds of generic material mean more to him than others. The interactive and prepared programmes point to contemporary, constructed and formatted popular factual content, whereas documentary is here to stay, it has longevity in the cycle of factual genres. He changed pet programmes at the last minute to place them in between documentary and natural history. In all probability, this viewer would have changed things again – where would he move *The Apprentice*? His prevarications are a natural part of working through factual genres, and to shuffle programme titles from one generic group to another, or move groups slightly one way or another, is exactly what viewers do on a day-to-day basis. His uncertainty about particular programmes is also something experienced by many viewers who aren't always aware of why they have responded in certain ways.

There are many examples of viewers working through factual genres during the act of classification. For example, this viewer began with a fairly traditional definition of factual programmes, but as she worked through the definition it changed to include a broad understanding of non-fiction television:

> Factual programmes should be those that deliver knowledge such as on Discovery Channels. Programmes such as nature series. Documentaries based on real events, even news could be considered factual, or DIY shows. In fact, any programme that reflects any real life situation is factual. *Top of the Pops* gives factual information about chart music (49-year-old British female consultant).

Another example highlights how hybrid genres resist categorization. This Swedish viewer worried over the term docusoap used in Sweden to refer to reality entertainment:

> Documentary portrays reality to the viewers then . . . *Idol* or *Expedition Robinson*, there you're supposed to get a picture of what is real, but it's an edited reality. Well it's called docusoap, documentary soap, soap opera, they are contradictions in terms, soap opera, documentary, so it's, well . . . like documentary shouldn't be there, that word (26-year-old Swedish male student).

Both viewers illustrate the uncertainty of working through what factual means to them. Although factual TV can be a simple definition for some viewers, as we saw in the previous chapter, the term also can be rather troubling, and these viewers begin to reflect on the intermediate space between fact and fiction in the act of classification.

For Bollas (1992) the intermediate space between consciousness and unconsciousness is a potentially transformative experience. If we take the idea of intermediate space and apply it to the spaces in between fact and fiction, then the hybridity that is so much a part of the changes taking place within factual television becomes an important focus of attention. When viewers reflect on the restyling of factuality in their discussions of various factual programmes and how they are part of a genre map, they touch on the transformative elements of an intermediate space. For example, this 23-year-old male shop assistant created new categories as a result of working through changes within factual genres:

> It's quite new categories here. I've categorized them quite specifically. To start with we've got the kind of ultimate reality television, like the originals like, *Big Brother*, *I'm a Celebrity . . .*, *Celebrity Love Island. . . .* Then I have *Faking It* out on a limb of its own, because I can't really place

it anywhere, and then we've got kind of lifestyle pushing programmes like *Supernanny, Wife Swap* and *What Not to Wear*, so these kind of social judgement programmes. *Plastic Surgery Live*, again couldn't place it. . . . And then we've got kind of late-night informative *Independent, Guardian* reader, kind of, *Crimewatch, Tonight with Trevor McDonald* and *Newsnight*. Followed by the trashy kind of eight o'clock rubbish that people just have on in the background, it's more entertaining than pushing a life-style: *Changing Rooms, Holidays from Hell, Pet Rescue* and *Airport*. And then the news programmes: *BBC News, 10 O'Clock, Sky News, Channel 4 News*. And then we've got *Walking with Cavemen*, kind of wildlife programmes that almost have an air of fantasy as well. People like to look at that, they can look at the world. *Panorama* and *Horizon* I think are real kind of heavy-going documentaries. Could go in to the *Crimewatch* pile but I think they are lower level. *Gardener's World* and *Antiques Roadshow*, simply because they're a real kind of cultural presence in the UK. They are two programmes that set that kind of real middle-class, conservative culture. Then *What the Victorians Did for Us* and *Jamie's School Dinners*, I think are kind of a new style of documentary, kind of like *Big Brother* meets *Panorama*, if you will. And that's it! Quite a lot of categories . . .

His confident explanation of the different clusters of programmes shows how aware he is of their changing status. His categories include 'ultimate reality television', 'social judgement programmes', 'trashy eight o'clock rubbish', all of which encapsulate his perspective of popular factual. Similarly, documentary gets broken down into 'heavy-going', 'fantasy' documentary, and a new style of documentary altogether – *Big Brother* meets *Panorama*. The last example reads like a film pitch, and it is precisely his in-house knowledge of factual programmes that enables him to creatively describe the topical, observational, constructed nature of *Jamie's School Dinners*. And yet there are also categories he found difficult to place, programmes such as *Plastic Surgery Live* that are out on a limb, resisting categorization. This rich discussion of the changes taking place in factual television illuminates the complexity of working through genres, where a chaotic mix of various different generic material is being collected by viewers on a day-to-day basis. Viewers process this generic material, making existing and new associations, adding personal meaning to the material, and in doing so are playing a part in the transformation of factuality.

Viewing modes

In this section genre work is considered in more detail in relation to clusters of programmes. Whilst audiences experience factual television as a whole, responding to the various different categories as part of non-fiction broadcasting, they also have distinctive modes of engagement for genres. This section draws on the immersive and reflective modes of engagement that Bollas argues are central to dream work: 'the psychic space we create when dreaming allows us to both experience the dream and at times witness ourselves in the dream' (1992: 18). The moment when we reflect on ourselves in the act of watching television is something explored in the qualitative research as a viewing mode that is both immersive and reflective. This aspect of genre work is helpful in highlighting the conscious and unconscious ways we deal with being a factual television viewer. There are relative distinctions between watching news and current affairs, documentary and reality TV, and these distinctions emphasize how viewers perceive themselves in positive and negative ways depending on their generic mode of engagement.

In research on Swedish viewers and everyday life, Bengtsson (2002) talks about the uncomfortable TV viewer. She points out that much research on television audiences has overemphasized the pleasures of watching television, underplaying the negative feelings, such as insecurity or guilt, that can arise from media experiences. Work by David Morley in the 1980s looked at the 'guilty pleasures' of watching television in the afternoon rather than getting on with household and family chores (1986). In a study of media and everyday life in Britain, Gauntlett and Hill found viewers felt guilty about watching television when they should be doing something more useful; so for example people in early retirement restricted their television habits so that they did not fall into bad habits, the fear of becoming a coach potato uppermost in their minds (1999). Bengtsson adds to this research by highlighting how people in her study did not want to be perceived as 'TV viewers', that there was a social stigma to being labelled as such in Swedish society. These viewers saw watching television through the lens of 'the cultural value of work' (2002: 227). They draw on a Protestant work ethic that is highly valued in Western Protestant societies such as Sweden or Britain. They also draw on the value of work in industrialized societies, where work has become a major part of people's sense of self – what some researchers call 'identity work' (see Giddens 1991, amongst others). With this context in mind, Bengtsson says 'watching television must have particular valuable direction to be accepted . . . which might be one explanation of why news, and other programmes with an orientation towards information, are much easier to legitimize than programmes more orientated towards leisure' (2002: 227). The uncomfortable feelings that arise from watching television are not uniform across all ages or social groups, with children, for example, happily watching lots of television compared to their parents.

In this section the idea of the uncomfortable viewer is explored in relation to genre work. That moment of genre work when viewers witness themselves watching television is significant to the reflexivity of media experiences. On the one hand, there is greater social and cultural value accorded to news and current affairs or documentary viewers, than reality TV viewers. It is therefore in the interests of viewers to overemphasize the legitimacy of watching certain kinds of factual genres connected with the 'public knowledge project'. There is an underemphasis on any value in watching reality TV, and within the framework of factuality reality TV is perceived as a 'waste of time' in the public knowledge project. If viewers were reflecting on watching reality TV in relation to entertainment, we might find different evaluative connotations, although the social stigma of reality TV is strong no matter what framework it is situated in (see Biltereyst 2004 for discussion of media panics in relation to reality TV). However, there is something about watching factual television that adds another layer of uncomfortable feelings for viewers. The challenge in responding to weighty generic material within non-fiction programming is that it confuses boundaries between fact and fiction, making the reflections of viewers bound up with the difficulties in responding to representations of reality. Thus, the reflections of viewers change depending on the kind of genre they picture themselves in the act of watching. Their reflections also change depending on the topic being represented within various factual genres. So, watching news may be a legitimizing act, but watching news of the London bombings in 2005 may be more complicated, and may bring about positive and negative associations.

News modes

Compared with other factual genres, news is something viewers recognize as all around them, available at fixed marker points throughout the day on broadcast television and radio, and via morning and evening newspapers, and always available on rolling news channels and internet sites. In this sense, viewers are working through news on a daily basis. News modes of engagement are based on a general familiarity with the genre in everyday life, and an awareness of its role in providing regular information on what's going on in the world. Most viewers know what news is, and have little difficulty in categorizing and evaluating it as a genre. But most viewers also know there is something more to news, that its presence in our lives is not only practical, but also emotional and psychological. In terms of genre work, viewers describe themselves as immersed in news, absorbing information and stories in a repetitive manner. When they reflect on themselves watching news, they mainly refer to its constant presence in their lives, a presence which can be reassuring and also anxiety inducing. When a major news event occurs, such as the London bombings, many viewers described the obsessive manner in which they immersed themselves in news. News genre work highlights the deeply immersive modes of engagement for this genre, and also shows awareness of our need for news, even if we are critical of it.

Michael Schudson, in *The Power of News*, argues that what makes news so significant to modern public consciousness is that it is a form of culture. We can better understand news if we recognize the production of news as the cultural production of public knowledge (1995: 2–3). He explains:

> news . . . is produced by people who operate, often unwittingly, within a cultural system, a reservoir of stored cultural meanings and patterns of discourse. . . . News as a form of culture incorporates assumptions about what matters, what makes sense, what time and place we live in, what range of considerations we should take seriously.
>
> (Schudson 1995:14)

The cultural processes of news production are part of the wider sociological processes of everyday life. If news is a form of culture, then viewers are part of this cultural process. When people watch the news, they also make value judgements about when news matters, how to make sense of it, and whether it should be taken seriously. The production and reception of news is part of news as cultural discourse. Schudson suggests that the producers of news are schizophrenic, believing in the ideals of news and its public and social value, and also recognizing the realities of news production and the difficulties in achieving such ideals. Rather than characterize this dual role as schizo-phrenic, another approach is to consider the immersive and reflective modes of engagement with news.

As Scannell has pointed out, it is the daily broadcasting of news that makes it so significant to our everyday routines (1996). This 45-year-old male primary school teacher explained: 'If I've got time I watch the six o'clock news and I watch the London news afterwards. . . . Sometimes I watch the 10 o'clock news and then later on I put on the BBC news programmes. . . . I tend to watch a lot of news, maybe I'm a bit nervous, I want to assure myself what has last happened and why.' The assurance of news in everyday life is part of what makes the genre so familiar and integrated into daily routine: 'There's something quite nice about that 10 o'clock slot, you can put your mind to rest and let go of the day' (36-year-old female social worker). The 24-hour news channels and websites also contribute to the familiarity of news, providing a constant reminder of the genre and what it stands for. The sense of news as always there can be reassuring but at the same time anxiety provoking. Silverstone (1994: 16) has suggested that news 'holds pride of place as the genre in which it is possible to see most clearly the dialec-tical articulation of anxiety and security – and the creation of trust.' For Silverstone, television is a transitional object, which is a term used by the psychoanalyst Donald Winnicott to explain the way certain familiar things can reduce anxiety, or can be a 'security blanket'.

Rolling news sites also point to changes in the genre and an increasing need to provide breaking news. As this viewer explained: 'It just keeps rolling, regardless whether there's news or not. It's always there. And if you walk in the door and you go 'what's the score last night?', 'did anything blow up in the Middle East?', you go to it, you feed off it' (38-year-old female office assistant). Another viewer explained: 'I always like to cross-reference with what other stations are getting at. You get some that are more accurate . . . and you get others where you've got much more choice, and you know it will be biased' (49-year-old female teacher). Both of these examples highlight the repetitive accessing and cross-referencing of news stories. The metaphor of feeding implies nourishment, in that viewers can feed off different stories and sources, but it also implies that news feeds into people's everyday lives like an intravenous drip. As Höijer (2000) has suggested, this can create a push–pull situation where some viewers don't want to know about negative news stories, and yet they feel a deep need to watch the news so they know what is going on.

An at times obsessive accessing of news mirrors the communicative mode of news to constantly update audiences. Ekström (2000) outlines three general modes of communication in television journalism. He calls these modes information, storytelling and attraction, and uses the metaphors of the bulletin board, bedtime story and circus performance to explain the journalism strategies in various news reportage. In relation to feeding off news modes, audiences will foreground the informative mode, but this can also crossover into other modes. For example, a major news event can be attractive to audiences because it presents information within a strong story-telling mode. Many respondents talked about the constant presence of news during the terrorist attacks in London on 7 July 2005. The repetitiveness of the news updates led to a constant accessing of news, providing a source of reassurance and anxiety in equal measure. One viewer explained his reaction to the news coverage of the London bombings:

> The repetition of it is strange, in a way. When it happened I turned the news on and they were reporting what had happened and then they were just reporting it again and again and again, every two minutes . . . until there is something else. It does give you that sense of 'it's still happening, it's still happening', but it just happened once. They just keep reporting the same news until more happens (21-year-old male artist).

The feeling that something is 'still happening' is very compelling during events such as this. Another example shows the power of news in connecting viewers with what is happening on the ground:

> Sky News or London Underground website, or BBC or whatever, they would kind of, you know, keep checking. Keep bringing it up, you know, just to see if there were any incidents on the underground or bombs or transport difficulties. So, there was that kind of like, constant alert-ness. . . . And then that whole flurry, you know, as soon as something happened, mobile phones were coming out, you know, you'd be ringing

round, your family, your friends: 'are you all right?', this may be happening, that may be happening. So, that whole sort of thing of instantaneous news and checking things out, and almost before it was news wanting to know and communicate with people (56-year-old female librarian).

I think, it's a similar thing, but it's going back to 9/11. I'm just reflecting on what she said. After 9/11, there's a kind of 'everything can happen in the next five seconds' (41-year-old male financial consultant).

Memories of 9/11 mix with the experience of the London bombings and highlight a 'constant alertness' to news production and reception practices. The emotional force of this news coverage is underscored by the need to share the experience, 'wanting to know and communicate with people'. Once again, there is reference to the total immersion in news, and its power to transform the appearance of time so that 'everything can happen' in no time at all. These kinds of news events can seem like a nightmare experience, one that viewers repeatedly re-experience in the never-ending cycle of the news stories.

Viewers can be both critical and uncritical of news, at times accepting its primary function to inform and at other times critiquing its portrayal of events. In Höijer's research using a survey and interviews with Swedish viewers, she found that news was perceived as 'real', with a focus on information, and although viewers criticized news items, none questioned its reality status (2000: 196). For a few viewers, especially younger adults, little distinction was made between different kinds of news – 'I've got the news pile' (19-year-old female sales advisor). For others, a distinction was made between news and entertainment, or sports news. Some commercial channels were known to viewers as providing news, but not as they knew it. For example, TV3 news in Sweden was perceived by viewers as tabloid, and therefore at the borders of the news genre: 'God, like TV3 news, that's difficult, is it news or not?' Lots of viewers adopted a tabloid and broadsheet distinction when describing the difference between news bulletins on different channels. For example, one viewer explained: 'Well, I suppose I am fairly addicted to Channel 4 News. I think that's a different class from any of the news' (56-year-old male researcher). He was critical of other flagship news bulletins from BBC and ITV precisely because they were 'tabloid': 'they've become really patronising soft entertainment, delivered by people with inane grins.'

It is also the case that viewers are aware of the influence of news on other genres and vice versa. The aesthetics of news, and perceived changes within news bulletins, were especially noted by older viewers who objected to stylistic trends. In one focus group discussion of viewers aged 40–55, criticism of the intense graphics used in news – 'things are moving, maps are going and the weather chart is going' – led one male viewer to reflect on how these aesthetics dilute the witnessing function of news:

It's mad. To me *that* is reality TV. I don't know why we call this other stuff reality TV, because it has got nothing to do with reality TV. But when you see television regularly, it happens really rarely, when you see an interview or something conducted by somebody really perceptive, really intelligent, and you feel a witness to something that television allows you to witness, that's when it's really, really a fantastic medium.

There can be no more perjorative term than reality TV, but for this viewer it signifies how news can witness reality, and has the potential to give viewers a rare feeling of witnessing an event for themselves. It is what Corner refers to as the 'see it happen' function of news, a promise that the genre struggles to deliver as the 'look' of news is one of fragmentary narrative (1995: 75). Once in a while, 'television allows you to witness', and news is the primary genre for this. However, the term reality TV also signifies how news has been 'tabloidized' for popular audiences, where the style of news takes over news content.

News is connected to other factual genres. As one viewer explained:

I keep changing them around [laughter] while I hear the others talking about them. Erm, for me, *Sky News, Panorama, ITV News, Tonight With Trevor McDonald, BBC 24* are all sort of about what's going on in the world. So, they belong to one category for me. And *Channel 4 News*. I have difficulty with *Jamie's School Dinners* and *Horizon*, because I think they're also about what's going on in the world, but they kind of blur into documentary (60-year-old male design consultant).

They adopt a broad umbrella approach to news, clustering all different kinds of news on broadcast and satellite channels along with current affairs strands, and specific documentary programmes about topical issues in science, health or education. These programmes all feel like news, they are about 'what's going on in the world'. Perhaps, this phrase, more than any other, sums up news modes of engagement, where audiences turn to news on a regular basis to know what is going on in the world. Despite criticisms of news provision, and a perceived overemphasis on style, it is the significance of news as something we immerse ourselves in on a daily basis, which fulfils a deep desire to know what is going on, that makes it so powerful a genre.

Documentary modes

Audiences have a general understanding that this genre is based on a degree of fact, and documents the world, to a certain extent and under certain conditions. The large range of documentaries, including investigative journalism, specialist documentaries on history or science, observational documentary, or docudrama, makes it difficult for viewers to adopt a single mode of engagement. The various stylistic techniques used within different types of documentary, such as the interview, eye witness testimony, caught on camera footage, reconstruction, also add to the ambiguity associated with documentary. It is more useful to think of documentary as a genre that requires multiple modes of engagement. Documentary genre work highlights how viewers quickly switch between various modes, reflexively responding to the intermediate space of fact and fiction that is such a feature of this genre.

Documentary films share certain characteristics that make them a genre, but also can be divided into different, sometimes overlapping, modes. In his overview of documentary, Bill Nichols (2001) suggests there are six primary modes of documentary film making: poetic, expository, observational, participatory, reflexive and performative modes. Each of these modes has a distinct set of characteristics that come from a particular time and place of documentary film making. For example, the observational mode 'emphasises a direct engagement with the everyday life of its subjects as observed by an unobtrusive camera' (34), and can be located historically in particular documentary films made in the 1960s, known as direct cinema, or cinema verité.

For Nichols (2001: 40), 'documentaries invoke a desire-to-know' (epistephilia). However, such a desire to know is bound up in more complex modes of address and engagement. When we watch documentary 'we bring an assumption that the texts, sounds, and images have their origin in the historical world we share', we expect documentaries to have an 'indexical relationship to the events they represent (2001: 35).' But at the same time we understand that the evidence used in a documentary has been re-presented to us, 'that the film as a whole will stand back from being a pure document or transcription of these events to make a comment on them, or to offer a perspective on them' (2001: 38). If we extend Nichol's argument about documentary modes to television viewers, there would be a common relationship between viewers and documentaries based on an assumption that the programmes use facts to tell us something. This comment from a viewer illustrates the general way documentary appeals to its audience: 'I have what I would call the looking at something, they look at something that you don't know about, and it's fairly objective documentary . . . *What The Victorians Did for Us, Walking with Caveman*, wildlife, *Life of Mammals*' (60-year-old male design consultant). Documentary television can also be broken down into different modes, for example investigative documentary, or observational documentary (see Chapter 2). A general expectation about documentary television does not preclude different modes of engagement from the viewer. In fact, documentary viewers are fast on their feet, responding quickly and instinctively to different modes in any one programme or series. For example, the development of digital reconstructions in historical natural history documentaries (*Walking with Dinosaurs*) demands multiple modes of engagement as this is an historical drama documentary using expository and performative modes. Austen's research on documentary audiences highlights how contemporary documentary film and television mixes various modes, and viewers are aware of this (2007). For example, he argues that the film *Touching the Void* uses two distinct documentary modes; that of the reconstruction of a mountain climbing accident and accompanying interview material with those involved. He found in interviews with viewers that they negotiated the two modes in order to enjoy the film's dramatic storytelling, underpinned by authentic testimonial.

Most television documentary has undergone a dramatic restyling, often using a variety of techniques to tell fact-based stories. As this viewer explains, responding to the changing nature of documentary means opening up the term:

> I find it a bit hard to understand what documentary is because that concept has widened, the meaning of the concept has gotten enormously wide. So I was a bit confused when you said 'tell us some examples' [laughing], so I don't really know what it is, but I watch *Pop Idol*, does that belong with the documentaries? (41-year-old Swedish female project manager).

Her playful reference to a reality format indicates how documentary blurs boundaries with other popular genres. Another example illustrates this further:

> Right, I put news and news documentary stuff together in one group. Because it seems to be reasonably based on a degree of fact. That's probably a very contentious statement. . . . I watch a wide range of documentaries, I think, I feel there's a bit of a sort of crisis in style, there are still some magnificent documentaries that are made for grown ups, and there are also documentaries where the presenter really, really, really, gets in the way and there's intrusive music and intrusive facts and it seems to be a great ego trip. . . . I put *Walking with Cavemen* separately in its own category, because I think it was a documentary, but the special effects of *Cavemen* was so incredibly irritating, so that goes back to what I was saying, that documentaries just drive you crazy and you can't watch them (56-year-old male researcher).

The 'crisis in style' is connected to the sound, images, presenters and digital effects that bombard the viewer. It is also connected to the different documentary modes that overlap and confuse viewers. All these different modes can make for a frustrating experience – 'documentaries just drive you crazy' – and can lead to confusion about what constitutes contemporary documentary. His comments on news and documentary emphasize how audiences negotiate genres, adjusting their evaluation of genres, their classification of factual content, to address the restyling of factuality.

Documentary has always explored the borders between fact and fiction (Winston 1995). It offers an especially rich range of generic material for viewers to work with on conscious and unconscious levels. When watching documentary, viewers can switch between different modes, immersing themselves in the fact-based experience of a documentary, recognizing different documentary modes, such as exposition or observation, and adjusting their responses accordingly. They can also critically engage with the modes of address used with documentary, at times critiquing the various techniques used to communicate with viewers. But, there are also ways of responding to documentary that come from deep within the psyche. The uncertainty that comes with watching documentary is part of the process of 'looking at things'.

Reality modes

Audiences have a general understanding of reality TV's presentation of real people and their experiences in an entertainment frame. This creates a contradictory viewing experience. On the one hand, viewers criticize reality programmes for being sensational and staged. They criticize themselves for watching reality programmes, for consuming what they perceive as fast food television. On the other hand, there are aspects of reality TV they like. For example, the attractions of reality TV include crossing boundaries between fact and fiction, a playful approach to ordinary people and celebrities, the spectacle of negative emotions, the intensity of experiences. There are certain kinds of reality programmes that are perceived as 'good' because they are so 'bad', inviting 'a guilty pleasure' in watching them. And there are also certain kinds of programmes that are perceived as 'good' because they deal with particular issues in a way that viewers can relate to in their everyday lives. Reality genre work highlights the dreamlike quality of watching reality TV, and how viewers reflect on the lighter and darker sides of the reality experience.

In previous research I conducted on reality TV audiences (Hill 2005), the main finding was that viewers were like computer games players, in that they had learned to play the game of reality and expected the rules of the game to change on a regular basis. The other key finding was that viewers possessed a default critical mode when talking about reality TV, often criticizing the genre for being 'mindless entertainment', and criticizing themselves for watching it. There is a game-like quality to trashing reality TV. Viewers delight in coming up with different negative associations: 'car crash TV', 'tabloid TV', 'lowest of the low', 'brain dead TV', 'pastiche TV', 'prostitution TV', 'humiliation TV' are just some examples. The art of name calling is part of the reality TV game. There is 'downmarket' reality TV (*Celebrity Love Island*) and 'upmarket' reality TV (*The Apprentice*). There is 'ugly reality TV' (*Big Brother*) and 'not ugly reality TV' (*X Factor*). One viewer described a cluster of reality programmes as her 'fake group'. Junk food provided a common reference for reality TV. As this viewer explained: 'Reality TV, I get this ghastly feeling occasionally, you know, you just sometimes feel like eating a large bag of crisps and some bars of chocolate. It's junk food television' (56-year-old male researcher). For some reality TV viewers, it is appealing because it is junk: 'I like how inferior reality TV is.'

Alongside general criticism of the genre, viewers are aware of variations within popular factual programming. Given the large range of formats within reality TV it is hardly surprising that viewers make distinctions between different types of programmes. But what is distinctive to reality TV is the general feeling that most of it is 'crap'. For example,

> I divided them into three basic categories: crap I would never watch, crap I might watch, and then crap I would definitely watch. The last bit is actually stuff I actually quite like. So, the crap I would definitely not watch – *Big Brother*, an absolute load of bollocks. I mean, people are whoring themselves, which is why I don't like it. Anyway, crap I might watch – *Airport*, I can relate to it. And then, of course, there's the *X Factor*, *Supernanny*. I wouldn't want anyone to know this . . . but I actually watch that (33-year-old male student).

The three categories of 'crap' contain a range of titles. The first incite strong feelings towards the participants in reality gameshows, the second represent programmes about everyday things this viewer can relate to, and the third are examples of shows they watch but are embarrassed about. If all reality programmes are crap, then it is hard to justify watching them. By saying they are all inferior, this viewer is able to distance themselves from the genre, contributing to the dominant critical discourses surrounding reality TV. The fact that they watch some of this 'crap' is a sign they can differentiate between different kinds of popular factual content. This is a very common position for a reality TV viewer to take, dismissing the genre as a whole as low quality entertainment, but at the same time differentiating between good and bad programmes based on personal preferences (Hill 2005).

Another example highlights how differentiation within the reality genre is connected to identification with real people and their everyday experiences. If viewers can relate to people in certain reality programmes, then the way they perceive themselves and the viewing experience changes:

> *Celebrity Love Island, Big Brother, I'm A Celebrity* . . . they're kind of salacious. . . . I would use the word crap. I think the interesting thing about *Wife Swap* is that there is often something to learn from it . . . about the way relationships are and how people have them. And you have to look at your own behaviour in some ways. Although, it's meant to be entertainment. I mean, it is entertainment. And it is in these categories. I

slightly pulled it out, as I have *The Apprentice*. They're both salacious, they're both suspicious. But they both contain things about the ordinary drive of life. Ambition, envy, relationships. What actually does go on in reality in some people's lives. I think they're quite hard to dispose of as rubbish. . . . There is something to get from them (60-year-old male, design consultant).

For this viewer, most reality programmes fit into his 'crap' category. But a format like *Wife Swap* is difficult to dismiss as entertainment. The comment that 'there is something to get from them' is very important to what reality TV can offer viewers. The phrase 'the ordinary drive of life' sums up the potential of the reality genre to connect with viewers on conscious and unconscious levels. When viewers witness the 'ordinary drive of life' in reality programmes, they are immersed in the experience of watching and also reflecting on how this relates to them, storing information and ideas, collecting generic material along the way.

Reality viewers find themselves twisting and turning in their effort to make sense of things. The speed with which the reality genre keeps changing adds to the general confusion. The various different hybrid formats, and the additions within ongoing formats, mean viewers are subject to increasingly complicated generic content. For example, the 2006 version of *Celebrity Big Brother* in Britain contained a fake celebrity who went on to win the show. This is an example of production and reception working side by side; the producers add a new twist to an existing format, and viewers take it to the next level in the reality game. In terms of genre work, when viewers perceive themselves watching reality TV (there's me in front of the TV!), they can reflexively respond in positive and negative ways. The following discussion amongst a mixed-gender group of 30–40-year-old viewers illustrates the twists and turns that characterize reality genre work:

JOHN: I kind of like reality TV, but I think there's good reality TV and there's bad reality TV. Like, I love the *X Factor*, I'm totally addicted.

JACKIE: Absolutely. But then there was this terrible programme on Channel Five the other day which was called *Drastic Plastic*, which had the very extreme kind of plastic surgery. And I did think 'why am I watching this?' It's just the worst kind of car-crash television.

SHARON: Which is why you watch it.

JACKIE: Absolutely, I couldn't stop watching it, and at the same time I was seriously questioning my intelligence.

SHARON: There's one I regret not being able to watch, cos I think that was just the most fantastic concept, just the title of it, it was *Celebrity Shark Bait*. I thought that was absolutely genius . . .

ANGELA: *Plastic Surgery Live* . . . the way they've got regular people to sort of have cosmetic surgery there in the studio. . . . I just find it fascinating probably because it is other people having it done and it's interesting to see, you know, how far could you go? [. . .]

SHARON: There's almost a pleasure in being grossed out by something. It's a weird way of putting it, but there is always a sense of enjoyment, you know, why do we go on fairground rides when they freak us out, but there's enjoyment at it and I think certain people get a pleasure from watching those programmes, and they go 'oh, oh, that's horrible!' and they are kind of being pushed to the edge a little bit.

The opening statement about the quality of different reality programmes leads to an extended discussion about 'bad' programmes and what this says about reality viewers. Whatever is good about *X Factor* is lost in the quality debate. Some reality programmes have crossed the line. Indeed, plastic surgery was a common reference point for many viewers, who worried about the extreme lengths programme makers and participants were pre-pared to go to make factual entertainment. The feeling of 'being pushed to the edge' is partly to do with what makes watching reality TV exciting. *Celebrity Shark Bait*, where celebrities swim with sharks (under controlled conditions), is a good example of a format that plays with the attraction of some reality programmes to push social or cultural boundaries. There is also a way that reality TV pushes generic boundaries, taking viewers to the edge of fact and fiction. But whereas in *Celebrity Shark Bait* there is no real danger to the participants, there is a concern amongst viewers of the impact of these programmes on themselves and other people. There is a sense that when reality TV crosses a line, in terms of fairness or taste and decency, it pushes some viewers to the edge of their own personal boundaries.

In another example from a typical discussion on the reality genre, these viewers from a mixed-gender focus group (aged 30–40) explain the self-critical position of the reality TV viewer:

ALEX: *Big Brother*, I find it painful to watch. It's sort of like, brain rot. And I feel I'm just sort of wasting my life by sitting there and watching it.

ELIZABETH: But that's quite annoying, though, that you're actually wasting your life if you turn on the TV.

SAM: It's ironic because you're actually wasting your life watching other people do really ordinary things that you do yourself. It's really quite weird. The whole thing is a quite weird process.

EMMA: Well, we all have things that we are living for, a dream. And they're kind of just exposing them on TV, but . . . I don't know. I suppose it's like a mad dream, that they kind of try and achieve through telly.

The 'weird process' of watching reality TV is partly to do with the banality of particular kinds of content in series such as *Big Brother*, but it is also to do with the process of genre work. If the work of watching *Big Brother* doesn't seem of much value then it is difficult to explain why anyone would watch it. As the above quote suggests, the process of genre work makes viewers feel uncomfortable when dealing with reality shows. Participants in reality shows are also part of this 'weird process', attempting to realize their dream of becoming famous through a reality show. But this is a 'mad dream', played out on television, with the contribution of viewers to the final outcome.

Reality modes of engagement are perhaps best explained as dream-like experiences. Sometimes the experience of watching reality TV can be positive, but more often it seems like a 'mad dream'. Between fact and fictional genres, and the public and private, viewers are caught in intermediate space. Drawing on dream work, this intermediate space can be transformative, creating a powerful self-reflexive experience. The fact that many viewers feel uncomfortable when they perceive themselves watching reality TV is indicative that some reality formats have occupied a troubling intermediate space between fact and fiction that is personally unsettling to audiences.

There is a moral as well as psychological dimension to what is so unsettling for viewers. As this viewer explains, when watching reality TV, it brings out 'characteristics in humans which I don't think you should bring out' (23-year-old female, day care worker). The attraction to reality TV has a dark side, where viewers worry about a lack of morality in the programmes and criticize themselves for their own morally dubious position. As this viewer reflects:

> It's very ambiguous . . . I see it as a bad side of me that I enjoy watching people getting exposed to difficult things on *Robinson*, but it's part of an ambiguity and then the question is, those who produce this, those who get an enormous amount of money from licence fees among other things to produce TV, should they take advantage of this? Somehow I don't think they should take advantage of my bad side, because it's in all of us in some way, some little bit of malicious pleasure (31-year-old Swedish male sub-editor).

It is as if television producers are practising dark arts, taking viewers into uncharted territory. Jung (1978) refers to the shadow as the dark side of the human psyche. The shadow is the hidden part of the unconscious, something we try to ignore but which is a powerful aspect of ourselves. To be conscious of the dark side of the psyche is important for self-development. This viewer's reflection on his 'bad side' highlights how reality TV can be the kind of generic material viewers search for in order to explore the more troubling or negative aspects of their self-experience.

In another example, two viewers worry about the development of the reality genre, which they see as having reached the limits of the genre and the limits of moral values:

DAVE: I think it's gone further, actually. Perhaps it's gone more comedic, more freakish, more chaotic . . . a lot more painful, actually, and that's where watching really . . . you know you just think, 'well that's not me' or you think 'actually that's me but worse' . . . and I think that's why people watch it, because it changes for the worse.

RACHEL: I think there's something a little bit worrying about reality TV itself. I mean if you take *Big Brother*, for example, it does cross the boundaries every year, you can see steady continual things getting a bit more . . . on-edge, it makes you feel like 'oh, maybe we shouldn't be watching this' or 'maybe we shouldn't be broadcasting it'. It's about identity isn't it, *Big Brother* as well, we watch it, we can remember these characters who we can identify with . . . or maybe they're characters we don't want to, we hate them because we can see a bit of ourselves in them . . . and I think, . . . where is TV going to take us?

The earlier discussions regarding 'bad' reality TV take on a moral dimension. What is so painful about watching certain kinds of reality programmes is how viewers feel bad about themselves and the choices they make. On the one hand, such criticism of television production is a useful way to place the blame on someone else. On the other hand, the self-reflexive aspect to criticism of reality TV is part of a general soul searching amongst viewers and their understanding of themselves.

Conclusion

Genre work is the process of collecting generic material for viewing experiences and also reflecting on what genres mean to us. It draws on the idea of dream work (Bollas 1992). It involves immersive and reflective modes of engagement. We experience watching the news, and at the same time notice ourselves watching the news. We can be deeply immersed, and at times we can also slightly withdraw from full participation as a viewer and reflect on the experience. Just as Ellis (2000) argues that television witnesses the world, and we witness television's representations, so too do we bear witness to ourselves as viewers. Genre work takes place in conscious and unconscious moments in our lives; we know about genres, but don't always know why a genre can be classified or evaluated in a certain way. Uncertainty, or prevarication, is part of genre work. It is connected to what Ellis calls an age of uncertainty, where broadcasting in a multichannel environment bombards us with images, sounds and information that we cannot fully process. Genre work is one of the ways audiences process the knowledge and experiences represented on television and also the relationship between these representations and viewers' own knowledge and experiences. The processes of genre work are not always clear, indeed they are often ambiguous, and they are related to different kinds of genres and representations that engender multiple modes of engagement and experiences. Genre work also is a never-ending process, an integral part of being an audience.

There are different modes of engagement with factual programmes, what we might loosely group as news, documentary and reality modes of engagement. Viewer work across these different modes, sometimes drawing on other viewing modes from fiction along the way. All these modes of engagement involve some form of seeing, listening or witnessing, and reflecting on this. The experience of watching a factual programme can feel like being in a dream, working through what is real or not, occupying a space between fact and fiction, participating in the constructed real world of the programme, and also reflecting on the nature of this real world and how it has been recreated for us to watch. Being a factual viewer means taking on multiple roles, as witness and interpreter, and occupying multiple spaces, between fact and fiction. The intermediate space of factual genres can be transformative, and at times we will personally connect with something in a programme, reflecting on what that person or real event means to us, creating a powerful self-reflexive space. When viewers watch, talk about and reflect on news, documentary and reality TV, they are transforming the basic elements of genres into something far more powerful than their original component parts.

The relative differences within genre work highlight the complexity of the psychosocial profile of television and its audience. The witnessing function of television is both something audiences see as objective and also something they see as subjective, so that witnessing is a multilayered process leading to different degrees of trust or distrust in the viewer. Responses to different kinds of factual genres connect with distinctive modes of engagement, news modes producing greater trust than reality TV for example. There is a certain uneasiness in fully trusting television as a witness, one that is most obvious in the uncomfortable experiences of some reality TV viewers, but is also detectable in some discussions of news and certain kinds of documentary. Viewers' awareness of the restyling of factuality has had an impact on their trust in television as a device for witnessing the world. They negotiate the generic changes taking place within various factual programmes, having to adjust their evaluation of a genre and its factual properties. Viewers' criticism of the 'crisis in style' in news, or documentary, indicates their increasing frustrations with television as a tricky witness, for example that certain kinds of political news stories have a hidden agenda, or that historical documentary is overly concerned with dramatic effects. At the same time, some viewers rather like the new styles used within factual genres, and enjoy the more dramatic aspects of television as witness. The different degrees of objectivity and subjectivity in factual programmes are also something viewers learn to negotiate, shifting positions as factual television changes.

Some genres occupy an intermediate space between fact and fiction. Those programmes that push the boundaries of fact/fiction can be exciting to watch, appealing to viewers' sense of adventure, taking them into uncharted territory. The playfulness that is so much a part of reality TV can be a creative environment for viewers. For example, a celebrity reality gameshow can provide opportunities for viewers to think through issues surrounding the production of celebrity. The hybridity of the format can create a certain energy that is appealing to viewers, as it pushes boundaries around a certain issue, or communicative style, it gets viewers' attention. But there is another side to this, a darker side, where in the process of reflecting on reality TV viewers confront perceived negative aspects of themselves. Some formats are thought to have gone beyond the limits of factuality, to have pushed boundaries of taste and decency. For example, a live show about plastic surgery can feel too challenging for viewers, as they question their motivations for watching and feel guilty about the reasons why. Reality TV viewers describe themselves as looking into a mirror and not liking what they see. Genre work therefore highlights how the restyling of factuality has produced generically and psychically weighty material for viewers to process.

Chapter 5

Truth claims

'It looked quite natural to me.'

Truthfulness is a defining characteristic of factual television. As one viewer explained, factual programmes contain 'a completely honest sight of something happening'. When programme makers produce factual television they offer audiences the promise of real events and experiences. Although these real happenings may be produced in different ways, using various modes of production common to television broadcasting practices, it is nevertheless the case that factual television is based on the premise that something really did happen. The truth claims made within factual content are therefore a major part of audience research in the restyling of factuality.

Research in news and current affairs, documentary and popular factual television has tended to use several approaches to understanding actuality. Studies in news and current affairs often foreground impartiality and accuracy of information within the production of news, especially located around journalism. Documentary studies have long made actuality, or realism, a central part of theoretical and production-based research. Work on reality TV has tended to use a combination of documentary theory and drama to examine realism in hybrid genres. Another approach used in this research is based on the sociology of nature and performance (Szerszynski *et al.* 2003). Audiences think about actuality in terms of nature, that is to say nature is made of real material things and is bound to natural or unnatural processes. The binaries of nature/artifice are part of how audiences understand truth claims. Viewers place news, current affairs and certain kinds of documentary at the top of a truth rating and reality TV at the bottom. Conversely, viewers apply a performance rating with reality TV at the top and news at the bottom of the scale. A truth/performance rating is a simple and effective way for viewers to judge the referential integrity of various factual and reality genres.

Drawing on the sociology of nature, the reality genre can be understood as a feral genre, a genre experiment that has a disruptive influence on truth claims within factuality. Viewers' critical engagement with the truth claims in news, documentary and reality TV indicates awareness of a 'reality effect' on many aspects of factual programming. One of the consequences of a feral genre is that it draws attention to the fertile environment, the natural creativity of factual television. More reflexive modes of engagement with factuality explore aesthetic issues and the impact they have on evaluations of truth claims. The restyling of factuality has therefore opened up abstract concepts like truth. Discussions regarding truth claims within news and current affairs, documentary and reality TV show how audiences have to be fast on their feet if they are to take into account the changing nature of factual genres.

Actuality

There are several ways of defining and studying actuality. A common approach is that of realism. According to Grodal, realism means the 'relationship between representations and a physical and social "reality"' (2002: 68). Viewers perform 'a series of mental operations in order to assess the reality status' of fiction or non-fiction content (ibid.: 68). Assessing the reality status of audiovisual representations is complicated because there are value judgements regarding what is real or might be true, and what we can see or hear with our own eyes, or is represented to us. For example:

> The experience of 'realism' is linked to perceptual specificity, but also linked to mental schemas that provide typical and familiar 'recognisability'. . . . Some types of realism focus on external reference, whereas other forms . . . want to portray the general 'essence' of things, yet other forms . . . activate subjective-associative references.
>
> (Grodal 2002: 67)

Thus, realism can mean something can be real, it can appear realistic, and it can also feel familiar to us. It is also the case that our experience of reality can lead us to question the realism of representations in fiction or non-fiction.

Authenticity is another way of looking at actuality. Similar to realism, authenticity can mean different things. If something is authentic it signifies the genuine article; but it can also mean that something is just like the original, or is authorized by the originator, or is true. When something or someone is thought to be true, what is authentic is 'to be true to the essence of something, to a revealed truth, a deeply held sentiment' (Van Leeuwen 2001: 393). When audiences talk about actuality in factual content they usually mean what is authentic and true to life about the programme. For example, 'a factual programme presents the actual or reported facts, so the viewer can make a reasonably informed decision as to the truth or otherwise of a process or event' (female, aged 65+, SES B). Although viewers use terms like 'real' to define factuality, their use of real is closely associated with authenticity and they judge the realism of most factual programmes by using a criterion of truth. Mepham refers to this as an ethic of truth telling (1990). Grodal (2002) calls this notion of realism perceptual specificity. He also makes the point that the 'mental operations' viewers perform can lead them to an anxious state of mind where nothing seems real. This postmodern position suggests authenticity is meaningless and realism is all relative. In the empirical research in this chapter there are many examples of audiences questioning the reality of factual TV and reflexively responding to their experiences of the real. Perhaps because of a general anxiety about judging what is true or not in life audiences turn to familiar and traditional notions of authenticity and truth. Especially when it comes to their experiences of reality TV, most viewers draw on a familiar understanding of actuality as meaning true to life.

Looking through

The previous chapter examined how genre work involved immersive and reflective modes of engagement. Similarly, evaluation of the truth claims made within factual programmes involves multiple modes of engagement. Corner describes this as 'looking at' and 'looking through' (2005: 54). He draws on research in visual arts to differentiate between first order observation (looking at something), and second order observation (looking through something). Looking through involves a reflexive mode of engagement. It is observation of ourselves experiencing something; through second order observation we can transform the experience, taking it to an 'imaginary space' without losing touch with what is real about the experience to begin with (ibid.: 52). For Corner, documentary is concerned with the dialectics of 'referential integrity' and 'aesthetic value'. This creates a documentary experience 'at once sensual and intellectual, referentially committed yet often possessed of a dream like quality for the indirectly suggestive and associative' (ibid.: 53). The 'intermittent aesthetics' of production design can have a 'cuing function', and so the different ways of looking at documentary as real and associative respond to the different aesthetics common to documentary production (ibid.: 54). Nichols also makes a related point that documentary documents the world and also offers a perspective on it (2001: 38). In two key works on documentary, Winston (1995, 2000) argues that documentary production has historically been concerned with aesthetics, and although the model of documentary as empirical observation has been dominant for the past few decades we should not ignore documentary aesthetics.

The aesthetics of news and current affairs, documentary and popular factual programming all have a 'cuing function'. One of the most important functions is that they cue viewers to expect certain degrees of actuality. Factual genre expectations have a significant impact on the way viewers look through and look at the truth claims within the programmes. News and current affairs, documentary and reality modes of engagement require different degrees of objective and subjective responses. In the next section, there is a discussion of 'truth ratings', where audiences place news first and reality TV last, with other factual categories somewhere in-between. One of the reasons why audiences apply such a rigid truth rating to factual genres is that they are 'looking at' these genres, and using a crude criterion to quickly assess their truth claims. This criterion is based on the promise of news to allow us to witness events as they happen and to present facts impartially and accurately. It is also based on the dominance of investigative journalism and documentary in audience evaluations of the truth claims within factual broadcasting (see Hill 2005; Winston 2000). As this viewer explained:

> I consider a factual programme to be one with the primary purpose to inform, enlighten or educate the viewers through the presentation of verifiable facts in a balanced manner giving a flavour of all sides of any issues. Comment, interpretation and speculation must be clearly seen as such and under editorial control (male, aged 45–54, SES C1).

These are the ideal values of news and the public service role of investigative journalism (see De Burgh 2005; Schudson 1995). This is a definition of factuality that is all about referential integrity rather than aesthetic value. It is perceptual realism, rather than affective or emotional realism. And yet such a position is hard to maintain across different types of factuality, and audiences quickly have to 'look through' factual genres if they are to respond to the aesthetics within them. There is a more flexible, critically engaged position, where audiences work through different kinds of factual genres and their disruptive influence on attitudes to actuality.

Another criterion for judging truth claims is that of performance. According to Gary Carter, a media consultant and former executive of Endemol International, reality entertainment formats such as *Survivor* or *Big Brother* are based on a 'continuum of performance' (2004: 255). Reality TV is an extreme example of performative factuality, but a 'continuum of performance' extends to other kinds of factual content as well. Performance works alongside authenticity as a criterion that allows viewers to subjectively respond to creativity within audiovisual representations. Performance is a rich area for viewers to draw upon because it refers to the repetition and variation within factual genres. Each time they watch a factual programme, it is similar to others and yet a variation on previous experiences. It is a creative act with an audience and it is also an everyday act within the context of daily life. Goffman's idea of the performance of the self in everyday life (1959) is one common to audiences as they reflect on authenticity and performance in factual programmes. This discussion between two viewers on the authenticity of reality TV participants highlights how performance is a criterion for assessing truth claims:

JAMIE: You can still see people's characters, even though they do it in a way
that is quite extreme, but you know if somebody is crying, they are
crying, if somebody is laughing, they are laughing and if somebody's
acting selfish or kind they are still people. They are *real*. It's just that the
situation is set up, so perhaps it can turn to something a little bit more
entertaining. But, I think it is the fact that they are normal people that
people like to watch it.

JOHN: Just think about it, there are people who act their way through most of
their lives.

The notion of performance is embedded in audience assessment of real people
and their experiences, especially emotional responses. An understanding of
'normal' everyday life is juxtaposed by an awareness of the performance of
selfhood, where people 'act their way' through life.

Nature/artifice

Jon Dovey argues that 'factual TV has moved from empirical observation to
the observation of simulated social situations' (2004: 233). By this he is
referring to the high degree of simulation and game playing so integral to
reality gameshows. Simulation is a 'representational mode based on making
models of complex structures and behaviours'; it is a mode that moves away
from realism or authenticity as described above and embraces the simulation
of 'social reality in performative models' (ibid.: 233). For Dovey, changes in
factual television symbolize a cultural logic of an 'order of simulation' (ibid.:
232). Factual television becomes a 'playful ludic zone, where performance,
challenges, rule sets and games of all kinds dominate the structure of the
programmes' (ibid.: 243). He refers to the work of the sociologist Anthony
Giddens, who has argued that we live in an age of reflexive modernity where
tradition and nature can no longer be relied upon, and where life politics and
identity work are fundamental to our 'reflexive project of the self' (1991).
Reality gameshows are part of reflexive modernity due to an emphasis on
simulation, performance and identity. They mark a move from trust in
empirical observation to 'a generalized sense that public culture has lost any
claims to seriousness that it may once have made and instead has become the
domain of playfulness, games and pleasure' (Dovey 2004: 233).

The idea of simulation and play as central to factual television challenges
audience assumptions about authenticity as a defining characteristic of factuality. Viewers do see the constructed environments of reality gameshows
like *Big Brother* or *Celebrity Love Island* as simulations of social experiences.
However, the use of simulation as a paradigm for all factual content doesn't
address the more organic processes involved in the production and reception
of a range of factual genres. Reality gameshows have effectively played themselves out of factual television and into an entertainment environment. But

it is important to audiences that other kinds of factual genres are perceived as true to life. Although simulation as a structured model can assist in real world knowledge, and is used in politics, science and many other areas of life as a method for learning about the world, it is a model that can only go so far. At some point we need to go beyond simulation to connect with the world.

Sociological theories of the environment and society provide another framework for understanding audience responses to actuality. In the edited collection *Nature Performed* (2003), Szerszynski *et al.* comment on the 'performative turn' that has taken place in the study of the environment and society. Their work builds on previous research by Franklin (2001), MacNaughton and Urry (2001), amongst others, on nature and social theory. A performative turn suggests 'a growing understanding of the dynamic quality of both nature and society' (2003: 1). Nature interacts with other individuals and processes; it is a mutual performance where practices are co-produced in an ever-changing, evolving environment. In discussing mutual improvisation in the natural world Szerszynski *et al.* point out that 'one loses a sense of nature as pre-figured and merely "played out"; instead the performance of nature appears as a process open to improvisation, creativity and emergence' (2003: 4).

Nature as a metaphor for the 'real', what is natural, organic, healthy, substantial, life itself, is a powerful concept for factuality. We understand and make judgements all the time about authenticity, or actuality, as natural and real. News presents itself as a witness to events, natural or man-made. Undercover journalism promises to go beneath the surface to get at what is really going on. Natural history documentaries document the real world. Observational documentary claims to be a fly on the wall. Aesthetic judgements are made all the time about natural footage, editing, presenting and performance of professional and non-professional actors. The binaries of nature/artifice, real/staged, genuine/fake, all help to construct cultural discourses of factual genres as true to life.

In his article 'Feral Ecologies', Nigel Clark (2003) focuses on nature, geography and colonialism. Long before concerns about a 'risk society' (Beck 1995), and 'biotechnological modes of reproducing and manipulating living beings', the European colonial project sought to replicate 'European life' in other parts of the world (Clark 2003: 163). Clark points out that biological forces are wildly opportunistic, and whether introduced intentionally or illicitly, quickly adapt to their host environment. He suggests that 'amidst all the forms of disorder and "deterritorialisation" accompanying colonialisation, biological forces stand out as the most irruptive and unpredictable – and the least amenable to re-containment' (ibid.). Feral ecologies are suggestive of the 'prodigious performance' of transplanted life (ibid.: 164). In contemporary society the 'intensive trade between distant parts of the globe has turned the trans-location of living organisms into a still greater threat to ecosystem integrity and biological diversity' (ibid.). Genetically modified organisms, unmanageable proliferation and interbreeding threaten the very existence of nature. Some environmentalists and social scientists have claimed that in a reflexive society, or risk society, nature has fallen, and we can now predict an 'end of nature'.

Clark's reference to colonialism and species invasion reminds us that there is another side to this story: 'what the achievements of the invasive organism highlights is the extraordinary – or perhaps merely ordinary – ability of living things to improvise in new settings' (2003: 165). In particular, Clark focuses on 'the idea of variation emerging out of repetition' to further understanding of evolutionary dynamics (ibid.). There are opportunities and constraints: 'the host environment may be altered irrevocably by the presence of a new organism but so too, inevitably, is the one who runs wild transformed by the terrain in which it insinuates itself' (ibid.: 166). So the performativity of life leads to the reproduction of organisms, but also the evolution of organisms as they transform in their natural or host settings. Clark is careful to acknowledge the generally negative consequences of species invasion, as evidenced from the European colonial project: 'in the majority of cases, the long distance trans-location of life – in all its forms – has induced damage and loss.' He urges accountability and caution in human engagement with nature. But he reminds us that 'the introduction of a species – or cultural trait – from a distant territory is less an absolute rupture with an essential nature than an intensification of a potential for making and remaking territories that inheres deep in the working of the world' (ibid.: 178).

The suggestive possibilities of feral ecologies can help to understand the changing nature of factuality. If nature is a common metaphor used to explain what is true to life about factual programmes, then species invasion is a way of explaining the impact of reality TV on other more traditional factual genres. Reality TV is a feral genre. It is a generic experiment tested across countries and continents. One viewer described it as 'a chemical experiment where you add different characters that react with each other' (25-year-old Swedish male student). It is wildly opportunistic in the media marketplace. It is deterritorial in its ability to cross generic boundaries. It is disruptive in the production and scheduling of existing factual genres; and it has overtaken, and in some cases all but wiped out, existing factual genres. Above all, reality TV is resistant to re-containment. The international trade in reality formats has allowed the genre to flourish, making it a transnational genre unlike any other. The construction of cultural discourses surrounding reality TV as artificial, unnatural, threatening, invasive, as a moral and cultural risk to society, highlights feral properties that threaten the integrity of factual broadcasting and act as a barrier to genre diversity (see Hill 2005; Kilborn 2003; Winston 2000, amongst others). Rather than see reality TV as 'the end of factual TV', it highlights the natural ability of genres in making and remaking factuality. Invasive organisms are an extreme form of the natural 'ability of living things to improvise in new settings' (Clark 2003). If reality TV does have the properties of an invasive genre then this serves to highlight television as a feral operator. The 'new world' of reality TV is one example in a long line of feral genres. The rest of this chapter considers the disruptive influence of reality TV on attitudes towards actuality. As reality TV has developed, its performativity has ensured generic re-location into entertainment.

Truth/performance

Truth and performance are central to audience evaluation of factuality. This section analyses the results of the quantitative data in relation to attitudes towards notions of truth and performance in various factual genres. In Corner's discussion of documentary as containing both referential integrity and aesthetic value we shall see how it is the referential integrity of factual genres that is primarily used in evaluating a range of genres (2005). Indeed, viewers draw on referential integrity as a quality indicator, a baseline from which to judge the authenticity of different representations of reality. The use of nature as a metaphor for the real is referred to in this section in order to understand the powerful and repetitive framing of factuality according to its 'claim to the real' (Winston 1995). Truth and performance therefore become understood in relation to notions of nature and artifice, with what is natural or true to life about a factual programme becoming the driver in genre evaluation. The evaluation of performance in factual genres therefore becomes a negative evaluation in this particular understanding of factual television as true to life.

The survey and focus groups contained questions on actuality in different types of programmes. One question related to the truth claims made by programmes, specifically attitudes towards the portrayal of events as they happened. Another related to the issue of the performance of non-professional actors in different types of programmes, in particular attitudes towards the degree to which ordinary people can 'be themselves' or 'act up' in front of the camera. For each of these questions in the survey, respondents were also asked how important it was to them that different types of programmes were true to life, and portrayed real people. Together, these questions formed a basis for mapping respondents' attitudes towards actuality. For the questions in the focus groups, participants were asked to discuss their responses to the truth claims made within different types of programmes, including short clips from various news and current affairs, documentary and popular factual programmes (in Britain and Sweden, respectively).

The perception and value of actuality in different factual genres is framed according to pre-existing categories and hierarchical structures. The framing device of nature/artifice is used in a similar way to the device of public/popular, as discussed in Chapter 3. The binary of nature/artifice allows viewers to classify factual genres, and to evaluate them according to commonly understood value judgements. There is a 'truth rating' to factual genres, with news at the top and reality TV at the bottom. Conversely, there is a performance rating with reality TV at the top and news at the bottom. The truth/performance rating is a simple and effective tool to quickly evaluate factual content. As one viewer explained: 'I consider factual programmes to be any programme that is shown which features real people that are not acting. However, I do think that some shows are edited to the programme makers' own ends to make it more acted' (female, aged 25–34, SES DE). We shall see how the comparisons across various factual and reality genres highlight audience awareness of the restyling of factuality, as they use a truth/performance rating to push popular factual television off the factual map into entertainment.

True to life

Figure 5.1 details the degree to which respondents' perceived particular categories as true to life, comparing Britain and Sweden. There was a hierarchical scale used, with news at the top of the scale (90 per cent) and reality gameshows at the bottom (less than 10 per cent). There is an association between actuality and factual modes of address, specifically those genres with informative or investigative approaches to real life, and more observational or constructed approaches. Therefore, perceptions of the truth claims made in programmes cluster according to news and current affairs and documentaries, with the exception of nature programmes, which are second to news in a hierarchical classification. There is a medium rating for politics programmes, which is also linked with perceptions of politicians as performers (shown below). The more constructed or staged programmes are also clustered at the bottom of the true to life scale. The results match the public/popular value

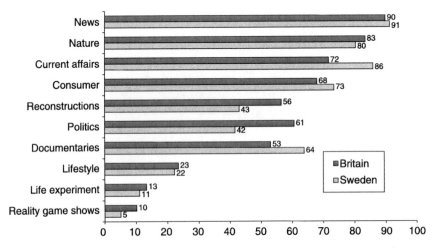

Figure 5.1 Perception of factual and reality TV as 'true to life' in Britain and Sweden (per cent 'agree').*

* British survey unweighted sample 4,516, Swedish survey unweighted sample 944.

attached to these genres, highlighting the significance of pre-existing cultural categories and social values for genre evaluation (see Chapter 3). There were some minor age differences; younger adults were somewhat more critical of traditional informative genres, whereas older viewers were slightly more critical of popular factual programmes. This relates to the age profiles for watching factual programmes and highlights the basic point that familiarity with genres helps to create slightly more positive value judgements (see Chapter 3).

Figure 5.2 shows the perceived importance that a certain genre is true to life. These figures were based on those respondents who claimed it was 'very important' that certain genres were true to life, comparing Britain and Sweden. The results followed a familiar pattern, resulting in high social value for traditional informative content (more than 80 per cent for news) and less importance attributed to popular factual genres (less than 20 per cent). There was generally a higher degree of importance attached to actuality by Swedish respondents across most factual genres, in particular public service content. There is a further criterion for Swedish respondents equating true to life factual genres as natural to Swedish broadcasting (see later section).

Figures 5.3 and 5.4 compare the perception of factual programmes as 'fairly true to life', with a 'fairly important' value rating. The use of the 'fairly' rather than 'very' category allows for a variation in the analysis of attitudes towards the truth claims in different factual genres. With the exception of news and nature programmes the value and perception of actuality differs. That is to say, viewers are critically engaged with the truth claims within different factual programmes, and are assessing the ideal of truth alongside

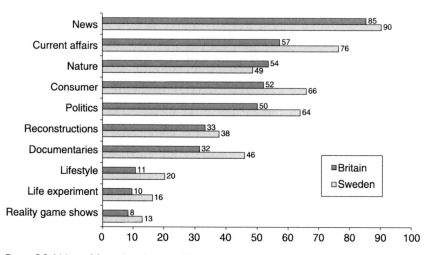

Figure 5.2 Value of factual and reality TV as 'true to life' in Britain and Sweden (per cent 'very important').*

* British survey unweighted sample 4,516, Swedish survey unweighted sample 944.

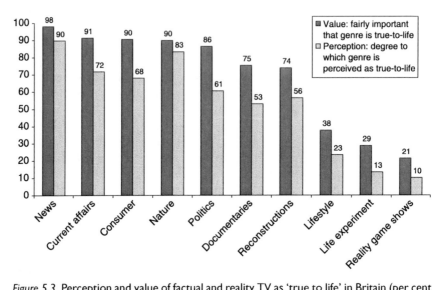

Figure 5.3 Perception and value of factual and reality TV as 'true to life' in Britain (per cent 'agree' and 'fairly important').*

* British survey unweighted sample 4,516.

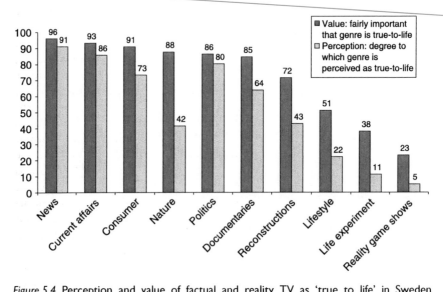

Figure 5.4 Perception and value of factual and reality TV as 'true to life' in Sweden (per cent 'to a fairly high degree' and 'fairly important').*

* Swedish survey unweighted sample 944.

the actual content on their television screens. Viewers have relatively different opinions as to the referential integrity of current affairs, for example in comparison with lifestyle. It may be important to viewers that current affairs ought to be true to life, but they may also criticize the genre for its current practices. The most marked example of viewers' criticism of a factual programme for not being as true to life as it ought to be is politics programmes. The difference between the value and perception of politics programmes as true to life was 88 per cent and 42 per cent in Sweden, and 86 per cent and 61 per cent in Britain. Thus the differential underscores viewers' position that politics programmes ought to be true to life, but they are a long way from reaching that ideal.

It is no surprise to see such a marked difference between Britain and Sweden with regard to attitudes towards truth claims in politics programmes. Voting turnout is high in Sweden, at around 80 per cent, and they therefore take politics programmes seriously and expect them to fulfil public service criteria in terms of information and education. Still, in both countries politics programmes are viewed with some suspicion, pointing to a general distrust in politicians (see below). There is little value or perception of actuality in reality TV, or lifestyle, or life experiment programmes, indicating a close association with these genres in both countries. The low truth rating for reality gameshows is indicative of the relocation of this type of hybrid format into entertainment, as it is almost off the truth scale altogether and viewers place little value on its truth claims.

Some of the differences across both countries are connected with the production histories and genre developments in each country. For example, in Britain there is a worrying trend in low truth ratings for current affairs and documentary. There are also differences in the value and perception of actuality in current affairs and documentaries (approximately 20 per cent difference). These figures suggest viewers pick up on cultural discourses surrounding these genres, specifically debate about tabloidization in current affairs and fakery scandals in documentary. To take documentary in more detail, in the British survey distinctions were made between history and science documentaries, and also observational documentary. Sixty-six per cent of the sample agreed with the statement 'I think history and science documentary programmes are true to life', with a slightly lower truth rating for observational documentaries (46 per cent). Comparing perceptions of truth claims with performance, the differences in attitudes towards documentary modes becomes clearer. Over half of respondents considered ordinary people acted up for television cameras in observational documentaries (53 per cent). The same amount said that it was important to them that ordinary people did not act up for cameras in these programmes (52 per cent). The hierarchical framing of factual TV in general is reproduced on a smaller scale within the documentary genre. Within the various types of documentary considered in the British survey, natural history was at the top and observational documentary at the bottom of a truth/performance rating. In the case of observational documentary, the hybrid genre of the docusoap has impacted on audience evaluations of this documentary mode. The docusoap is a hybrid genre which takes a fly-on-the-wall approach to everyday institutions or people within a soap opera narrative structure (see Bruzzi 2000). Its popularity with audiences, its high profile fakery scandals, and the celebrity status of some of the ordinary people featured in certain docusoaps, contribute to audience understanding of observational documentary. Ellis suggests that the documentary crisis of the late 1990s in Britain was 'almost forgotten' in the drive to re-position documentary as trustworthy (2005: 356). But, he says, these ephemeral moments in the history of documentary have a fundamental and enduring impact on the structure of the documentary genre (ibid.). We can see this in audience evaluations of truth and performance in observational documentary in Britain.

In relation to Swedish documentary, there is a distinction between those made in-house and those imported from different countries. The cultural specificity of evaluation of actuality is addressed later in this section, but the point here is that the relatively higher truth rating for documentary in Sweden is partly explained by the production history of documentary. Swedish documentary is still mainly associated with SVT, and thus debates about its truth claims are closely connected to public service ideals. Foreign documentary, on the other hand, can be subject to more criticism, especially as it is mainly associated with American imports, and shown on commercial channels. For example, this viewer explained: 'it's about which channel it's on . . . if you watch something on SVT 1 and 2 you think it's more serious, you notice the quality of the different programmes, but TV3 and Channel 5 I wouldn't even call that documentary' (23-year-old female student). Younger adults tend to be a bit more critical of the truth claims in documentary because they are more familiar with imported documentary on commercial channels (see Chapter 2).

Performance

Many of the results in the previous section become clearer when attitudes towards performance are taken into account. The nature/artifice framework to genre evaluation of factuality means attitudes towards truth claims need to be seen alongside those for performance. Viewers are critically engaged with levels of performance within different factual programmes, and are assessing the ideal of a natural, or authentic, performance alongside the actual performances on their television screens. Viewers have relatively different opinions as to the levels of performance in natural history documentary in comparison with reconstructions. It may be important to viewers that reconstruction ought to contain authentic performances, but they may also criticize the genre for its current practices.

Figures 5.5 and 5.6 show the percentage of respondents perceiving that people are acting up for the camera and the social value attached to performance. It compares those respondents who claimed that ordinary people were acting up to 'a fairly high degree' in Britain and Sweden. The hierarchical scale is inverted for this table, with news and nature programmes at the bottom of a performance scale and popular factual genres at the top. Traditional factual

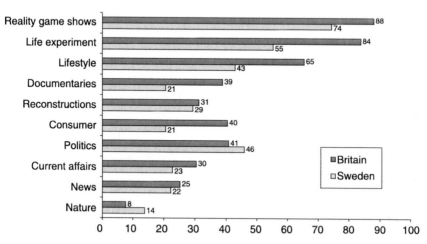

Figure 5.5 Perception of performance in factual and reality TV in Britain and Sweden (per cent 'agree' ordinary people act up for the camera).*

* British survey unweighted sample 4,516, Swedish survey unweighted sample 944.

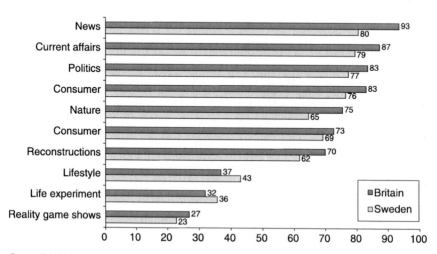

Figure 5.6 Value of performance in factual and reality TV in Britain and Sweden (per cent 'very/fairly important' ordinary people do NOT act up for the camera).*

* British survey unweighted sample 4,516, Swedish survey unweighted sample 944.

genres were least associated with people acting up for the cameras and they were also genres within which respondents claimed it was important people did not act up. Nature documentaries were at the bottom of the performance scale for obvious reasons to do with perceptions of the environment and wildlife. Politics programmes were criticized by respondents for high performance levels, matching low truth ratings for these programmes. Consumer programmes and reconstructions were in the middle of the performance scale, matching attitudes to actuality. Reality gameshows were thought to contain high levels of performance and respondents attached little value to this. Respondents expected reality participants to be reality performers, differentiating between ordinary people in different factual and reality genres (see Chapter 7).

The difference between the value of not acting up and perceptions of performance in various genres was particularly illuminating. For example, the differential of more than 60 per cent for news and natural history shows just how important these genres are to British viewers. We should also note that respondents wanted politicians to be more 'natural' in politics programmes. Similarly, documentary was another genre in which respondents wanted to see less performance from ordinary people. Reality gameshows also had a differential of over 60 per cent but this was the reverse, with a low value rating and high performance level. Once again, we can see how reality gameshows are in an entertainment space far removed from news. The performance indicators for life experiment and lifestyle programmes tell us that viewers were critical of the degree of performance in these programmes, and that they associate them with a performative turn in factality.

Cultural differences correspond with those in the previous section, where Swedish respondents gave a higher truth rating to traditional factual programmes than in Britain. In Figures 5.5 and 5.6 British respondents gave a higher performance rating than the Swedes for popular factual programmes. Once again, documentary stood out, with a higher performance rating in Britain than Sweden, indicating that the development of documentary, and associated fakery scandals, have had some impact on audience responses to the referential integrity of these genres. One difference was related to lifestyle, where Swedish viewers were less critical of performance levels than British viewers. This is not surprising given the performative turn in makeover lifestyle formats in Britain (see Dover and Hill 2007).

Finland

In an online survey in Finland, similar results were found for the perception and value of actuality in news, documentary and reality TV (see Appendix for details). Eighty-nine per cent perceived news as true to life, 61 per cent for documentary and 22 per cent for reality TV. The genre hierarchy occurred for the value attached to actuality, with those respondents who thought it was important that factual programmes were true to life placing news at the top of the truth scale (97 per cent important), documentary close to the top (91 per cent) and reality TV at the bottom (13 per cent). We should note that documentary received a higher social value rating than in Britain, and slightly higher than in Sweden. There were no significant differences across age or gender groups, except with regard to a general tendency that older viewers were more critical of popular factual programmes.

There was a similar response to the question of performance. Eighty-two per cent of respondents claimed people acted up in reality TV programmes, and only 28 per cent claimed it was important that people did not act up. For documentary, 47 per cent of respondents claimed people never acted up, 33 per cent claimed they sometimes acted up and 85 per cent said it was important people did not act up in documentaries. For news, 62 per cent claimed people never acted up, 20 per cent sometimes and 89 per cent said it was very important people did not act up in news. We can see that whilst it is expected that reality TV participants perform for the cameras, it is not acceptable for people to perform in news or documentary. Respondents were especially critical of documentary, with a third of the sample claiming people did act up sometimes, and yet the majority wished this were not the case. Just as before, there were few differences across age or gender groups, except that older viewers valued reality TV less than younger viewers, which was also the case for the general findings in the main study.

Feral genre

The notion of nature and artifice is also a device for understanding factual television from different cultures and broadcasting structures. Nature as a metaphor for the real becomes caught up in notions of nature as natural to a particular habitat. The idea of a feral genre discussed by Clark (2003) in the early part of this chapter becomes particularly helpful when considering the differentiation between news and current affairs, and documentary, as public service genres with some degree of referential integrity, and popular factual genres as having very little indeed. For many viewers reality TV doesn't belong in their classification of factual television as true to life. Reality TV therefore takes on the properties of a feral genre, a genre experimentation that has gone so far that it no longer can be contained in its original habitat.

This sense of factual television as something natural to public service broadcasting is evident in the previous section, as well as in Chapter 3. The similar trends in Britain, Sweden, and also Finland, point to common perceptions and values for factual and reality genres. The public/popular framing device used to judge the social importance of factual genres can also be mapped to nature/artifice. It is no surprise to see news at the top and reality TV at the bottom of the truth scale, and vice versa for the performance scale. News is perceived as a 'natural' genre for public service broadcasting and its ethos to educate and inform its audience. Popular factual content attracts audiences but these same audiences criticize its 'truth claims', and see it as a performative genre. This is one of the reasons why reality gameshows have been relocated to an entertainment space. This development is also happening with makeover and life experiment formats, such as *Extreme Makeover* or *Wife Swap*. Although for some producers, *Big Brother, Survivor* or *Idol* have always been classified as reality entertainment (Carter 2004), there is a shift in audience perceptions of reality TV; once these formats could be located in border territory between fact and entertainment but over the past few years have migrated into entertainment territory (Dovey 2004; Hill 2005). Although the contestants in the first series of *Big Brother* (UK) sang 'it's only a gameshow' audiences weren't quite so sure. By *Big Brother* 6 producers and audiences had taken 'the real' out of reality TV.

The reality genre adapted especially well in Swedish commercial broadcasting. After SVT received so much criticism for *Expedition Robinson* in the late 1990s they did not continue to show many reality formats, leaving it to the commercial channels to almost exclusively cash in on the popularity of reality gameshows. In the mid-2000s, *Expedition Robinson* was perceived by Swedish viewers as 'quality' reality TV compared to the 'trashy' reality formats found on commercial channels. The high proportion of imported reality programmes and formats from America and Britain has also influenced perceptions of, and values attached to, popular factual genres. We saw in the previous section how reality TV is perceived as artificial and performed, what one viewer described as 'recreated scenery'. In this section there is further evidence to show how in relation to Sweden the reality genre is also perceived as a cultural invader.

In the Swedish research the question of foreign and home-grown factual programming was addressed in the survey and the focus groups. The British research did not specifically address this as the majority of factual genres on peaktime schedules were made in Britain. The cultural specificity of genres did emerge within the British focus groups, as some respondents perceived a negative influence of American commercial programming on factual television. For example, this 23-year-old male shop assistant commented: 'It's because we have an American approach to factual programmes, a staging. Even the people who are meant to be in a reality programme are given a script and they encourage them to act in certain ways . . . this really, really fake approach to reality television.' The majority of respondents however tended to associate reality TV with a commercial or tabloid genre that was British in origin.

Figure 5.7 indicates that programmes from Sweden and other Nordic countries were perceived as 'fairly' or 'very' true to life by Swedish respondents (95 per cent Sweden, 94 per cent other Nordic countries). Britain, with its strong public service broadcaster, was also thought to produce mainly true to life programmes (91 per cent). Respondents were more critical of Britain when it came to 'very true to life', with only 31 per cent agreeing with this statement compared to 53 per cent for Swedish programmes. Other European

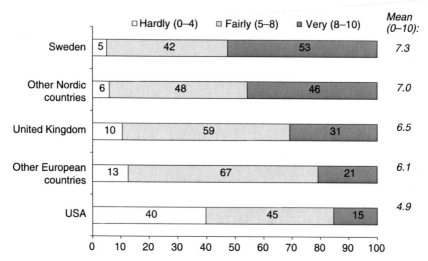

Figure 5.7 Perception of factual TV as 'true to life' in programmes from different countries (per cent 'hardly', 'fairly', 'very' – Sweden).*

* Swedish survey unweighted sample 944.

countries were also thought to produce programmes that were 'fairly' or 'very' true to life' (88 per cent). American programmes were thought to be the least real, with 40 per cent of respondents claiming US programmes were 'hardly true to life', and 45 per cent 'fairly true to life'.

Younger viewers were more likely to be critical of all programmes made in the selected countries than older viewers. Whereas in the previous section, only minor variations in age and perceptions of actuality were apparent, in Figure 5.8 age became more significant when using the 'very true to life' category. In terms of a truth rating, all age groups were in agreement that American factual programmes were at the bottom of the scale (15 per cent). Other European countries also received a low rating of less than 20 per cent. There was a general agreement across the age ranges from 16–65 regarding British factual programmes, which received a fairly low rating of around 20–25 per cent. The over 65s however were far more positive towards British factual programmes (42 per cent). This could be partly explained by the high proportion of British imported programmes on SVT, a channel with an older profile. The differences were even more apparent across various age groups for Swedish factual programmes. For example, 37 per cent of younger viewers (16–29) thought Swedish programmes were true to life compared to 68 per cent of older viewers (65–80). Once again, this could partly be explained by the high proportion of Swedish-made reality formats on commercial channels which have younger age profiles. The incremental trust in truth claims follows a stepped pattern according to age and life stage. At the

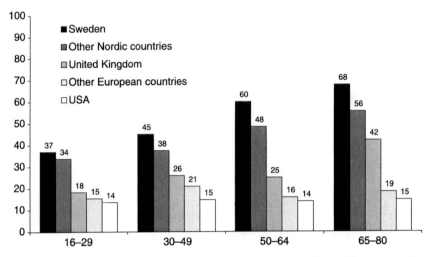

Figure 5.8 Perception of factual TV as 'true to life' in programmes from different countries by age (per cent 'very' – Sweden).*

* Swedish survey unweighted sample 944.

end of this chapter critical engagement with factual genres is addressed in more detail, but here the point to make is that younger reality TV viewers have carried over their criticism of this genre to other factual genres.

An open-ended question in the survey asked respondents to reflect on their attitudes towards Swedish and foreign factual programmes. Whatever criticisms of Swedish factual programmes that appeared in attitudes towards truth claims in Figure 5.8 were not apparent in the open question, which was dominated by criticism of American imports. The vast majority commented on American programming, often in very negative terms. American programming was described as sensationalist and overly commercial. A few respondents also mentioned British programming, which mostly was regarded as of high quality. Only a couple of respondents referred to 'European', or 'Scandinavian' programming. International programming was therefore mainly constructed as American and a negative cultural invasion of Swedish broadcasting. Home – grown programming was described as more true to life and as better reflecting a 'Swedish' mentality of 'down-to-earth-ness' and honesty.

A range of responses from the open question in the survey highlight the similarity of opinions regarding Swedish and foreign programmes:

> You feel more at home with the Swedish language, which means you trust what they are saying more (male, aged 16–24, plumber).

> Programmes from the USA are so exaggerated. It's just about being

the greatest, the best and the most beautiful. In Sweden we are more down-to-earth and want to keep to reality (female, aged 16–24, student).

Programmes from the USA tend to give very peculiar images of reality – perhaps because we are so different, but more likely because it is more sensationalism and ratings figures that are the controlling factors there – at least more so than in Europe and especially Sweden (female, aged 35–44, project manager).

Too many programmes originate from or have been inspired by the USA. It gives a strange picture of reality and a peculiar understanding of the world (male, aged 55–64, postman).

I can more easily identify with the Nordic culture (female, aged 65+, carer).

The language used by respondents to define differences between Swedish and foreign programmes indicates their value judgements regarding public service versus commercial dominated cultures, and national culture and identity. There is a sense that respondents perceive foreign programmes as not only importing foreign content, but also importing foreign social, cultural and moral values. The comment that American factual programmes 'give a strange picture of reality' highlights the general feeling that American TV distorts representations of reality.

We can see from the results of the survey that reality TV, especially American reality TV, has the properties of a feral operator. It is an influential genre in the restyling of factuality. Audience evaluation of truth claims in factual television highlights some of the consequences of genre invasion. Feral genres cross geographical borders, relying on the international trade in formats to travel to many parts of the world. In Sweden, the consequences of the reality genre have been felt by broadcasters and audiences. The schedules have been invaded by reality formats, budgets have been devoted to reality series, and younger audiences have turned to commercial channels rather than public service ones (see Chapter 2). SVT has attempted to address its declining younger audiences by, amongst other things, devising its own Swedish reality formats. This move by SVT, as well as TV4 and independent production company Strix, to create more popular factual programming based on Swedish cultural values addresses the negative consequences of over-relying on foreign imports or formats. *Farmen* (TV4) is a Swedish reality gameshow set in a summer house on a lake, a typical national leisure activity. The historical reality series *Riket*, meaning 'realm', was created by SVT in a deliberate attempt to make a public service reality entertainment format. The series was a hybrid of a reality gameshow and an historical educational series, using ordinary people to go back in time to seventeenth-century Southern Sweden, and also using historical facts and collaboration with museums to give an informative dimension to the series. There is a challenge for Swedish broadcasters, in particular SVT, to find a way to produce Swedish popular factual content that can be clearly distinguished from other reality formats. There is also a more difficult responsibility in ensuring Swedish popular factual television contains what are perceived as national moral, cultural and social values. For Swedish audiences, a public service broadcaster can play a significant part in containing genre invasion and maintaining referential integrity within genre experimentation.

In Britain, the perception of reality TV is a result of somewhat more internal genre experimentation amongst public service and commercial broadcasters, and independent production companies, such as RDF or Endemol. Transborder crossings took place between broadcasters and production companies, and reality formats were introduced into factual and learning departments, quickly taking root in peaktime schedules. It is no exaggeration to claim that during the 1990s reality TV ran rampant throughout British broadcasting (see Holmes and Jermyn 2004; Kilborn 1998). The kinds of heated debate about the consequences of reality TV on British culture and society took on moral dimensions, as various reality programmes were accused of distorting moral values. In the early 1990s, it was the BBC that received the main criticisms regarding the impact of reality TV on British television, after they showed 999, loosely based on the American emergency services reality format *Rescue 911* (see Hill 2000a; Kilborn 1998). It was the cultural invasion of reality TV and its alleged negative consequences on the integrity of British culture that dominated discussion. In the mid-1990s, audiences did see connections between a so-called Americanization of television and this 'new' reality genre (see Hill 2000). By the 2000s, there had been so much reality programming on television that the foreign aspect of the genre became less apparent. The BBC's major role in the success of docusoaps such as *Airline* or *Driving School* added to the generally national feel of these programmes. In 2000, Channel 4 acquired the foreign format *Big Brother*, but by this time audiences saw reality TV as mainly a result of internal genre experimentation.

In other countries the feral properties of reality TV have also been met with criticism. The debates about *Big Brother* created what Biltereyst calls a 'media panic' (2004). Drawing on the more traditional term of moral panic, a media panic refers to: 'the historical phenomenon that the introduction of a new mass medium or a "new" genre can cause strong public reactions, sometimes leading to a spiral of fear' (ibid.: 92). Biltereyst contends that this reality format simulated a media panic in order to create controversy and to gain an edge in a competitive media landscape. His argument touches on Dovey's view that reality TV is about simulation rather than social reality (2004). Here, the very hype and press discussion surrounding reality TV is as simulated as the reality gameshow itself. Heated debates around the world on various reality formats highlighted concerns about quality standards, privacy, moral and cultural values, dubious pleasures, and the damaging effects of reality TV on contestants and audiences: 'stories about the "dangers" of reality TV were so powerful that they quickly became crucial reference points in the critical coverage by the European quality press, as well as in wider public debates' (Biltereyst 2004: 93). These public debates differed from country to country, with Southern European countries expressing more moral outrage and religious concerns than Northern European countries. Mathijis (2002) showed how in Belgium, critical responses to *Big Brother* quickly moved from moral outrage to questions of genre and aesthetics.

In the next section, viewers' critical engagement with the truth claims of news and current affairs, documentary and reality TV indicates awareness of a 'reality effect' on many aspects of factual programming. Although this is closely connected to questions of style, there are also other issues at stake. There is a common perception amongst viewers that broadcasters have failed to contain the impact of reality TV on other genres. The lack of containment of this genre experimentation has consequences for trust in the truth claims of factual television.

Critical engagement

When Corner describes the process of watching documentary as looking through and looking at the genre it provides a useful way of characterizing viewers' critical engagement with factuality (2005). The double act of viewing, what I call the processes of genre work, involves varying degrees of engagement. That is to say, the audience is both immersed in factual television, 'looking at' it, and reflecting on the act of watching factual television, 'looking through' it. Corner draws his reference to looking through and looking at from arts aesthetics. The idea of genre work is taken from psychodynamic theory and practice. Whatever the intellectual framework for the double act of viewing, it is a feature of genre evaluation and the assessment of truth claims within factuality. This last section of the chapter considers the way viewers negotiate the meaning of truth, nature, artifice and performance in their engagement with various factual genres.

Critical engagement signifies high levels of media literacy as viewers not only show an understanding of the media but are also able to critically reflect on particular genres (Livingstone and Thumin 2003). The immersive and reflective modes of engagement that are part of genre work allow viewers to flexibly respond to the issue of actuality. For example, when watching news there is an immersive mode where viewers engage with information about the world, with particular events, feelings and experiences that are represented in the news content, and with the presenters and journalists who make the news. There is also a reflective mode where viewers at certain moments and under certain conditions critically engage with the news, drawing on genre classification and evaluation, alternative information about news events or personal experiences to bring greater awareness to the role of news in their own lives, and also more broadly in society and culture.

Different factual genres have cuing functions, inviting viewers to trust in their truth claims or not as the case may be. In Brunsdon and Morley's study, *Everyday Television: Nationwide* (1978), they analyse the discourses of nation and everyday life in a popular news magazine series. Their analysis shows how the construction of the programme invited viewers in to a familiar world of domestic news. In one section on subjects and experts they discuss a 'structure of access' (ibid.: 65). A structure of access is used by the programme team to control access to the discourses within the news stories, and more generally to control access to wider economic and political spheres routinely absent from news stories. The open and closed functions of various factual genres operate as a structure of access, attempting to control modes of engagement with truth claims. Generally speaking, news asks its audience to trust in its truth claims, creating a structure of access that is relatively closed to viewers. Reality gameshows invite the audience inside the genre and have a structure of access that is relatively open to viewers. There are ways that programme makers control access to discourses, and wider socio-political issues. Nevertheless audiences respond to the apparent openness of reality gameshows by readily critiquing the genre, a strategy they can carry over into other genres. Using the broad genre headings of news and current affairs, documentary and reality TV, the rest of this section draws on discussions in the qualitative research that illustrate critical modes of engagement.

Reflections on truth claims in factual genres illustrate dynamic viewing practices. As discussed at the start of this chapter, studies in the sociology of nature can help to explain the idea of nature as performance. By using a similar idea for factuality, factual programmes interact with other individuals and processes. An understanding of actuality therefore is not only about the cuing functions of various factual modes, but also is related to the mutual performance between programme makers and viewers. Viewing practices for truth claims in factual programmes illustrate the mutual improvisation of factual processes; there is no longer a sense of actuality or truth as 'pre-figured' or 'played out' but instead there is something open to change (Szerszynski 2003: 4). These viewing practices therefore connect with the restyling of factuality, and the ways audiences deal with change.

News

Immersive and reflective modes of engagement for news can be characterized by 'looking at' and 'looking through' the truth claims in the news genre (Corner 2005). Trust in the news is a very important part of the genre and its social and cultural function: 'I think there is a trust in the news. I think there is a cultural thing you know, this is the news!' (22-year-old British male artist). Social acceptance of the truth of news is closely linked to genre expectations and public service broadcasting. The news presenter is also an important source of trustworthiness, a personal reminder that viewers can relate to the integrity of news professionals: 'We have to trust the newscaster and feel confident because that way, when you watch the news and you know that you feel confident that it's true, and that it is correct' (37-year-old British female art-seller).

Audiences want to trust the news, but they also know that news is a representation of reality and therefore cannot be totally trusted. The following comment explains the difficult position of being a news viewer:

> I kind of believe what I see when I watch the news. But I sometimes think it's also being picked. You know, like, what's important and what's not important. And you never know, you know, it can be subjective in that way. They show certain bits of a war, for example, and you don't know really what's going on with both sides. Cos they might show more of that side or. . . . And you kind of think 'oh yes, yes, yes', you believe what you see. But you don't know whether you get all of it, like, a full range (30-year-old British female multimedia developer).

This viewer wants to immerse herself in watching news, and 'believe' in what she sees, but at the back of her mind is an awareness of the construction of newsworthy stories and the issue of impartiality. In another example, one viewer explained: 'I think it is essential that it seems and feels authentic and that you can believe in it, and that you are not too aware of the editing processes' (36-year-old British female personal assistant).

Many viewers switched between trust and distrust in the news. An example of a typical group discussion illustrates this point:

> It's a picture of reality . . . well if you trust the person, or the people making the programme, then you can perhaps relate to it and think you get some kind of overall picture of some major event in society. But, I think you are fairly aware that it is a picture. I don't think you think you'd get some genuine knowledge of reality (29-year-old Swedish male student).

> Well, often you don't know anything else, but that is what you get to see, so then you believe that is what it's like. If there's been, like 'the president has died in Lebanon' then you believe that, you wouldn't think that's not the case. But if you watch other news, American news, then you can discover that it's angled differently from the Swedish news (29-year-old Swedish female desk officer).

The discussion centres on how trust in the truth claims of news does not necessarily mean news is treated uncritically. The phrase 'a picture of reality' encapsulates understanding of actuality in news.

Much criticism of actuality related to news editorial processes. For example, comments focused on editorial framing, or particular perspectives – 'they all angle it differently so you have to be careful with what you accept.' For some British viewers the news coverage of the London bombings on 7 July 2005, and the subsequent police investigations, left a lasting impact on their trust in the news. This discussion by a group of 18–30-year-old females was concerned with editorial processes and news coverage of the shooting of a suspected terrorist:

DIANE: Like if it's real, you can tell with certain programmes how they edit it.

CARMEN: Yeah it's like long cuts. Where they probably didn't say too much before, but these . . . snippety bits, where you don't know if they said something else afterwards that went completely against what they just said.

BETH: The thing is when they shot the guy who was suspected to be a terrorist. I watched a news story and . . . they just show you what they want you to see, they don't really show you the whole story. . . . It's just somebody else's story. If you work out the truth, you know, he was an innocent man and, you know, I don't know about the truth in the news.

The editing of representations of reality which is necessary to create a news story is also cause for suspicion, the 'snippety bits' perhaps hiding the 'real' story. The case of the man who was mistakenly identified as a terrorist and shot by police on the London Underground is a shocking example of how reality can be distorted. The inability of the police to admit their mistake in the first few days after the shooting contributed to public suspicion of the police and the way it was being reported in the press. As this viewer commented: 'You don't know how much they're telling you, how much they really know about' (21-year-old male writer). Other studies of news audiences have also found distrust in certain news coverage of events. For example, Philo and Berry in their study of the reception of news coverage of the Israeli–Palestinian conflict found that viewers were concerned about the quality of information and whether they were getting the 'whole picture' (2004: 211).

Some viewers looked for alternative news sources and compared various pictures of reality: 'I read a lot of news, I watch news programmes and things, to see how each one covers it. Cos I mean – there is no such thing as "truth" ' (25-year-old female photographer). Already connected in this viewer's mind were distrust in news representations and a wider distrust in truth as a normative concept. For other viewers, distrust in the news was connected to a perceived fall in quality standards. For example, 'it seems to me that TV doesn't have the same kind of trustworthiness as it used to have' (45-year-old British male primary school teacher). The perceived commercialization of news discussed in the previous chapter is also apparent in some discussions of news on different channels. This was more obvious for Swedish viewers, who made a point of differentiating between public service and commercial news. Most Swedish viewers cited the short commercial news segment on channel TV3 as an example of entertainment news. For example, this 28-year-old female carer commented: 'Well their thinking is not to present serious news but to present some kind of news entertainment. . . . I don't even trust their weather, it just feels like "no" there's nothing I want to watch.' Another viewer jokingly explained that her cynicism was a result of a somewhat dramatic reconstruction series also shown on TV3: 'I have become so terribly cynical, I don't know, but I don't believe in anything anymore. I have lost faith in people after watching *Efterlyst*' (44-year-old female computer technician). A few viewers connected their distrust in the news to specific world events, such as the London bombings or coverage of the Iraq war: 'I don't have much trust in TV these days. And have kind of lost my trust in TV over the war' (31-year-old British female pattern cutter).

Overall, a contract of trust in the news is co-produced by programme makers and viewers. As this participant explained: 'It's an acceptance of truth. It may not be, but it's this kind of social acceptance, and this, in particular, is kind of constructed in such a way that it must be the truth' (30-year-old British male gardener). The idea of news as something that 'must be the truth' signifies its intrinsic value as a public service genre. The news is perceived as a natural resource that should be responsibly treated and maintained in order to be for the public good. The social acceptance of truth claims within the news is reliant on a robust contract of trust which once broken is difficult to repair.

Documentary

The contract of trust is also co-produced for documentary. Like news, a documentary's truth claims need to be trusted if it is to function as a genre. As this viewer explained: 'You trust that you're seeing real stuff, you're not seeing a fake argument between two people that you can tell was generated. So, you get that trust established in the beginning in a good documentary, and then anything that happens after that, you believe' (38-year-old female office assistant). But also viewers have to work in order to immerse themselves in the genre. This 25-year-old female student explained: 'I think if you watch documentary, you kind of put yourself in a kind of ignorant point of view, you know, you kind of believe in the documentary. You're ready to believe in everything.' She takes an 'ignorant point of view' in order to immerse herself in the referential integrity of the genre.

Thus, in order to trust documentary's truth claims most viewers have to suspend disbelief in order to foreground its referential integrity. For example, this viewer explained 'documentaries are an illusion, but . . . you don't notice it too much' (30-year-old male gardener). Ellis suggests that there is a soft boundary between fact and fiction, where documentary invites 'two distinct regimes of response: those of the factual "our world" and those of fiction "a parallel world"' (2005: 351). For some viewers, the factual world is an idealized place of truth and objectivity: 'the purpose of a documentary film is to represent an objective image of reality in some way, or something you perceive as an objective truth' (25-year-old Swedish male product manager). The associations between objectivity, reality, truth and documentary are underscored, but there is also awareness that these integral elements to the genre are perceived as such by viewers. They notice the truth in documentary rather than the illusion. Another viewer explained: 'I think documentary, that's observation to me, that someone has observed something, and they try and represent it . . . then of course it's about how it's angled but it still starts with observation' (23-year-old Swedish female student). There can be a priority in the way audiences respond to documentary's truth claims and its aesthetics, with emphasis on nature rather than artifice. Of course, viewers 'understand they fiddle a bit to make a good documentary' but what is vital is that 'it still feels like a real situation' (26-year-old male student).

Justin Lewis (2004) addresses the boundaries between fact and fiction in his discussion of 'two epistemes' for television audiences. By this he is referring to two modes of existence, the real world we live in and the mediascape we participate in. These are 'two adjacent realities' that sometimes overlap and cause tension, and sometimes reform to delineate boundaries between fact and fiction (2004: 295). According to Lewis, 'our culture's notion of reality works within two parallel, but quite distinct frames of reference. It infers two discreet notions of truth', but significantly both are united in the ideology of 'real life' (2004: 301). As viewers we occupy a grey area between these two epistemes, flitting backwards and forwards between real life and the mediated world of real life. Although Lewis uses this argument to analyse reality TV it can also be applied to documentary. Indeed, the next section shows that for most viewers 'real life' has been removed from reality TV, suggesting delineation between everyday life and 'TV life'.

In terms of documentary, there is some awareness of competing perspectives on the world and the way documentary documents it. For example: 'If you're going to look for objectivity, it's a very difficult concept, but of course documentaries are, I don't know how to express it, it's localized knowledge, we have the knowledge we have when making the documentary and we watch the documentaries from our own perspective' (38-year-old Swedish female teacher). For this viewer, localized knowledge signifies the different and yet connected positions producers and viewers take in seeing reality. Once again, there is the awareness that documentary is co-produced, combining local knowledge to create a position of trust. Such knowledge can just as easily create a position of distrust, depending on the value attached to one perspective over another. Thus, another viewer's perspective on two modes of reality can distance one from the other: 'TV is still a TV, it can never be real, so however much we try to achieve it, it's not a reality like this, you can't really compare them' (41-year-old Swedish female project manager).

There is a less clear cut position for the viewer in responding to the essential ambiguity of documentary. This picks up on what Corner highlights as the ambiguous position of the documentary genre as both maintaining its referential integrity and its aesthetic qualities (2005). The documentary film maker Roger Graef claims there is a 'chain of trust' between the producers and the audience (cited in Ellis 2005: 353). The metaphor of a chain signifies the various documentary modes, where different kinds of documentary are links in a chain, connected by the central tenet of documentary to document the world (Nichols 2001). Different documentary modes therefore cue viewers to trust in the truth claims more than others. And as documentary often mixes up modes within one programme, or series, a documentary chain of trust is a constantly moving thing, forming and reforming. One viewer explained: 'It's just got to be grounded in reality, no, in truth. A documentary should document something, actually. "This is how this happened" or "this is what has happened". And it could be a little bit of drama in there' (51-year-old female librarian). For this viewer, as long as the genre has a strong foundation in truth a bit of drama along the way is acceptable. For another group of viewers, they debate whether the constructed nature of *Jamie's School Dinners* matters or not:

JANE: You know, it might not be Jamie who's behind the good thing . . . maybe it's the production team, the editor.
SHAUN: Yeah and that's why they're showing all these clips of his family, you know it is emotional blackmail.
JACK: Yeah, but then you've got the argument . . . does it matter that there was a team if it changed to something very good, if it's good for society then what's the problem with it.

The backstage team producing *Jamie's School Dinners* undermine the authenticity of his crusade against low quality children's school meals. His celebrity status also works to undercut the authenticity of his feelings and those of his family. But there is an ethical dimension to this, which says that if the illusion of documentary is there for a greater good, in this instance healthy school dinners, then it makes it worthwhile. Viewers have to be flexible if they are to respond to the truth claims in documentary, reflecting on the aesthetics of documentary genre and changes taking place within production and reception environments.

Reality TV

Reality TV is a disruptive influence on attitudes to actuality. The huge success of reality gameshows has meant that the term reality TV signifies a distinctive kind of format. For example, this 33-year-old female business development executive pointed out: '*Changing Rooms, Holidays from Hell, Pet Rescue* are not exactly reality TV . . . they're just this weird, kind of, they were there originally before *Big Brother* came along.' When viewers in this study use the term reality TV (or docusoap in Sweden), they are referring to an entertainment format. This 25-year-old photographer explained her perspective on the reality genre: 'The whole idea that they are reality TV shows is a bit defunked. Cos they aren't, so many are staged.' Or, as another 20-year-old male student put it: 'I don't think that any of those shows are real, they're all scripted, so we can sit there and watch people make fools of themselves!' One viewer called it 'fabricated reality TV', summing up the artifice that is at the heart of much reality programming.

Reality TV invites a critical viewing mode. The genre invites the viewer to engage in debate, to question what is authentic and what is staged, to judge the actions of non-professional actors faced with challenging situations. In many ways, reality TV was easy for participants to discuss in terms of actuality precisely because the genre invited viewers to judge truth claims. These Swedish male viewers (23–26 year olds) summarized a common mode of engagement with reality TV:

JOHAN: You think about it all along 'can this be real?'
LENNART: And that's maybe part of what's fascinating, that it could be real.
JOHAN: Yes.
LENNART: Even though it's probably not.

Most viewers expect reality TV to be artificial, and in a perverse way the explicitly constructed nature of reality gameshows is a form of truthfulness. With reality TV you know what you are getting up front. As this Swedish viewer explained:

> Well, if you're after what truth is, reality then . . . really there is nowhere in any of these programmes you can be sure of getting to see the truth or reality. And then in a way it's better with the docusoaps [reality TV], with them you know you don't expect the truth (30-year-old male civil servant).

His comment helps to explain the results of the survey, which showed that respondents placed little value on the lack of truth claims within the reality genre. Whereas with news or documentary there is a 'chain of trust' between the producers and the audience, there is a 'chain of distrust' regarding producers and audiences of reality TV (Graef, cited in Ellis 2005: 353).

The 'chain of distrust' for reality TV is partly to do with the formats themselves. If a programme such as *Space Cadets* is based on the premise that there is a space shuttle full of people who believe they are in space when really they are on a television set, then the format itself begins a chain reaction based on distrust. *Celebrity Love Island* may claim to be about romance but no one expects the professional actors, musicians, sports men or women who take part in the programme to be looking for love. It is also partly to do with editing, where the drama and characterization so common to the reality genre are clear to see. As this 22-year-old male student explained: 'The editing is the most creative thing about these programmes. The situation can be completely different, but the way they put it together is, well, the exact opposite.' Even with *Big Brother*, whose premise is that the contestants are filmed 24/7, audiences expect the footage to be edited into stories that construct certain characters or personalities. The construction of a non-celebrity as a celebrity in the 2006 version of *Celebrity Big Brother* in Britain is a prime example of this.

Another important factor in the chain of distrust is the people in reality programmes. Given the staged nature of so many reality formats it is hardly surprising that ordinary people act up for the cameras. Many viewers perceive the casting, editing, and performance of reality TV participants as part of the overall staged nature of the genre. For example: 'You're supposed to think "well, that's how people are." But they're not. You're getting these extreme personalities in a forced environment, just creating something that is really weird' (30-year-old female bar manager). In previous research I discussed how audiences learned to judge authentic performances within reality TV (Hill 2005). What Roscoe calls a 'flicker of authenticity' (2001) describes how reality TV contestants are expected to perform, but also how the performance may break down and we might catch a glimpse of the 'real personality' behind the performance. These moments of authenticity are connected to our understanding of the 'performance of the self in everyday life' (Goffman 1959). This viewer explained:

> There's this feeling that people aren't really themselves . . . there's always been this fascination to like see people and go 'I wonder if they go to the toilet like me?' you know when you watch it, and that's what *Big Brother* allowed us to do. . . . And we would imagine who they actually are and I think that fascination stems from this closure, crawling in to the home and not be truthful when you get outside the home (22-year-old male artist).

Thus, although *Big Brother* is about improvised performance these performances are familiar to some viewers. It is an odd experience when the artifice of *Big Brother* connects with everyday life: 'You do get this odd thing when the truth suddenly clicked in when they're making breakfast on the television and *you* are making breakfast . . . it's *bizarre!*' (22-year-old male artist).

It is precisely because the reality genre is based on a chain of distrust that audiences are so critically engaged with the truth claims within the programmes. Reality TV disrupts common assumptions about actuality. It challenges audiences to question authenticity and performance, inverting the binary of nature/artifice so that performance becomes part of what is natural to the reality genre. Paradoxically, audiences are more critically engaged with the truth claims within reality TV than news or documentary. Many viewers often have first-hand experience of the issues in the programme related to social and personal behaviour, relationships and emotions, and this invites easy criticism. For example:

> I think I get more passive . . . when I watch news . . . while I watch more actively when I watch docusoaps [reality TV], that is I try and think more about what the relationships between the participants are like . . . while the news is like taken in, worked on. You're probably thinking more critically when you're watching docusoaps because you know 'what can be true and what is scripted' compared to those who are on a square in Moscow [reporting] about the Russian presidential election (20-year-old Swedish male, unemployed).

This viewer judges what is true or 'scripted' in reality TV according to his knowledge of relationships. He is less critical of the news because of the need to 'take in' what is being reported by experts and journalists in the field. The structure of access for reality TV is more open than for news, allowing viewers in to the format. Just as Brunsdon and Morley (1978) point out, the structure of access is limited to personal issues in reality TV in order that it can appear so open to viewers.

On the one hand, reality TV is perceived by audiences as artificial. However, its very transparent artificiality allows audiences the opportunity to work through its truth claims. With regard to the documentary fakery scandal in Britain, Ellis points out: 'trust had to be re-established between audiences, institutions and filmmakers' and one way that this was implemented was to 'guarantee authenticity by increasing the level of explicit artifice' (2005: 354). Whilst for documentary, audience modes of engagement in its truth claims are fairly ambiguous, the explicit references to the construction of reality formats have in some ways freed viewers from the chain of trust altogether.

Conclusion

The issue of actuality is crucial to understanding factual television audiences. Realism is concerned with what is experienced as real, and therefore audience experiences of representations of reality are important. Most viewers use a criterion of truth when responding to factual genres. Here, realism means what is authentic about factual content. There is an understanding of actuality as true to life, a sense of representations of reality as natural and authentic, or as unnatural and staged. The binary of nature/artifice is part of how audiences understand truth claims within various factual genres. A 'truth/ performance rating' is a simple and effective way for audiences to judge the nature/artifice of various factual genres. The similar trends in Britain, Sweden, and also Finland, point to common perceptions and values for truth claims in factual and reality genres. Audiences use a hierarchy, where news is at the top and reality TV at the bottom of a truth rating. A performance rating places reality TV at the top and news at the bottom. There is no space for reality TV in this classification of factuality as true to life.

In assessing the truth claims within various factual genres audiences show an awareness of the restyling of factuality. They are critically engaged with the issue of actuality, and how they perceive it as a defining characteristic of factual television. The chaotic mix of factual and reality programmes is structured according to a rather rigid framework that relies on the referential integrity of factual television. A criterion of truth guides viewers in their evaluation of news and current affairs, documentary and reality TV. Certain genres receive a low truth rating because audiences are critical of the degree of artificiality in a programme. For example, politics programmes are heavily criticized by viewers in Britain and Sweden for not being true to life, and we can see that it is the performance of politicians that is one of the reasons viewers are so critical of this genre. The fact that many viewers would like to see politicians as more authentic is a sign of how seriously they take the criterion of truth in their assessment of politics programmes. This is, of course, an ideal position, and the practicalities of how politicians can perform authenticity is not a barrier to audiences thinking political programmes ought to be more true to life. Nature as a metaphor for the real thus becomes a touchstone, a guide to the labyrinthine world of fact and fiction, something to hold onto in the highly stylized representations of reality that dominate factual television. The changes in political culture outlined by Corner and Pels (2003) that has led to performative politics are also connected to the changes in factual television that have led to performative factuality.

The notion of performative factuality is a contradiction, and audiences work to separate fact from fiction by taking the most performative of factual genres and pushing them to the edge and beyond the limits of factuality. The perception of reality TV as a genre experiment in fact and fiction has meant that it has had a disruptive influence on attitudes towards actuality. Reality TV is perceived by audiences as having all the properties of a feral genre (Clark 2003). It is a genre experiment run wild, upsetting the normal expectations for the contract of trust by programme makers and audiences. The chain of trust created by news and documentary is a chain of distrust for reality TV. Reality TV cues viewers to be distrustful, providing a relatively open structure of access that invites viewers in to have a look at the construction of reality within a hybrid format (Brunsdon and Morley 1978). By comparison, news feels like a relatively closed structure of access, inviting viewers to observe rather than get their hands dirty. The obvious staging of reality TV makes it oddly transparent, a perverse honesty in its artificiality. Classifying reality TV as entertainment helps to restore order to established value judgements, but the disruptive properties of the genre cannot be fully contained and audiences are left with an uncertainty about how to handle truth claims in factuality.

The extent to which audiences use the metaphor of nature to understand actuality doesn't make things any easier. There is the use of nature/artifice as a framing device for different kinds of factual genres, a means to pin down the most authentic genres, and hold them to task if they do not meet audience expectations for what ought to be real. Then there is the use of nature/artifice as a framing device for public service and commercial factual content, a way of preserving what is perceived as a natural terrain of public service broadcasters, something that they need to hold onto in a time of increasing commercialization. There is also the use of nature/artifice as a national or cultural framework, a means to differentiate between home-grown and foreign factual programming so that audiences can claim what they perceive to be naturally their own and critique that which is foreign to them. The notion of true to life becomes severely tested as it is applied across these different issues. The apparent simplicity of evaluating factual television as true to life gives way to a far more complex take on factuality. Discussions regarding truth claims within news and current affairs, documentary and reality TV show how audiences have to be fast on their feet if they are to take into account the changing nature of factual genres.

The act of looking through and looking at factual genres is a double act. It involves applying a truth/performance rating to factual genres, looking at them as if they are real, and treating the process as a necessary act in the evaluation of factuality. It also involves reflecting on representations of reality, looking through factual genres to see the mediation of real events and people, and treating this process as a knowing act. The connections between actuality and performance can help us to understand factual TV audiences. Performance is concerned with repetition and variation. In the research in this chapter we can see how audiences perform factuality, repetitively responding to truth claims within factual genres, and also varying their responses to deal with changes along the way. In this sense, actuality is an ongoing product of performance, and no matter what their evaluative connotations of truth and reality, audiences are performing their understanding of these issues when they watch factual television.

Chapter 6

Knowledge and learning

'You will get something out of anything.'

Knowledge and learning are intrinsic to factual television. There are different kinds of information presented in multiple ways to different groups of viewers. There are formal and informal learning experiences, such as learning about world events or social issues, and learning about emotions or practical tips. What we learn from news may be quite different to documentary or reality TV. Our trust in the objectivity and truth claims in different factual genres will impact on evaluation of knowledge. Our experience of watching television, listening to radio, reading newspapers, accessing the internet, downloading mobile content, in historical and socio-cultural settings all impacts on our understanding of learning from the media in our everyday lives.

The politics of information has long been a topic of intense debate in scholarly research and in the media itself, especially regarding news and current affairs. The 'public knowledge project' (Corner 1998: 110) is concerned with the power of public service factual genres to inform and potentially influence the viewer. Drawing on the idea of the public sphere (see Chapter 3), traditional factual genres can inform viewers about political, economic and social issues, and can help in their development as citizens who take part in democratic processes. The historical context to public service broadcasting in Britain and Sweden, along with other countries with dominant public service broadcasters, shows the power of the public knowledge project as a defining characteristic of public service content, especially factual genres. Although public service broadcasters have undergone a period of intense change, forced to compete for audiences in a commercial and de-regulated media environment, the public knowledge project has not disappeared. However, the value of this project is open to debate, and as viewers work through factual genres they explore the meaning of knowledge and learning in terms of cultural, social and personal contexts.

Traditional notions of public knowledge are being transformed alongside more personal notions of learning. Knowledge as facts and information about the world is most commonly associated by audiences with news and current affairs, and some types of documentary. Viewers describe themselves riding a wave of information when watching news. This is an information-rich environment but one that is hard to connect with unless there is some personal investment in a news item. Learning as getting something from a programme, something for yourself, is most commonly associated by audiences with some types of documentary and popular factual. When watching such genres viewers can sometimes take out information that is personally relevant to them. Information can go into a learning reserve and can be drawn on when needed. Another type of learning is related to the media itself, with the majority of viewers displaying high levels of media literacy, and critical engagement with the presentation of knowledge or information, especially in more popular factual genres. This critical literacy shows just how resourceful the viewer is in learning about the media from the media (Buckingham 2003; Livingstone 2001).

The knowledge profile of factual television is rich and complex, with various news and current affairs, documentary and reality genres bringing different kinds of knowledge to viewers for their learning reserve. The relative separation between knowledge about the world, knowledge about the media and self-knowledge highlights the scale of the knowledge project, and just how varied and challenging factual genres can be in the presentation of knowledge. One factual programme can be addressing the viewer about different kinds of knowledge and learning at the same time. It stands to reason that viewers also gain knowledge and learn about people and experiences in different ways, learning a little or a lot from different genres, and sometimes avoiding learning altogether.

Understanding learning

Learning is a porous term that can mean various things depending on the context. Knowledge, learning, information, they all mean something similar and yet they are not quite the same. Learning can be understood as knowledge gained by study. Knowledge in this context signifies specific information about a subject, events or situations – knowledge as facts. Learning can also be something that occurs as a result of experience. Knowledge in this context signifies awareness gained through the experience of learning – knowledge as experience. Another interpretation of learning is that of information giving form to something. Our knowledge of a subject can be formed through information; self-awareness can come from formative learning experiences. Broadly speaking, learning can be both formal, something we get from educators or professional sources, and informal, something we get from our own and other people's experiences. Whether we learn by formal or informal routes, the facts and experiences that we gather help to form our body of knowledge about the world and ourselves.

The sociology of knowledge has sought to address the distinction between formal and informal knowledge. Early research by Karl Mannheim in *Ideology and Utopia* identified knowledge as encompassing 'intuitive impressions' and 'controlled observations', with the aim of a sociology of knowledge to systematically comprehend 'the relationship between social existence and thought' (1936: 278). For Mannheim, knowledge was situated within empirical observation but some types of knowledge were more situationally bound than others. For example, knowledge of science or mathematics was classified by Mannheim as more abstract than other kinds of knowledge. Following on from Mannheim, Norbert Elias, in *Involvement and Detachment* (1958), also argued for a scale of knowledge, with objective and subjective types of knowledge at different ends of the scale. The more objective types of knowledge led to greater detachment for the individual, the more subjective types of knowledge allowed greater involvement for individuals, and also greater psychoanalytic purchase. Similarly, Hammond proposed a 'cognitive continuum', with facts and analysis at one end of the continuum and intuition and experience at the other end (1980). In her overview of the divisions between formal and informal knowledge, Power calls for an end to these distinctions, referring to the anthropologist Mary Douglas's contention that sociologists should treat everyday and scientific knowledge as a single field of study: 'to argue for the treatment of knowledge as a single field is not to promote a totalizing programme, but to enable the continual raising of questions about "pre-constructed divisions"' (2000: 24).

It is the pre-constructed divisions between different kinds of knowledge and learning that is of specific interest in this chapter. The research design was deliberately broad regarding the issue of learning. The term 'learning' was chosen to signify a more informal approach to the topic; knowledge, information and education seeming more formal and less associated with watching television. Learning in this study meant social learning, such as general knowledge or information on world or national events, practical learning, such as household tips or advice, and emotional learning, such as learning about relationships. Respondents were asked in the focus groups 'what do you learn from these kinds of programmes?' They were prompted to discuss any of the broad range of programme titles used in the research as part of the categorization games, and in several clips from current affairs, documentary and reality TV programmes used during discussions. What emerged was an example of Elias's scale of knowledge, with pre-constructed divisions between knowledge as objective information and learning as a more subjective experience.

One viewer commented: 'I think I can learn out of everything or anything. So, I would not distinguish between information or reality TV, because it's all something that you see and you have your own way of thinking. So, you will get something out of anything' (25-year-old female waitress). The phrase 'get something' is one that occurs again and again to describe learning.

For this viewer, you can 'get something out of anything'. But the majority of respondents distinguished between knowledge as information and learning as 'getting something' out of a programme. Two 30-year-old female participants described their distinction between knowledge and learning:

ANJIA: It's just information, pure information.
EMMA: It's nothing emotional, not reflecting on it in any way.

Or, as another viewer explained: 'I think there's kind of a difference. You learn more like that from documentaries, and from reality TV things you learn more about yourself' (31-year-old female assistant curator). One viewer questioned 'whether we are actually learning anything or whether they are just filling us with stuff, facts. . . . Does knowing stuff actually make a difference to what you are about?' (60-year-old male design consultant). An audience perspective on learning from television is based on preconceived ideas of information as facts and general knowledge, and learning as personal and part of self-experience.

Viewers move from the general to the particular; general knowledge being associated with news and some types of documentary, popular factual being more associated with specific learning experiences, if at all. For example, this 29-year-old Swedish female desk officer explained how factual genres can offer general knowledge:

> You can learn languages, you learn about different cultures, about animals, about space and all sorts of things you wouldn't otherwise get to see, *När & fjärran*, you get to see from different countries, which you wouldn't otherwise, you may not ever go there, so you can get an idea of, some perception of what the world looks like which you wouldn't have otherwise.

Another example illustrates the world of facts made available to viewers: 'I just think documentaries or news is what you can really learn from, so you keep up to date on what's happening in general' (27-year-old Swedish female student). There is a difference between 'keeping up to date on what is happing in general', and learning that personally touches you. For example: 'sometimes things we learn are enlightening. . . . The things that enlighten you are the things that are obviously very personal to me' (45-year-old male artist). Another viewer described learning as 'when I feel enriched in some way'. Being enriched, enlightened, getting something from a programme, are all part of what makes viewers feel more engaged with learning experiences. This doesn't mean to say that general knowledge and the informative function of television aren't valued by audiences. In the next section the statistics match the valuation of factual genres from Chapter 3; those genres that are perceived as important and socially valued are also information rich, whilst those that are not so important are information poor. But the discussions about learning in the focus groups were the most lively when respondents referred to specific learning experiences that were personal to them. Elias's use of involvement and detachment as ways of distinguishing between different types of subjective and objective knowledge holds true for audiences who are most involved when responding to learning as a personal experience.

Divisions between different types of knowledge as facts and learning as experience help to make sense of the detached position viewers can sometimes adopt when considering the knowledge providing role of television. The following comment illustrates how, for one viewer, news is something distant from everyday life: 'If I'm watching news I'm trying to just understand what's going on. But I'm not trying to see . . . the bit that I would get in my normal life or everyday life' (26-year-old male office worker). Another respondent explained how the presentation of knowledge in news can be overwhelming:

> Sometimes I think, you know, when we have news which is just very big things, like, let's just say, bird flu, what can I do about it? Nothing. What can I do about this? Nothing. A lot of the news, I think, makes us feel hopeless and helpless and the problems are bigger than our capacity to solve them. And then, that can lead to, I don't know, despondency or, I don't know, giving up altogether of any involvement at all, and increasing alienation. So, I sort of think, when you can bring an expert in who talks with maybe some authority, at least you can connect with the ideas. Or maybe if news is very local to your area, or the area that you're interested in. You know, there can be small nuggets of information that might not be of interest to a wider group or a community, but it might be interesting to you (56-year-old female librarian).

This viewer felt alienated by the representation of news stories, by the sheer scale of world events, and the lack of involvement of ordinary people in helping to 'solve' problems. Her suggestion to make the news relevant to audiences is illustrative of the way more personalized information can be subjectively interpreted by viewers.

Her response is one common to many studies of news, where news audiences struggle to get a purchase on the enormity of world events. Costera Meijer (2006) found that young people felt the news was all around them, and they were detached or involved in news events depending on personal reasons. Philo and Berry, in their research on news reportage of the Israeli–Palestinian conflict, found that viewers needed to know about the history and context of the conflict in order to understand it: 'incomprehension led to detachment and increased the sense of powerlessness some people felt when watching terrible events and which they could not engage or relate to' (2004: 257). When news journalists do find a way to engage audiences, the power of news in representing suffering is all too apparent, as Seaton's historical analysis of violence and news makes clear (2005). Comments on news coverage of the London bombings in July 2005 in the previous chapter show how powerful news information can be when it engages viewers. This reflection on watching news coverage of 9/11 is a good example of the intensity of specific news coverage:

> I remember watching 9/11, like, happening live. It was pretty much one of the most powerful things in my life, actually. Which is kind of sad, actually, but in that moment, when it was actually happening, I was watching it on Sky and I was just thinking about that. How it's marked a day in my life, you know, I will remember that day with that image. It's amazing (35-year-old male printer).

News can appear alienating, the presentation of facts distancing viewers, but it can also at times have a lasting impact on people's lives.

In general, most respondents in the study found it difficult to engage with the information in news stories on a day-to-day basis. The public knowledge project that Corner (1998) identifies as so important to television seems somewhat remote in the following discussion of learning by a 21-year-old female student:

POLLY: I don't really think you learn anything. I just think they just inform you of what's going on in the world. . . . That's about it. I don't think I learn anything from watching the news.
INTERVIEWER: So, can you get headlines?
POLLY: Yeah, I just think that's what it is, really. I don't think it's a learning thing.
INTERVIEWER: Okay. So, what would turn it into something you might learn from, then?
POLLY: I don't think the news should be something that you learn from. I think you've got enough things to learn, like, I mean . . . other things. I just think the news is just to inform people.

The idea of the viewer as citizen learning from the media in order to take part in democratic processes is not apparent in this viewer's comments, where the news is not a 'learning thing.' One interpretation of this discussion would be to see this detachment from news as evidence of 'dumbing down'. This argument would assume that the quality of news has declined, and this in turn has influenced audiences who approach news in a less serious manner, who have lowered their expectations so that news is 'just to inform people', without any further qualifications or desire for it to be something else (see Dahlgren and Sparks 1992 for discussion of tabloid news). Another interpretation could be that learning is a different experience, one that is more personal to the viewer and therefore not something news would necessarily be expected to provide. This argument allows for different types of learning in different viewing contexts (see Buckingham 2003; Livingstone and Thumin 2003, amongst others). John Hartley (1999), in his book *The Uses of Television*, points out that audiences use television as a resource for all kinds of learning, in particular learning that contributes to cultural citizenship (see Chapters 1 and 8).

The knowledge project would therefore include a broad understanding of knowledge, information and learning, taking into account that knowledge and learning are not the same and mean different things to different people. Viewers describe knowledge as something you can access, accumulating it via various sources. Information is something you can accumulate, hence the metaphor of information rich or poor genres. Knowledge and information are all around, but to do something with it involves a process of learning. Thus, viewers describe learning as being conscious of the relevance of information in their lives, or understanding something so as to use this information. The presentation of information makes a significant impact on the evaluation of learning opportunities in factual content. Some genres seem more information rich than others. Information is also something that needs to be transformed in order to become learning. Just as with genre work, it is the viewer that works on the information they gather from watching factual programmes and, in certain cases under certain conditions, information is transformed into learning.

For example, one viewer explained the active process of learning:

> I think news is more information than learning. Just information, and it doesn't matter. You can have lots of information but not really understand things well. You just know a lot of things, but you don't really understand. The news gives you information but it's up to you how you understand and how you make connections and develop thoughts (31-year-old female pattern cutter).

News is information rich, but to get something out of it viewers have to make the connection with other kinds of facts and other things they have learned. Her repetitive use of the word 'understanding' highlights the role of the viewer in connecting knowledge and learning. Another viewer described news and current affairs as helping her to be conscious of world or national events:

> I don't know if you can learn, more than you become awake. . . . You know what's going on. Like . . . happy slapping, they can tell you it is happening but they can't tell you how to avoid it, so you're aware of what's happening out there, but you are not learning how to take yourself out of that situation. So the news, for me anyway, it's more knowing what's going on in the world (30-year-old female bar manager).

She referred to a current affairs programme that investigated how young adults were attacking strangers and filming their behaviour for distribution to other mobile users, commonly referred to as 'happy slapping'. The programme made her more aware of the phenomenon, but this didn't mean she learned from the investigation. Her comment 'you become awake' sums up the distinction between information about happy slapping and learning to do something about it. This 30-year-old female shop assistant explained: 'You can have a lot of information, numbers, and they're just basic facts, without making anything out of it.' For many viewers in this study, the process of learning is dynamic and multiform, where information can be consciously transformed by audiences into social action.

Much of the discussion about knowledge and learning by viewers is informed by their social knowledge of the value of learning, whether this is formal education, practical learning, or emotional learning. This comment highlights a general perception of the media, and television in particular, as only one source of knowledge: 'When it comes to general knowledge it's never-ending, but there's not much you can't learn somewhere else, it's not like they've got a monopoly on knowledge, it's at other places as well' (28-year-old Swedish male software developer). Another comment encapsulates distinctions between knowledge and learning, and television and everyday life:

> You know the whole thing of knowledge and learning . . . we are actually describing a process of knowledge and sometimes it can be really transcending and it's wonderful, but it's not actually the same as learning about things by doing something. You know, growing something instead of watching Gardener's World (49-year-old female teacher).

For this teacher, learning through experience in the real world is different from television as a knowledge provider – better to work your own garden than watch gardening on television.

Some participants, especially younger adults, associated television with entertainment, its knowledge providing role secondary to the job of TV as diversion. A discussion about documentary by one viewer highlighted the genre in the context of television as entertainer: 'This is what I call worldly television. It's kind of your old-fashioned, lots of money spent type, historical, nature television. Educational . . . yeah, I have to say, probably those programmes I watch the least [laughter]' (36-year-old female personal assistant). Her laughter at her own admission of guilt reveals common assumptions about the social value of documentary as good for you. Another comment shows the educational label as a turn off for some viewers: 'I tend to turn on a programme when I'm not doing anything else, and I don't want to learn anything when I'm that happy . . . if there's something that I think is educational I tend to record it and watch it later' (25-year-old female illustrator).

The association with leisure time and happiness works well together for television as entertainer, but not so well for television as educator. Her comment that she records educational programmes to watch later signifies the social weight of information rich genres as something viewers should watch but don't really want to watch during downtime. Another example sums up viewers' attitudes towards the entertainment project of television and how learning is something perhaps more closely associated with other social spaces: 'I don't think TV necessarily should be educational. When I was watching [*Wife Swap*] I don't want to leave it thinking "oh yes, there's a very interesting psychology behind it!" I don't study it and I don't expect to learn that off TV. I don't think that's TV's ultimate goal' (24-year-old male unemployed). The rest of this chapter examines both the positive and negative implications of the social and personal evaluation of learning experiences.

Learning from factual TV

Classificatory practices in the previous chapters show how audiences rely on familiar genre discourses regarding public and popular television when making sense of factuality. Similar classifications are at work in the evaluation of learning. The research in this section supports Elias's scale of knowledge, with preconstructed divisions between knowledge as objective information and learning as a more subjective experience. A scale of learning is mapped onto genres, with learning evaluated in relation to what are perceived as more objective or subjective factual genres. Classifying learning according to pre-existing genre evaluation helps audiences makes sense of learning. To adopt a position where learning is everywhere, and we can learn from anything, is a difficult position to maintain. In relation to learning and factual genres, viewers draw upon already familiar classifications concerning public and popular genres to make learning more of a manageable issue.

Questions in the survey related to perceptions of learning opportunities, specifically attitudes towards opinion formation. The aim of the question on opinion formation was to ask respondents to think about how watching specific content may help to form opinions on any subject. There was also a specific question on levels of learning. One question that was tried in both surveys but did not really work related to different types of learning. Respondents were asked 'For any type of programme that you have watched and feel you have learnt at least a little from, which of the following things did you learn about?' and were given six categories: 'world events, national events, social issues and public opinion, about real people's lives, practical tips, increased my general knowledge'. The answers to this question were confusing, in that respondents linked certain types of learning to types of genres in ways that can only be explained within social and cultural contexts to factual programmes. For example, in the British survey respondents

claimed to learn the most about world events from news (83 per cent), politics (77 per cent) and celebrity profiles (68 per cent), and national events from
current affairs (59 per cent), observational documentaries (54 per cent) and
reality gameshows (50 per cent). To make sense of these results would involve
looking at international celebrity stories as world news. The high percentage
for national events and reality TV may be related to the impact of media
reportage of reality gameshows, where *Big Brother*, or *I'm a Celebrity* . . .
regularly feature in the media as national cultural events. Similarly, we
might expect learning about real people's lives to be something respondents
associated with reality gameshows, but that was resolutely rejected (1 per
cent). This is a reaction to perceptions of non-professional actors in reality
gameshows, and expectations of high performance levels in these formats
– 74 per cent of the sample thought people acted up in reality gameshows.
The genres respondents associated with learning about real people's lives
are more closely related to investigative journalism – undercover investigative programmes (46 per cent), current affairs (45 per cent) and CCTV/
reconstruction shows (41 per cent). My previous research showed this is a type
of genre viewers trust because it often uses undercover filming and therefore
presents little opportunity for people to act up when they don't know they are
being filmed (Hill 2005). Other responses were more straightforward, such as
that respondents learned the most about general knowledge from natural
history (74 per cent) and history/science documentaries (51 per cent). But it is
too risky to interpret the results of the survey when so many contextual
factors need to be taken into account. Needless to say, the valuable lesson
from this tricky question and answer is that socio-cultural contexts to learning
are essential to understanding the issue, and the focus groups provided rich
territory for exploring this in more detail.

In terms of opinion formation, the results of the surveys in Britain and
Sweden indicate news scores at the high end of an opinion formation scale
(61 per cent Britain, 66 per cent Sweden) and reality TV at the low end of
the scale (9 per cent and 6 per cent, respectively). Figure 6.1 details the
hierarchical manner in which respondents classified programme categories
according to opinion formation. The public service function of news ensures
it is perceived as information rich, where general knowledge can help to form
opinions on issues. The more commercial and entertainment associations of
popular factual genres ensure they are perceived as information poor and not
an especially useful resource for opinions on issues. In the next section,
respondents contradict this result by having strong opinions on reality TV,
along with other genres classified at the lower end of the learning scale.
Although, as Hartley (1999) suggests, television is good at teaching people to
watch television, most viewers place little value on media knowledge. A
learning scale is therefore initially framed in relation to traditional understanding of learning as facts and general knowledge, which also maps onto
other genre discourses regarding public/popular television and the social

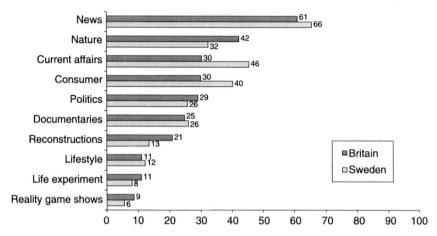

Figure 6.1 Opinion formation from factual and reality TV in Britain and Sweden (per cent
'always' or 'most of the time')
* British survey unweighted sample 4,516, Swedish survey unweighted sample 944.

value accorded different factual genres. The consistency of the public/popular
axis is further evidence of its powerful influence on genre evaluation.

Corner talks about the significant role of news journalism in national
knowledge orders, pointing out:

> In Britain, public service obligations on broadcast news have led to a
> situation in which it provides, for many viewers, the most serious and
> extended account of domestic and world events they will receive, given
> that they either do not take a newspaper or take a popular tabloid whose
> serious coverage falls well below network news standards.
>
> (1999: 118)

Figure 6.1 indicates television news is primary in British and Swedish
national knowledge orders. Any discussion of the value of news needs to take
into account the social value given to public service news content and the
perception of television news as helping the public to form opinions on what
matters to them. The fact that current affairs and politics programmes are not
highly placed in the knowledge order is of concern. In Britain, commercial
issues may help to explain the position of current affairs low down on the
learning scale (30 per cent Britain). In Sweden, it is somewhat higher (46 per
cent). In the previous section, respondents described how watching current
affairs may make them more aware of a topical issue, but that this doesn't
necessarily mean they learn from it in a practical sense. The distinctions
between knowledge and learning could in part explain the low position of
current affairs on the learning scale. The presentation of information in

current affairs would also be a factor in attitudes to opinion formation. The divergence between British and Swedish respondents highlights the different production styles for current affairs in both countries, and the social value accorded current affairs. The 'dumbing down' debate on current affairs in Britain (see Corner and Hill 2006) may have impacted on attitudes to learning. As Turner argues in his defence of current affairs in Australia, it is important for current affairs to retain public service credentials (2006).

Similarly, political programmes have suffered from a lack of trust in politicians and in both countries there is a cynical approach to politicians which affects the role of political television in national knowledge orders. The low rating for political debate programmes (29 per cent Britain and 26 per cent Sweden) connects with the low truth rating given for politics programmes and perceptions of high performance levels by politicians (see Chapter 5). It is likely that viewers' attitudes towards opinion formation are associated with issues of actuality; the less objective and trustworthy politics programmes are thought to be, the less likely the information in such pro-grammes will be trusted. With such a low rating, British and Swedish viewers may be getting political knowledge from other sources, such as newspapers or websites. Costera Meijer (2006) suggests that young people 'snack' on news from various media content, including rolling news and online news. There is also a lack of interest in politics, what Eliasoph (1998) calls a national trend in avoiding politics in America; similar trends in both countries in this study suggest that politics in the traditional sense is something viewers avoid (see later section).

With regard to documentary, natural history (42 per cent Britain and 32 per cent Sweden) is higher on the learning scale than general documentary (25 per cent and 26 per cent, respectively). In the British survey, this is also reflected in the similar rating for history and science documentaries alongside natural history, and a lower rating for observational documentary that is similar to general documentary. There are several reasons for these distinc-tions. First, these attitudes to learning reflect the various documentary modes at work in both countries. Specialist documentaries tend to appear on public service channels, and in Britain this is illustrated by the high position of natural history on the learning scale. For British viewers, natural history signifies large scale, high quality BBC productions such as *Blue Planet*. General documentaries is such a broad term that it would cover imported and home-grown documentaries, and the low rating perhaps reflects the lack of specificity of learning from any particular kind. However, the same rating for general documentary and observational documentary in Britain also suggests that the fakery debate in the late 1990s, and subsequent criticism of the truth claims within certain kinds of documentary, especially 'docusoaps', has affected the place of certain documentary modes in the national knowledge order. As Ellis (2005) suggests, documentary scandals can have lasting impacts on the documentary genre.

Age is the key differential in attitudes to learning. Although the pattern is generally similar for all age groups, there are some systematic age differences in how learning is regarded. Among older adults, traditional factual programmes were placed higher on a learning scale. Among younger adults, popular factual programmes were perceived as containing more learning opportunities than older adults. This would match the viewing profiles for these genres, and therefore greater familiarity with news or reality TV would lead to more chance of opinion formation. It also matches the age profiles for attitudes to actuality in the previous chapter in Britain and Sweden. If we take the case of Sweden as an example, the age differences for opinion formation for 16–29 year olds and 65–80 year olds for news were 56 per cent and 79 per cent, respectively, and for natural history documentaries 24 per cent and 55 per cent, respectively. With regard to popular factual, the learning rating was low, in keeping with the general scale, but slightly higher for younger than older adults – 18 per cent and 11 per cent for lifestyle, 10 per cent and 2 per cent for reality TV, respectively. Interestingly, politics was the only category in which each age group agreed on a learning scale (33 per cent).

In the surveys respondents were asked 'How much do you think you generally learn?' from types of programmes they had watched. Respondents applied a hierarchical classification of learning to factual genres, placing traditional factual genres at the higher end of a learning scale and popular factual genres at the lower end (see Figure 6.2). For example, 67 per cent in Britain and 80 per cent in Sweden claimed to learn a lot from news, with less than 10 per cent for reality gameshows. There is a clustering of traditional, information rich genres, as before, with those genres perceived as more

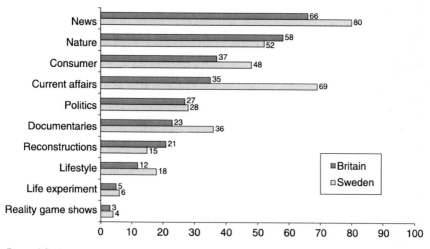

Figure 6.2 Amount of learning from factual and reality TV in Britain and Sweden (per cent 'quite a bit' and 'quite a lot').

subjective, such as lifestyle, being clustered with reality gameshows. The scale of knowledge is one that uses a hierarchy of objective facts and subjective experiences, as described and discussed in the previous section. The differences that emerge when comparing opinion formation and a learning scale suggest that forming opinions on a subject within a factual television programme occurs less often than general learning. For example, news becomes much more information rich for Swedish respondents when considering levels of learning (80 per cent), rather than opinion formation (66 per cent). Other differences that emerge across countries suggest production contexts also influence the evaluation of learning from various factual genres. For example, British respondents claimed to learn more from natural history and reconstructions, whilst Swedish respondents claimed to learn more from news, current affairs, consumer programmes and documentary. The association of these genres with the public service broadcaster SVT is a significant contextual factor in the cultural differences in attitudes to learning.

If the categories for learning also include learning an average amount, the percentages on the scale increase, but the hierarchy remains the same (for example, news increases to over 90 per cent, reality TV to 10 per cent). Thus those genres associated with the public knowledge project become more information rich if viewers consider an average amount of learning; news, current affairs, politics and documentary all provide more occasional opportunities for learning, with a differential of between 20 to 30 per cent for learning a lot and learning an average amount. For example, politics programmes increase from around 30 per cent (learn a lot) to 60 per cent (learn sometimes). Popular factual genres separate into two areas, with reconstructions and lifestyle offering more occasional learning opportunities (a differential of around 20 per cent), and life experiment and reality gameshows hardly altering at all on the learning scale. Public service factual genres therefore are perceived as having greater potential for knowledge and learning. On the one hand, this is a positive opportunity for programme makers and broadcasters in the development of 'the public knowledge project'. On the other hand, the question of why viewers don't learn more often from news or current affairs needs to be addressed. The different interpretation of knowledge and learning is one answer. If viewers transform information into learning experiences then it stands to reason this process will occur less frequently. Another answer is that viewers, especially younger adults, are not watching news or current affairs that often, and when they do they find it difficult to engage with. Whatever the answer, the ambiguity of what knowledge and learning is, and how often viewers can learn from factual genres, contributes to the challenges in 'the knowledge project'.

There is a consistent pattern of responses to a learning scale across age, gender and socio-economic status. This doesn't mean to say that everyone learns the same things from different genres, but it is yet further data that supports the dominant genre discourses concerning public and popular factual programmes. Using the British survey as an example, age is the most significant variable, with a similar pattern to the Swedish age profiles for opinion formation. Younger adults (aged 16–24) placed popular factual genres at a slightly higher level than older adults (65+), for example lifestyle (10 per cent and 5 per cent, respectively). Both age groups were in agreement on the position of politics programmes on the learning scale (28 per cent and 30 per cent, respectively). In terms of gender, male and female respondents shared the same pattern of responses, with the only variation being that whilst both agreed on news, current affairs and documentaries, female respondents were slightly more positive to the idea of learning from popular factual genres. As with age, familiarity with specific genres will make a difference to attitudes to learning. With regard to socio-economic status there is little difference, with the most striking thing being the pre-established distinctions for public and popular genres cutting across class. Comparing the socio-economic status of upper middle class and lower working class in Britain (AB and DE), respondents were mainly in agreement on the following selection of genres: news (69 per cent and 64 per cent), politics (30 per cent and 25 per cent), lifestyle (8 per cent and 13 per cent) and reality gameshows (1 per cent and 5 per cent). The minor variations are as much to do with age and viewing preferences as with class differences. Although the content of different factual genres addresses specific class issues, and more qualitative interpretations of the content may be read along class lines, it is the case that genre is linked with a knowledge scale in ways that unite audiences in common classificatory practices.

Learning and genre work

According to Elias (1958), the sense of knowledge as facts or objective information can lead to feelings of detachment. If learning is a more subjective experience, then viewers should feel more involved in the processes of learning. Drawing on the idea of genre work outlined in Chapter 4, a reflective mode of engagement is apparent in discussion of learning, including personal or emotional learning that can increase self-awareness. There is also a self-reflexivity in talk about learning that highlights the way viewers see themselves watching television, and think of themselves as an audience. Livingstone's reference to the resourceful viewer in *Making Sense of Television* (1998) is particularly apt here, as viewers draw on their social knowledge of the idea of learning alongside their genre knowledge, creating a multilayered approach to learning.

Factual television can be a resource and certain genres such as news provide information that can be used to help form opinions on a variety of subjects. This traditional sense of public service factual content as a resource for public opinion is one shared by respondents in this study. Not only do the statistics support this, but also comments such as the following by a group of 30–40-year-old respondents emphasize TV as a resource for furthering knowledge:

JAMES: It kind of triggers an interest. Like I said, if there's something you had not seen before and it kind of intrigued you and, you know, a lot of documentaries you watch, they kind of trigger you to go and look further into it . . .

FAYOLA: Yeah, but you were saying that you have to relate to the programme. But again, the way it relates to you is that you learn something about something that you wouldn't know exists.

MARION: Extend your knowledge.

Documentary is a particularly common genre viewers refer to as a 'trigger' for further interest. This relates to the point made in the previous section that different documentary modes can score higher or lower on the learning scale depending on the connection they make with viewers. As this viewer explained: 'I watched this documentary on autism, for example. Something like that sticks in my mind and *Jamie's School Dinners* taught me masses actually, but again it just depends on the documentary' (36-year-old female personal assistant).

There is also the sense of television as a resource for personal improvement, something much discussed in research on lifestyle where the genre plays a role in 'producing, circulating and promoting ideas of taste and lifestyle' (Bell and Hollows 2005: 9). This comment from a 22-year-old female bar worker showed how practical tips could be gleaned from lifestyle:

> I think there's a certain satisfaction you can get by watching them because you can maintain some tips for yourself, you know go away and go, 'right, I should eat broccoli' or something, you know . . . or 'I should maybe not wear vertical lines because it won't make me look as slim'.

However, there was an absence of comments like the above example. This is partly because of the research context, where learning is not the easiest topic to discuss without reference to specific examples. But it is also because of the production context to lifestyle television, where viewers perceive the makeover as often highly stylized, what one person called 'telly rooms'. In an article on the production and reception of lifestyle television in Britain, research shows that the development of the makeover, and its dominance in peaktime schedules, has ensured real life has been taken out of lifestyle (Dover and Hill 2007). Bonner (2003, 2005) makes the point that genres and subgenres within lifestyle need to be examined and culturally specific understanding of lifestyle encouraged. Certainly, for British audiences there is a reluctance to acknowledge learning from makeover TV, as opposed to more instructive lifestyle formats (see Brunsdon *et al.* 2001; Hill 2005). As this comment illustrates, other people might learn practical things but most viewers don't want to admit to learn about the kinds of lifestyle portrayed on television makeovers:

> I think *Plastic Surgery Live* is quite good, actually. I think it's quite educational, to a certain degree, where it just shows you how it's done, and . . . and I think that for some people that want to do that kind of thing, that might be a good thing for them as well. So, I think that can be quite educational to a certain degree (21-year-old female student).

The hesitations and qualifications suggest a reluctance to claim such a programme can be personally informative. There are other kinds of popular factual programmes where audiences do learn practical and emotional things, such as animal care programmes (see Hill 2005) but, as with documentary, it depends on the mode of lifestyle and its presentation of knowledge. This respondent was reluctant to say she learned from watching factual TV: 'I don't think people watch those kinds of shows to learn something. For me, if I've had a really long hard day, I could just sit in front of the television and almost switch my brain off' (34-year-old female educational support worker). But as she worked through the various programmes she found one that was personally useful to her: 'I think after watching a few *Supernanny* techniques, I will kind of use those with some of the kids I work with, actually. I think "No, Supernanny wouldn't do that!" So, yeah, I think there is a certain element of taking stuff on board.' This is a typical example of an attitude towards TV as entertainer, not educator, and also an approach to learning as getting something from a programme for personal use in everyday life.

Learning as experience is a common presentational device in popular factual programming. In life experiment programmes such as *Faking It* or *Wife Swap*, watching other people go through challenging experiences can be a source of emotional learning. These two 30-year-old female participants commented:

EMMA: You have these families that are really dysfunctional and have no idea why. I mean, it's hard to see yourself from outside. And so you can sit down and see this family and see all the mistakes they're making and it's just so crystal clear. And it's interesting, how a little bit of work really helps. It's almost like therapy, you know.
ANJA: I think it's interesting because, yeah, you can kind of recognize these people . . . and it's interesting to see how they change.

Observation of participants in *Wife Swap* can sometimes lead to awareness of psychological issues, both within the programme and also for viewers' own lives. There is an emotional mode of engagement where viewers can learn through the intensity of the experience of participants: 'I think about people that are going through emotions in preparing for something. . . . And you can see their sort of self-belief and anxiety and things like that, and how they work towards something, that's kind of inspiring' (46-year-old unemployed female). When a programme inspires viewers it often does so because it has shown people trying to do something to the best of their ability: '*Faking It* – actually, you look at it and you think, well, they're never gonna be able to do it, and then they go out and do it. There are quite a few things that I actually felt inspired by quite a few times' (30-year-old male sales clerk).

Gossip about participants in popular factual genres is another example of learning. When viewers gossip and debate about these programmes they become part of a social, sometimes national, event. One viewer described how they watched reality TV in order to be able to discuss them socially:

> Above all through watching TV in today's society you learn to keep up to date on what's happening, I mean coffee break talk is to a fairly large part caused by what's happening on TV . . . it's like when *Robinson* started, if you didn't know what *Robinson* was . . . you'd get totally alienated, you can't communicate with people, they're like 'what, haven't you watched *Robinson?*' (29-year-old Swedish male student).

This viewer 'always has something to discuss with someone' through watching reality TV, indicating the all-purpose usefulness of television for general social interaction. The kind of peer pressure that accompanies high profile popular factual series adds to the sociability of these genres and the general social learning that comes with regular gossip on the latest activities of reality performers (see Mathjis and Jones 2004; von Felitzen 2005). One viewer described gossip about reality TV as 'your own personal kind of environment of information' (33-year-old female bar worker). An environment of information is created by the programme makers, reality participants and audiences, all working together to maintain an environment where information about the reality show has personal value. However, the social value of gossip is not especially high for the majority of viewers in this study, who take a common position that gossip is trashy. The following discussion by 20–22-year-old respondents shows how viewers debate the value of learning about reality performers:

CHARLIE: I think [they] are there as a kind of prop to social communication. Do we need to know these things really? Do we want to learn from them?
JACK: You're learning how a person reacts to a certain situation.
RACHEL: But, it's almost like gossip isn't it?
CHARLIE: That's learning, though.
SARAH: It's kind of comfort information, I think, that goes in one ear and goes out the other, like reading a tabloid paper.

Although viewers are aware that their knowledge of a particular reality series can be a source of conversation, an easy way to communicate with people in public and private spaces, it is also a source of embarrassment, as there is a stigma attached to gossip and to reality TV, a double negative that outweighs the pro-social aspects of media knowledge.

There is a politics to the 'environment of information' created around a specific factual programme. Part of a reluctance to admit to learning from television is to do with social or common knowledge of television itself, whereby audiences have come to criticize themselves for taking television too seriously and indeed for watching it in the first place. As this 34-year-old female teacher quipped: 'You can learn to switch off. I'm sure of that!' There is a reflexive mode of engagement when watching certain factual genres that highlights people's awareness of themselves as viewers. This Swedish participant reflected on learning from reality gameshows:

> You can't learn from a docusoap really, except that you learn that you'd never want to take part in a soap, that's the only thing you learn. . . . But, well of course I think that autumn when we were watching *Farmen* practically every evening, it's been rolling here, and you've followed this psychologist or therapist, or whatever he was, who was the most dif-ficult person you can imagine, and then he wins the whole lot. Then somewhere, of course, when you see his actions and behaviour, and you get to see reflections afterwards where they might regret what they said and did and so on. When you watch it you put those things in your little reserve in there and then you remember that this was a bad way of doing it, you should not have done it that way, and it's much easier to sit here and say 'shit, how can you say that, how can you do that and that' . . . I think, well of course, you learn something whether you think you've learnt something or not. When this whole series has passed, you get impressions whether you want it or not (33-year-old male production designer).

First this viewer makes a throwaway remark about learning, joking that the only thing to learn from watching a reality gameshow is not to take part in one. On reflection, he begins to explore his own viewing experiences. His description of a 'reserve' is significant, as it shows how he can 'get impres-sions' and learn along the way without explicitly acknowledging learning from this programme. In the learning reserve are ideas and impressions about social behaviour, right and wrong ways of living and relating to people. As a viewer, he may draw on these ideas and impressions from his reserve as and when he needs them. An understanding of learning as getting something from a programme is here illustrated by the metaphor of a learning reserve.

The psychological aspects of learning are also apparent when viewers critically reflect on themselves. This respondent explained how he has learned not to expect to learn anything from reality TV:

> My mother's husband is watching *Robinson* and *Farmen* and really does
> hope that he'll learn something, and does get really sincerely pissed off
> that there isn't enough of farming in *Farmen* and not enough of survival
> in *Robinson*. Whereas if I watch that programme I can get a sadistic
> pleasure in watching people act like idiots, and you can sit here at home
> feeling 'how good it is that I'm not as stupid as all the rest' (30-year-old
> Swedish male student).

The mocking tone signifies on the one hand genre knowledge, he knows what
to expect of reality TV, and on the other hand self-awareness, as he mocks
himself for the 'sadistic pleasure' he gets from criticizing reality performers.
The reference to watching people act like idiots is one that comes up again
and again when referring to reality TV – 'that's why you think of it as idiotic
because there are idiots who apply to be able to be on TV'. In the next chapter
this is examined in relation to attitudes towards participants in factual TV. In
terms of genre work it is a technique for self-criticism:

> You learn about yourself – 'why do I sit here and watch?' You think 'I'm
> really not someone who watches that kind of crap' . . . and then you sit
> there for fifteen minutes, and you sit and note that 'now I sit here and
> watch that kind of crap' . . . and then you start to think 'but why do I still
> sit here?' (30-year-old Swedish male civil servant).

His philosophical questioning of himself as a viewer highlights an immersive
and reflective mode of engagement. In seeing himself watching television the
picture is all wrong and we get the sense that he wants to change the channel
inside himself as well as the remote control.

Genre work highlights viewing practices concerned with learning about
the media. The Communications Act (2003) requires that the British media
regulatory body, the Office of Communications (Ofcom), promote media
literacy. In a report of 2004, Ofcom defined media literacy as 'the ability to
access, understand and create communications in a variety of contexts'. In
this chapter it is critical engagement that is relevant to how viewers have
learned about the media from various factual programmes. Buckingham
argues that media literacy is social, in that we provide evidence of our
media literacies in social situations with particular audiences in mind, and
also it is critical, in the sense that 'it involves analysis, evaluation and
critical reflection' (2004: 38). For Buckingham, media literacy is a form of
critical literacy. Two related reports presenting a literature review of adult
media literacy in Britain comment that there is a lack of empirical evidence
(Livingstone and Thumin 2003; Livingstone *et al.* 2005). According to
Livingstone *et al.*: 'research on the audience's understanding of television
content is divided between evidence pointing to a creative, sophisticated,
"media-savvy" audience and evidence pointing to an often forgetful,

confused, biased or inattentive audience low in critical literacy skills' (2005: 4). Although 'literature suggests that respondents understand, enjoy and trust many broadcast genres, it is less clear that audience trust is always associated with good understanding or critical judgment' (2005: 4). In addition, they suggest 'barriers to media literacy include the changing forms of media representation (especially hybrid genres that blur reality and drama)' (2005: 4).

Genre classification and evaluation, modes of engagement, criticism of the truth claims or information within factual genres are all evidence of media literacy, and in particular a strong position on changing forms of media representations of reality. In relation to learning about the media from the media, the low rating for popular factual genres and opinion formation is not matched by viewers' forthright opinions on hybrid genres. There is an argument that viewers' detailed reasons for not learning from popular factual television is evidence of critical literacy (see Hill 2005). There is a general position which runs along the lines that, as one participant put it, 'you can learn that you don't trust the media'. Trust is a key word in the idea of learning from television: 'I think we'll always learn something even if we learn not to trust it and not to watch it again' (40-year-old male unemployed).

Viewers have critical positions for specific genres. The following discussion highlights a push-pull mode of engagement, where news should be trustworthy, but viewers' knowledge of news events and the news genre work to undermine trust in news reportage:

FARIA: Yeah I do learn stuff from the news, but I also learn that it's like, it's constructed and . . . because that thing with New Orleans, it was constructed just to show that "oh, look how they're acting. We knew they were that kind of people" . . . It's just constructed to have millions of images upsetting people (19-year-old female student).

CLAIRE: You can have your own idea about their idea, so you can see what's going on and if it's really true or . . . (21-year-old female artist).

DAWN: You can't say that, though, because in the news you take it for true and you think that is happening and that no matter what they say over the footage you believe it because it's the news (19-year-old female sales advisor).

For these participants, they can learn 'stuff', but how much should they trust it to be true? The sense of learning as an active process is significant, as it is only when they have an idea about the ideas in news that learning takes place.

To learn to trust the news or not trust the news is a crucial part of media literacy. One common technique is to trust certain news sources, thus using knowledge of media production contexts to filter news into commercial and public service sources:

> I think that a lot of the time you just see a story on the news like, 'your children might die after this', some sort of shock thing. And you can tell if you're watching it, you can tell it is a shock thing. . . . You know, they blow it up and then you see the next channel a week later doing something very similar. And you know it's a rating thing, and that's why I kind of like the BBC because they're not going for ratings. . . . They'd have some person who has earned their stripes and possibly knows what they're talking about. And they can do stories that are not 'Shock! Sex! Demolition!' you know, the headline grabbing things, because they're not worried about the ratings (38-year-old female office assistant).

For this viewer, as for many others in the study, they have learned to trust public service factual content and therefore their genre expectations are contingent on the presentation of knowledge within public or popular contexts.

The critical literacy skills that are applied to news are amplified many times when considering popular factual genres. Reality TV is a rich site for media literacy, as it encourages audiences to get into the production process and see for themselves how representations of the real are constructed (see Chapter 5). Reality TV scores low on the learning scale because knowledge is understood as facts, but if it was understood in relation to media literacy then it would score very high indeed. The following comment illustrates a sophisticated understanding of reality performers in *I'm a Celebrity . . .*:

> I think it's fantastic that people have learnt what to do in there, so it seems to that awful Jordan and Peter . . . they're staying together because they *know* about the magazine deals they are going to get, so I think *they* learn. They learn how to make careers out of it and things like that (34-year-old female educational support worker).

Another viewer explained how media knowledge is one of the main things people get out of watching television: 'I think you learn more about the sort of media and its techniques than you do about the actual subject matter itself. I think that's what you take from them' (36-year-old female personal assistant). This is a resourceful viewer, often able to see through media techniques. The question of what kinds of knowledge and learning are part of 'the knowledge project' is vital if there is to be further understanding of how audiences engage with factual content. In the final section of this chapter the resourceful viewer is considered in relation to wider concerns about the apathetic audience.

Avoiding learning

In *Avoiding Politics*, Nina Eliasoph (1998: 10) asks, 'how do citizens create contexts for political conversation in everyday life?' The background to the question is political apathy and her work is an attempt to understand 'how so many Americans manage to make the realm of politics seem irrelevant to so many everyday enterprises' (1998: 6). Eliasoph's argument is that 'apathy takes work to produce'. Whether we like it or not we are engaged with politics: 'few Americans vote, many tell survey interviewers that they have little faith in government, many are astonishingly ignorant about the most basic political issues: yet all are touched by this untrusted, ignored government' (1998: 6). She uses qualitative, ethnographic research with different types of volunteer and recreational groups to understand how the processes of everyday talk can lead to political conversation. She observes when people are in public places they avoid talking about politics, but in private spaces they engage in 'public spirited' conversations:

> In making these constant, implicit distinctions between public and private, participants simultaneously create a context for interaction and a relationship to the wider word. People create the realm of politics in practice, when they create, and recreate, and recreate again, this kind of 'grammar' for citizenship, constantly drawing and redrawing the map that separates 'public' from 'private'. The public sphere is something that exists only between people, and comes into being when people speak public spiritedly. Speaking public spiritedly creates the public sphere.
>
> (Eliasoph 1998: 16)

A grammar for citizenship can be located in the spaces in-between the public and private, and looking at political avoidance can illuminate political engagement because it is through these more private opinions that citizenship can emerge. Although Eliasoph calls the public sphere a 'dry and dismal' place, she believes that through talking in a public spirited manner the American people can bring it to life (1998: 263).

The argument in this chapter has been that we need to open up our understanding of knowledge to include both formal and informal learning, and to acknowledge that learning means different things in different contexts. Eliasoph is also suggesting that we need to open up understanding of politics, and embrace a more informal, private politics if we are to encourage political engagement. There is a sense that viewers are apathetic to learning as knowledge, that it is 'just information, and it doesn't matter', as one respondent put it. These are viewers surrounded by information, riding a great wave of information from the media and other sources, living in what is sometimes called 'an information society'. And yet, they are avoiding this information, seeing it as the realm of public service content that is important to society but not always meaningful in their everyday lives. There are similarities to the argument for a grammar of citizenship and a grammar of learning. Audience understanding of learning is that it is a more personal process, guided by self-interest. Similarly, Eliasoph argues that self-interest drives Americans to remain apathetic and detached from politics. Just as Eliasoph observed that during informal conversation her participants were lively and engaged in political issues, even if they wouldn't call it that, so too were participants in this study the most opinionated and animated when talking about genres they perceived as information poor. Through talking about not learning from popular factual genres, viewers showed they learned a great deal from watching these programmes and carried over their critical viewing to other genres, using their critical literacy skills again and again.

The use of public and popular genre classifications is also something that relates to the spaces in-between public and private spheres. Through the processes of genre work, audiences use pre-existing distinctions between public and popular factual genres, and formal and informal knowledge and learning; at the same time, they open up these distinctions, working through public/popular content, transforming knowledge into learning experiences. One of the main goals of the public knowledge project is to inform the viewer as citizen. Concerns about 'dumbing down' and political apathy can be counteracted by considering the resourceful viewer, the media literate viewer. There is evidence to suggest that the public knowledge project has changed, but this doesn't mean to say it is dead. Rather, audiences have learned to live with the media in an information rich society by selecting what is useful to them, by getting something from factual content that contributes to their learning reserve. The process of learning may be informal and personal but it can also lead to civic engagement, just as public spirited conversation can contribute to political debate. Dahlgren's (2005) concept of civic cultures supports such a position, as discussed in Chapter 1.

There are also differences between Eliasoph's research into Americans avoiding politics, and British and Swedish viewers avoiding learning. The first, and most obvious, is that the notion of a public sphere is well established in public service broadcasting. Critics argue that the BBC or SVT do not fulfil their public service duties, that they do not create a public sphere in the sense that Habermas intended. Nevertheless the idea of public service factual content that serves a public good, is trustworthy, informative and educational is not only alive and well but dominant in the generic discourses examined here. Indeed, the discourses of public and popular, public service and commercial, are so dominant in audience evaluation of factual genres that they positively get in the way of alternative approaches. This is a form of social and cultural knowledge that comes from the experience of living in two Northern European countries with strong public service traditions.

Another difference to point out is the lack of framework Eliasoph describes for 'sorting through facts or finding patterns'; with one recreational group Eliasoph describes how a lack of political conversation created a world of politics that 'seemed to be a collection of spare parts that did not fit together and was probably best avoided' (1998: 132). The world of factuality described here is one that is based on pre-existing frames of reference, where a ready-made analytical framework is available for sorting through the multitude of factual programmes available to viewers. It is precisely because there are so many different kinds of factual and reality genres and programmes that viewers get a handle on this ever-changing world by putting it all into some kind of order. Classification is a performative act; it is not only evident through talk, but also takes place in social settings and involves social action. It is because classification is a performance that the repetitiveness of categorizing things changes as we do it, so that new classifications and subcategories emerge (Waterton 2003). The presence of pre-existing frames of reference contributes to an understanding of factual television as a resource for knowledge and learning. The framework of the public and popular, knowledge and learning, may be prescribed in one sense, but it is also gradually transforming as a result of changes in broadcasting and viewing practices.

Conclusion

There is a rich and complex knowledge profile for factual television, with news and current affairs, documentary and reality genres bringing different kinds of knowledge to viewers. The communication of facts, information and analysis, and personal experiences varies not only across factual genres but also within one type of programme. In order to make sense of this knowledge profile, viewers make distinctions between knowledge about the world, knowledge about the media and self-knowledge. They also make a distinction between knowledge as facts and learning as experience. There is a distinction therefore between objective and subjective knowledge and learning, one that matches Elias's scale of knowledge (1958), where people can feel detached from knowledge as facts and more involved in learning as experience. The understanding of knowledge as objective facts ensures news is at the top of a learning scale and reality TV at the bottom. This evaluation of knowledge and learning maps onto other pre-existing categories used by viewers, in particular public service and commercial broadcasting. Audiences draw on their social knowledge of broadcasting contexts alongside their genre knowledge to evaluate the knowledge profile for television.

Audiences also reflect on traditional notions of public knowledge alongside more personal notions of learning. They describe themselves as riding a wave of information, one that is difficult to navigate, that can seem overwhelming in its range of facts and information from different sources. News and current affairs are therefore perceived as information rich genres, but viewers feel at times detached from the knowledge provision. Learning as getting something from a programme, something for yourself, is most commonly associated by audiences with some types of documentary and popular factual. This mode of engagement with the knowledge profile of television highlights the dynamic processes of learning. This involves transforming an environment of information into learning experiences, taking facts and doing something with them.

This is an understanding of learning as personal and social action, where the viewer uses factual television, as with other kinds of media, as a resource for their learning reserve. The value of factual television as a resource for learning is especially apparent when information can be gathered from a variety of media and non-media sources. The fact that viewers struggle to find purchase and relate the news to their personal concerns is significant to the development of the 'public knowledge project' (Corner 1998). Popular factual genres, alongside certain modes of documentary, can offer more informal learning opportunities where viewers feel they can connect with the experiences represented. The 'environment of information' shows that the knowledge profile for television is contextual to viewers' understanding of factuality.

There is much evidence to support the finding that viewers are media literate, that they have a high degree of understanding and critical evaluation of different factual genres, in particular hybrid genres. If there were a scale of knowledge based on media or genre knowledge, then reality TV viewers would be at the top of the scale. The very fact that they dismiss the idea of learning from reality TV is evidence of their critical evaluation of this genre. Their reluctance to acknowledge learning from popular factual genres highlights the social knowledge they draw on in assessing themselves as reality TV viewers. Genre knowledge seems to have little importance to them, and yet in their perceptive and reflective comments on the restyling of factuality viewers show how much information they have absorbed and processed in order to make such comments in the first place. As we saw in a previous chapter, through the process of genre work viewers can at times reflect on themselves in the act of viewing. In this context, the image of themselves as a knowledgeable viewer of reality TV is not especially flattering, and they make disparaging comments about learning not to watch reality TV, as one viewer said 'you can learn to switch off'. Thus, the knowledge that comes with watching reality TV comes at a price, as viewers would prefer to perceive themselves as knowledgeable about many things other than reality TV. Their awareness of the restyling of factuality is doubly important in the construction of themselves as knowledgeable viewers. They can show an awareness of the public knowledge project for television, critique the impact of hybridization on factuality, and in a self-deprecating fashion distance themselves from the messy business of reality TV.

Different developments within all the genres under discussion in this project have opened up the notion of knowledge and learning. The more viewers negotiate the restyling of factuality, the more knowledge they gain – there is no going back to a one-dimensional notion of knowledge as facts. Viewers contradict themselves, saying news is packed with information that can help them form opinions on a variety of things, and then dismissing news as 'just information'. They say reality TV can't help them to learn about things, and then come up with all sorts of sharp observations on reality TV participants. The more emotional or psychological kinds of experiences so dominant in popular factual television also feature in other kinds of factual genres – news, politics, historical documentary and reconstructions all use people's experiences as narrative devices. Viewers have picked up on this, but haven't quite worked out what this means to them in the wider contexts of other kinds of knowledge and experiences. There is an uncertainty in dealing with the changing nature of knowledge in factual television. Different kinds of facts, information and learning can bump into each other in factual programmes. Viewers negotiate this environment of information as best they can.

Chapter 7

Participation

'You always want to be treated like everybody else is treated.'

There are various ways of participating in media production and reception practices. Participation can involve the making of a TV or radio programme or website, whether as part of a professional organization, a private company or for personal use. It can involve taking part in a programme, or multimedia platform, by participating as a professional/non-professional, as a member of the public, being part of a studio audience or generating content such as photographs. It can also involve watching, listening to and talking about a programme, as well as interacting with certain elements, such as voting, gaming or online communication. Media production and reception practices operate in a big loop, connecting people who are media professionals of one sort or another with members of the public, some of whom participate in the media. The different levels of involvement in the production and reception of factual television highlight ethical issues to do with the treatment of people by programme makers, the motivations of people to participate in pro-grammes, and audience responses to this.

In this chapter, the focus is on audience attitudes towards fair treatment of people who participate in the media, specifically non-professionals, public figures and celebrities. Are there right and wrong ways to treat people in factual TV? This question is central to values and ethics in factuality. Fairness is associated with ethical practices within media professions, such as journal-istic ethics, or documentary ethics. In particular, it is the legal and regulatory matters of 'informed consent' and the public's 'right to know' that frame ethical treatment of people. Programme makers are expected to gain informed consent unless there is a wider public issue at stake. The behaviour and motivations of people who participate in factual programmes are also a factor in assessing fair treatment. Reasons for participation vary considerably, such as witnessing a news event, sharing uplifting or tragic experiences, asking for help from experts, wanting to overcome a challenge, or win a prize. Becoming famous is perhaps the most well-known motivation, with the

Warhol phrase 'fifteen minutes of fame' summing up what many people believe to be the underlying reason for members of the public participating in television. The motivations of viewers in watching people on television also need to be factored into fair treatment. Audiences routinely watch professionals and non-professionals in factual programmes, and have come to expect certain kinds of representations (the eye witness account, undercover filming and the confessional video diary) that all involve people in challenging situations. Politicians have a right to be treated fairly by journalists, but audiences have come to expect them to be given a hard time, in the interests of the public's right to know. Audience attitudes to fair treatment are contextual to all of these issues and more, and should not be treated in isolation from wider cultural and social settings.

Although the production and reception contexts to fair treatment are important, nevertheless there are certain patterns in attitudes to the treatment of different social groups in news, documentary and reality programming. Overall, viewers in this study think that programme makers treat different social groups fairly well. However, there is a moral and social ordering to attitudes to fair treatment. They value the fair treatment of all social groups in all genres, but they value fair treatment more in relation to children rather than celebrities, and in news rather than reality TV. This difference is partly explained by context. Viewers perceive a difference between the types of people who are asked to offer their opinion or share their experiences in news and documentary, and people who apply to take part in reality gameshows. There is no universal position on fair treatment, but rather a context specific position that draws heavily on people's motivations for taking part in factual programmes, and on the professional practices within different genres. Audiences expect those genres they associate with public service broadcasting to treat people better than those genres with a more populist agenda. Similarly, audiences expect members of the public to deserve better treatment than public figures and celebrities. The moral and social ordering of groups in factual genres indicates an awareness that just as there are different kinds of people in the public eye, for example sports personalities, actors or politicians, there are different kinds of 'ordinary people', and that all of these groups have various reasons for being on television.

Fair treatment is an ethical minefield. From an audience perspective, there is an ideal position on fairness that falls short in the production and reception process. In the case of reality TV, many viewers feel in conflict as they think everyone has a right to be treated fairly, but then again the people in reality shows know what they are getting into. In Sweden, some viewers call reality TV contestants 'media hot', a pejorative term that implies something un-Swedish. Similarly, British viewers like to disassociate themselves from reality participants. Many viewers in both countries refer to the reality genre as 'humiliation TV' and also 'wannabe TV'. If reality performers are shamed and humiliated, then viewers also feel ashamed by their pleasure in watching. Their personal interest in seeing people put in emotionally difficult situations, in watching how shameless reality performers can be in their pursuit of fame, makes reality TV both attractive and repulsive to viewers. In some ways, viewers adopt a shallow ethical position, placing self-interest first, seeing reality TV participants as a resource to be managed for entertainment. In other ways, viewers adopt a deep ethical position, feeling guilty about the treatment of participants, and moving towards a more universal position on the rights of participants. Overall, audience attitudes towards the fair treatment of social groups in various genres highlight different ethical positions, from shallow to deep ethics.

Participants and audiences

Participatory media is a term commonly used to refer to multiplatform content and interactive audiences. It is also a term that implies public participation, and is therefore something connected with public service broadcasters such as the BBC, public orientated media platforms such as Myspace.com and open formats such as *Big Brother*, with its catchphrase 'who stays, who goes? You decide'. Participatory media encapsulates contemporary media experiences, where the audience/user is invited to interact with content at home, at work, in the programme itself and related media content. Participation in the media is a specific example of participatory media practices, and it has been something people have been doing for a long time. Since the beginning of television and radio, people have been taking part, as professionals, members of the public or public figures. Griffen-Foley charts the history of participatory media in America, Australia and Britain from the nineteenth century to the present day, tracing a direct line between readers' contributions to Victorian periodicals, popular confessional magazines in the 1920s and women's magazines, talkback radio and reality genres in the latter half of the twentieth century (2004).

Factual television is a rich environment for participation, and we have come to expect to see 'real people' taking part in news and current affairs, documentary and popular factual television, alongside media professionals, such as journalists, presenters, actors and celebrities. It is participation in its most traditional sense that is the focus here. As this book is about audiences, the actual participants are not part of the research, although audiences can be participants, just as participants can be audiences. The distinction is somewhat artificial, but usefully shows how many viewers differentiate between themselves and the people who take part in television – there are those people who know they will never do it, there are those who do it, and those who would like to do it if they had the chance. Viewers observe and judge participants in factual TV, and in turn they observe and judge programme makers in their treatment of people on TV.

Fairness is of general concern to anyone who wants to be treated justly and in the same manner they would treat other people. It is part of an ethic of rights, and an aspect of modern moral philosophy that attends to human and animal rights. Social and political campaigns and movements concerned with violence and abuse, racism, slavery, women's rights, animal welfare and ecology, all have grounding in rights ethics. The philosopher John Locke argued that everyone has a right to life, liberty and property; everyone has a right to the pursuit of happiness. His general ethical position is still evident today in universal human rights law. Fair treatment is also associated with an ethics of care, where compassion and responsibility towards others is fundamental to both personal and public caring ethics. Kittay points out that we have a duty of care; we are obliged to care for others because we have all been the recipient of care at some point in our lives (2001). Fair treatment is therefore based on social ethics and rights ethics, and it is concerned with reciprocity – we treat people fairly in order to be fairly treated in return.

Informed consent

In relation to television, fairness is associated with ethical practices within professions, such as journalistic ethics or documentary ethics. In particular, it is the legal and regulatory matters of 'informed consent' and the public's 'right to know' that frame ethical treatment of people in factual television. Informed consent means someone has given their permission to be part of a programme, and has been given some knowledge about the purpose of their involvement. When a person has been doing something that the public has a right to know about, for example a politician misusing public money for personal gain, then their consent is no longer necessary. The normative concept of fairness when applied in particular production contexts is something that is subject to interpretation and dispute. Fair treatment is not only about social and rights ethics, but also situated ethics and moral issues common to specific professions.

In two studies by the former regulatory bodies in Britain (The Independent Television Commission and Broadcasting Standards Commission), the issue of informed consent was examined using multimethod research, including interviews with ordinary people who had taken part in popular factual and light entertainment programmes, and a survey and interviews with a representative sample of British viewers. The two reports, titled *Consenting Adults?* (Hibberd *et al.* 2000) and *Consenting Children?* (Messenger Davies and Mosdell 2001), both recommended that greater measures were necessary to ensure informed consent. Regarding adults, the researchers found 71 per cent of their respondents thought that 'programme makers should both inform participants about what is involved in making the programme and advise them about the possible consequences of transmission' (Hibbard *et al.* 2000: 7). Respondents were also supportive of participants' rights, including the right to feedback prior to and post transmission, and the right to complain to an independent body. Informed consent not only included those directly taking part, but also indirect participants, such as those filmed by surveillance footage. The study found that respondents made a distinction between entertainment and investigative programmes, supporting investigations in the public interest. Attitudes towards the motivations of adult participants indicated that respondents questioned motives, for example the most popular response to the question 'what do you think motivates people to appear in public participation programmes?' was 'to be famous' followed by 'don't know' (Hibbard et al. 2000: 27). However, there was also a sense that some people would benefit from appearing in a programme, to resolve conflict or to show strength of spirit in difficult circumstances (ibid.: 28). The research found motivation to be a major factor in whether viewers liked programmes or not, and presumably the participants in the programmes:

> There was a wide gap between participants' motives for contributing and audience perceptions of their reasons for appearing on television. Participants' motivations included the desire to share with the wider public an experience they had gone through, or to raise awareness of issues that can affect other people's lives. On the other hand, the audience characterisation of participants' motives included being labelled 'show offs' or 'exhibitionists'. In short, viewers questioned the motives of both producers for the way they used people, and of participants, for wanting to appear on television.
>
> (ibid.: 8)

The participants' motives for wanting to share their experiences may be true, but so too is the suspicion of audiences that these people want to get into TV. The report also found that half of the participants they interviewed had appeared on television two or more times – they were 'repeat performers'. When looking at the experiences of these performers, the researchers found that there was a lack of information on general production matters, and a lack of awareness of how editing and post-production techniques could change a participant's contribution. Overall, the report recommended an explicit code of rights for participants, and redefined informed consent to include 'permission based on a participant's knowledge and understanding of (a) a programme's format, aims and objectives, (b) how their contribution will be used, and (c) the potential consequences for them or for third parties of their taking part' (2000: 7).

Brian Winston argues that 'full scale ethical systems' do not work with 'the realities of the media industries or the demands of free speech' (2000: 148). He points out how documentary is both journalistic and creative. It has always relied on 'everyday little white lies and omissions that often characterise the "bargaining" between film maker and participant' (2000: 138). For example, in the making of the landmark documentary *Nanook of the North*, film maker Flaherty and the main participant Allakariallak had an arrangement which Winston calls a 'conspiracy to misrepresent' (2000: 139). He explains: 'Allakariallak connived at his own representation as a technical naïf (which he wasn't), living in an igloo (which he didn't) and re-enacting his father's generation's experiences (when he had a contemporary Inuit lifestyle)' (ibid.). Despite this arrangement, Winston argues that responsibility lies firmly with the film maker, and that any 'ethical shortfall' belongs to the film maker no matter how much the participant may be involved in a conspiracy to misrepresent. He also points out informed consent needs to take into account the different motivations of participants. Some people have positive experiences, such as Pat Loud, the mother in observational documentary *An American Family*, who wrote a book and began a literary agency, or Jeremy, an employee of Heathrow Airport, who went on to be a television presenter after the success of the docusoap *Airport* (ibid.: 138–9). Other participants may 'benefit a little and regret a lot', yet others still 'consent without understanding there will be no benefit for them' (ibid.: 143–5). When participants complain, the individual arrangement made prior to filming, and the kinds of benefits that participants may expect through their involvement, make the consent defence specific to each participant and film maker. Although Winston feels that 'inequality remains the besetting ethical problem of the documentarist/participant relationship', ethical systems are not the answer (ibid.: 147). He refers to the guidelines drawn up by media professionals, in particular journalistic ethics and documentary ethics, which are focused on work practices. These guidelines value social responsibility, the public's right to know, truth telling and freedom of expression. They are useful guidelines but fail to address the contradictions between what Winston calls 'the fundamental amorality of the concept of free speech', professional ethical imperatives and the constraints of working in cultural industries (ibid.: 119). Ultimately, it is difficult to draw an ethical line regarding fair treatment, but he recommends a relativist situationist ethic, where the media professional is primarily responsible for participants, and uses personal judgement alongside moral principles (ibid.: 127–8).

Whilst an overriding ethical system for fair treatment would be hard to implement in light of working practices, the research into participants and audiences of popular factual genres does highlight the grey area of hybrid genres which rely on created situations rather than observable behaviour. What of a professional code of conduct for those working in lifestyle or reality gameshows? The nature of fair treatment comes into question when a conspiracy to misrepresent is often part of the format itself, such as *Space Cadets* (Channel 4, UK). News and investigative journalism, and documentary, share public service values, and their justification and purpose can override general ethical conduct regarding informed consent. However, popular factual genres can rarely claim to be in the public interest. According to Winston: 'all moral fall-out firmly falls onto the film-maker, despite the clear consent and collaboration of participants who, after all, are engaged in situations not remotely of their making' (2000: 140). The research by Hibberd *et al.* (2000) found that audiences questioned the motivations of people in popular factual genres more so than programme makers. It is certainly the case that respondents in this study found fault with reality participants, and were quick to situate fair treatment within the contexts of reality formats, arguing that participants have prior knowledge and have learned to play the game of reality perhaps better than programme makers. Research by Syvertsen (2001) in participants in a dating gameshow highlighted how these participants cleverly used the opportunity to be in a television production to suit their own personal motivations, such as going on holiday or having an afternoon out of the office. These gameshow contestants knowingly played the game, and worked with the programme makers rather than being exploited by them. The perception of the balance of power shifts from film maker to participant, and is a reversal of the ethical position Winston argues for.

Ordinary and celebrity

One of the reasons for this ethical position is the perception of participants' motivations for taking part in different established genres. Frances Bonner's *Ordinary Television* refers to lifestyle, reality and light entertainment genres which contain non-professionals. She points out: 'ordinary television needs ordinary people to agree to collude to produce the appearance of being ordinary' (2003: 60). Those marked out from the ordinary include presenters and actors who regularly appear in a series, and also less regular appearances by celebrities and experts. Celebrities are defined by Bonner as 'people who have a high recognition index' and experts as having specialized knowledge (2003: 85). The difference between the two is that 'celebrities need to be willing to move outside their areas of expertise and hold up aspects of their private lives to the public gaze, while an expert need do neither' (2003: 86). When experts reveal private matters this is usually a sign they are transforming into celebrities, such as the transformation of fashion journalists Trinny and Susannah from experts in *What Not to Wear* to celebrities appearing on chat shows. Although not common to ordinary television genres, we should include public figures in the selection of those marked out from the ordinary. These participants hold publicly accountable positions in society, such as politicians, the mayor of a city, or public officials in charge of health or security matters.

Ordinary people is a category that includes participants who are used as 'examples' of an issue under consideration, who 'function to personalise the issue as one involving people just like them' (Bonner 2003: 89). Bonner notes the high numbers of ordinary people applying to get on gameshows, chat shows and reality gameshows. Reality talent shows such as *Pop Idol* include the application process in the format itself, with queues of people waiting to audition for a part in the show, only to be a part of a show already. Ordinary people 'representing themselves' differs from members of the public in news or documentary programming where they are 'framed in some manner as exceptional or exemplary, and where they are expected to ignore the televisual apparatus' (2003: 90). Bonner uses gameshows as an example of people unreflexively being an 'ordinary' man or woman, as they have been given an opportunity to 'produce a television persona within the constraints of a programme's format' (ibid.). It is not always the case that members of the public can manage their personas, and many popular factual formats construct specific subject positions where the ordinary person is at a disadvantage. For example, Clifford Giles suggests that participants in lifestyle makeover series have to adopt the aesthetic tastes of the experts and presenters if they are to ensure an equal footing (2002). Reality gameshows operate on a similar principle, although they provide the opportunity for ordinary people to manage themselves over a period of time. As reality gameshows became popular, participants learned to play the game, often by creating conflict, a staple of this format. They also have learned to play the fame game, with winning not necessarily essential to their success outside of the programme: 'only one person wins, but the gift of exposure is given to many and this is, after all, what television gives most freely' (Bonner 2003: 92).

Graeme Turner argues 'celebrity – as a discourse, as a commodity, as a spectacle – is marked by contradictions, ambiguities and ambivalences' (2004: 109). Turner draws on Rojek's model of celebrity as something someone is ascribed through blood relations, achieved through work or attributed through the media. He also takes Rojek's term 'celetoid' (someone whose fame comes fast and is short lived) and applies it to the rise of the reality gameshow where the goal is the construction of the celetoid. For Turner, reality television producers have 'taken control of the economy of celebrity by turning it into the outcome of a programming strategy'; and reality television participants pursue 'celebrity as an objective rather than as a by product of personal activity' (ibid.: 54, 63). This leads Turner to reflect on the role of ordinary people within celebrity industries and culture. If ordinary people have greater access to celebrity through such formats as reality gameshows or talk shows, then celebrity becomes less an elite experience and more an everyday expectation.

If we take this a step further, the complexities of celebrity can equally be applied to ordinary people. We cannot assume a common understanding of 'ordinary people', nor that people who watch reality gameshows want to be on TV. Reality television is so diverse that there are different constructions of the 'ordinary', and it is so fast moving that our understanding of the 'ordinary' changes with it. Thus many *Big Brother* viewers no longer expect to see an ordinary person on the show, nor would they associate themselves with the kind of people who are contestants. Bonner claims that for the most part 'the people who appear on ordinary television seem just like those who watch it, just a little better looking, a little more articulate, a little luckier' (2003: 97). This may be the case with certain genres, but with regard to reality gameshows this is no longer always the case. The Swedish term 'media hot' is a negative description of ordinary people who participate in reality gameshows (see later discussion).

Coming back to informed consent, the way viewers in this study place responsibility on reality participants is associated with their genre knowledge and their position as reality game players. Winston's suggestion that film makers should be responsible for ethical fallout resulting from the use of participants in reality formats is a position that works as long as audiences are knowledgeable about media production practices. Hibberd *et al.* asked their respondents to list the kinds of information participants should be told about before they agreed to be on popular factual programmes, and the most popular response was 'don't know' (2000: 33). It isn't necessary for audiences to know about production practices in order to like or dislike a programme, but it is necessary if their views are to be taken into account in ethical issues concerning fair treatment. The next section considers audience attitudes towards the moral and social ordering of participants in different factual genres.

Fairness

The topic of fair treatment of different social groups was the basis for a series of questions in the survey related to attitudes towards treatment of non-professionals, public figures and celebrities. The different groups of people included a range of social groups. The range was not exhaustive, and the intention was to gauge whether respondents perceived programme makers as treating some people differently to others. The selected categories included young children, teenagers, men, women, elderly, ethnic minorities, people with mental health problems, people with disabilities, politicians, experts and celebrities. The British survey also included royals, the treatment of which is a topic of heated debate in Britain, especially since the death of Princess Diana in the late 1990s. Respondents were asked if they thought programme makers treated these different groups of people fairly in three broad factual categories: news, documentary and reality programmes. These broad genre headings were used instead of a longer list of programme categories and titles, as the intention was to see if genre played a part in attitudes to fair treatment of different groups of people. Rather than have a long list of programme categories, there was a long list of groups of people. They were also asked how important it was to them that these groups of people were treated fairly in the three genre headings. In the focus groups, participants were asked 'are there right and wrong ways to treat people who take part in factual programmes?' and prompted to consider a variety of factual categories, including the large variety of titles used in the categorization game.

Perception and value of fair treatment

The results of the surveys show a generally positive perception of fair treatment in news for all social groups. Figure 7.1 outlines British perceptions of fair treatment in news and reality genres. These two categories confirm the influence of genre evaluation on social and cultural attitudes to fairness. Documentary has been excluded from these tables as the results were very similar to news (see later in this section). Respondents perceived men (68 per cent), women (66 per cent), children (66 per cent) and the elderly (61 per cent) as very/fairly well treated in news, followed by ethnic minorities (59 per cent), experts (58 per cent) and teenagers (54 per cent). Half the sample thought politicians (50 per cent) and people with disabilities (49 per cent) were treated very/fairly well, whilst 45 per cent thought celebrities, royals and people with mental health problems were treated very/fairly well. Comparing perceptions of fair treatment in news with reality TV, respondents thought people of all groups were treated much less fairly in reality TV (approximately 20 to 30 percentage points lower).

Figure 7.2 shows that British viewers value fair treatment for all social groups in news. For example, 74 per cent valued very fair treatment of the elderly, 73 and 72 per cent, respectively for people with disabilities or mental health problems, and 69 per cent for women and young children. Men,

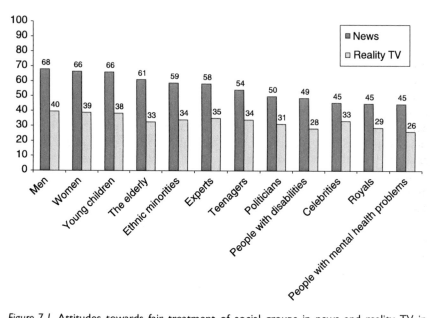

Figure 7.1 Attitudes towards fair treatment of social groups in news and reality TV in Britain (per cent 'very/fairly well treated').

* British survey unweighted sample 4,516.

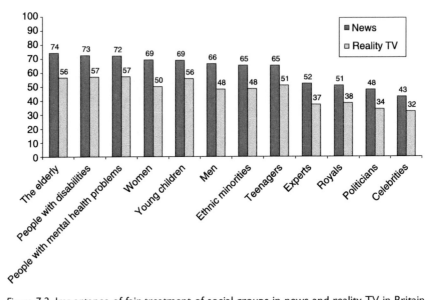

Figure 7.2 Importance of fair treatment of social groups in news and reality TV in Britain (per cent 'very important that people are treated fairly').

* British survey unweighted sample 4,516.

teenagers and ethnic minorities also scored highly in the value scale, with around 65 per cent. Experts (52 per cent), royals (51 per cent), politicians (48 per cent) and celebrities (43 per cent) scored lower due to their public personas in the media. If we compare these figures with those for reality TV, respondents placed less value on the fair treatment of all groups (approximately 15 to 20 percentage points lower) but the ranking is about the same. The difference between perception and value of fair treatment indicates a critical take on this issue. For example, respondents highly valued the fair treatment of the elderly in news (74 per cent) but perceived fair treatment to be less than they would wish (61 per cent). Whilst the elderly, men, women and children scored fairly highly in Figures 7.1 and 7.2, people with disabilities and mental health problems scored significantly lower in Figure 7.1 (approximately 30 percentage points lower). These statistics indicate that viewers are particularly critical of the way programme makers treat people with disabilities and mental health problems. In terms of celebrities and politicians, they remain at the bottom of the scale, with viewers perceiving their treatment by programme makers proportionate with the value placed on fairness for these public figures.

Figures 7.3 and 7.4 show the results for the Swedish survey. The results are similar in that there is a difference between the perception and value of fair treatment in news and reality genres, and also an order for social groups. In

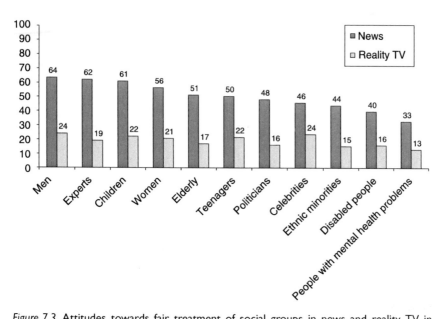

Figure 7.3 Attitudes towards fair treatment of social groups in news and reality TV in Sweden (per cent 'very/fairly well treated').

* Swedish survey unweighted sample 944.

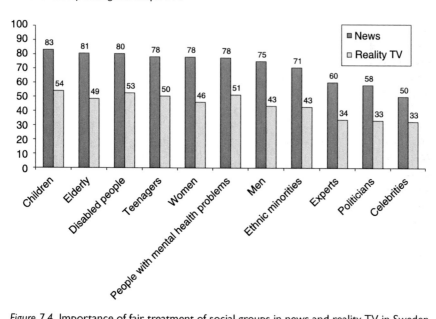

Figure 7.4 Importance of fair treatment of social groups in news and reality TV in Sweden (per cent 'very important that people are treated fairly').

* Swedish survey unweighted sample 944.

terms of perceptions of fair treatment in news, the differences between the two countries indicated Swedish respondents were generally more critical than British respondents. For example, there was approximately a 10 per cent difference for women, the elderly and people with mental health problems or disabilities. There was almost a 20 per cent difference for ethnic minorities. The other groups were perceived similarly to Britain. It is likely that the differences are due to social attitudes towards these specific groups, and their representations in the media in both countries, but research would be necessary to look into this further.

What can be interpreted from the results is that genre evaluation and fairness are dependent on the production and reception contexts in both countries. In Sweden, fair treatment in reality TV is perceived as very low compared to Britain. Whereas there is a slightly lower rating for fair treatment in news, the differential for reality TV ranges from 20 to 40 per cent, almost double that for Britain. Swedish respondents were therefore especially critical of reality programme makers and their ethical treatment of participants. If we consider the production contexts for reality genres in Sweden, then the high proportion of foreign, in particular American, reality formats should be taken into account. Also, the *Expedition Robinson* scandal in the late 1990s was concerned with the suicide of an ex-participant in the first version of *Survivor* (see Chapter 2). Such media scandals and public debate on ethical treatment of participants would perhaps be a factor in respondents' attitudes, although it is more the general perception of reality TV as humiliating people that makes Swedish respondents so critical of the genre. In general, Swedish viewers are more critical of current ethical practices in factual and reality television compared to Britain. This compares with the generally higher positive evaluation of traditional factual genres in the results for social value, or attitudes to truth claims, or knowledge.

Both countries share similar moral and social ordering for the value of fair treatment. A distinction emerges for those groups thought to be more vulnerable in society, who may need other people to act on their behalf in terms of rights. Children are one such group, and the results are similar to those found by Messenger Davies and Mosdell (2001), where viewers want children to receive high levels of care whilst participating in television. In particular, people who are cared for privately, or publicly, for physical disabilities or mental health problems are near to the top of a value scale. An ethics of care becomes significant here, as those people whom we have a duty to care for, especially a public duty of care, are exactly the people viewers worry about in terms of their treatment by programme makers. The degree of criticism of existing fair treatment by viewers is a signal that programme makers are being asked to be more transparent about how they look after these groups. It may be that once the public understood more about existing practices, their concerns would diminish. Or it could be that a high degree of concern for such groups is part of general social attitudes in a welfare state. Either way, it is evident that audiences are looking for a public ethics of care with regard to specific social groups and their representation in factual television.

Both countries also share attitudes towards people in the public eye. The results suggest viewers think politicians and celebrities get the treatment they deserve. As we saw in the research on perceptions of truth claims, and levels of performance, in politics and celebrity programmes there was an all-round cynicism to these genres and the participants. These attitudes reflect national trends in distrust in politicians or celebrities and their motivations for being in the media, and correspondingly public awareness of performance and political spin. With politicians, the right to know defence is an influencing factor, as viewers think it is the job of investigative journalists to give politicians a hard time (see next section). With celebrities, current research on 'celebrity bashing' in tabloid papers and magazines, and television, radio and websites, links negative attitudes to class and power. Ordinary people take pleasure in the representation of celebrities as flawed, a 'how the mighty have fallen' position that makes non-celebrities feel better about themselves (Turner 2004). Johannson found that tabloid readers enjoyed negative stories of celebrities because it made them feel morally superior, and reduced the impression of celebrities as 'better than us' (2006). However, the context to the representation of celebrities and their motivations for participating are closely bound up with attitudes to ethical treatment in the media. The authenticity of their emotions, their personal reasons for participating, are important to the way audiences judge celebrities.

Age, gender and class

There is a similarity of attitudes across age, gender and socio-economic status. Whereas we might expect to find particular respondents being more or less critical of fair treatment of their own representational group, this is not the case. For example, in the British survey, perceptions of fair treatment of teenagers in news were the same for young adults aged 16–24, and older adults aged 65 + (47 per cent). Perceptions of the elderly were also similar for both age groups (57 and 50 per cent, respectively). If we compare responses based on gender or socio-economic status (using the AB/DE grades, see Chapter 1 for details), the results are the same. For example, in terms of the elderly, around 50 per cent of male and female respondents, and AB/DE respondents thought they were treated very/fairly well in the news. The value of fair treatment was also similar. In terms of gender, perceptions of fair treatment of women in news were similar for male and female respondents (62 and 57 per cent, respectively). Once again, the value accorded to fairness was similar.

Perceptions of fair treatment of ethnic minorities in the news shows similar results across age (48 per cent 16–24, 42 per cent 65+), gender (47 per cent males, 44 per cent females) and socio-economic status (49 per cent AB, 42 per cent DE). Taking people with mental health problems as another example, there was a 10 per cent difference in perceptions of fair treatment in news for younger and older respondents (44 per cent 16–24, 34 per cent 65+). The value attributed to fairness also altered accordingly (49 and 33 per cent, respectively). Two other groups also were perceived a bit differently by younger and older respondents, with a 5–10 per cent difference for the perception and value of fair treatment of politicians and celebrities, suggesting older respondents were a bit more critical of their treatment than younger viewers.

Turning to reality TV, we might expect younger adults and women to perceive fair treatment differently from older adults or males because of their greater familiarity with the genre. We might also expect respondents from lower socio-economic groups to have somewhat different attitudes to other groups based on their frequency of viewing, and also because class is so often cited as a major factor in the content of reality programming (see Holmes and Jermyn 2004; Murray and Ouellette 2004, amongst others). However, whilst there are some minor variations, attitudes are remarkably similar. Perceptions of fair treatment of teenagers in reality TV were somewhat different for young adults aged 16–24 (38 per cent) and older adults aged 65+ (28 per cent). If we compare responses based on gender or socio-economic status, around 30 per cent of male and female respondents, respectively, and 25 and 39 per cent of AB/DE respondents, respectively, thought teenagers were treated very/fairly well in reality TV. The value of fair treatment was the same across the variables. The results indicate that those respondents less likely to watch reality TV were a bit more critical of programme makers' treatment of these groups, but that all respondents were in general agreement on the value accorded fairness.

In terms of gender, perceptions of fair treatment of women in reality TV were similar for male and female respondents (35 and 37 per cent, respectively). Once again, the value accorded to fairness was also similar. Perceptions of fair treatment of ethnic minorities in reality TV shows similar results across age (35 per cent 16–24, 30 per cent 65+), gender (30 per cent males, 31 per cent females) and socio-economic status (28 per cent AB, 33 per cent DE). Taking people with mental health problems as another example, there were similar perceptions of fair treatment in reality TV for younger and older respondents (27 per cent 16–24, 22 per cent 65+). The value attributed to fairness was also similar (57 and 59 per cent, respectively). There was also agreement across gender and socio-economic variables for this group. Politicians were perceived a bit differently by younger and older respondents (32 per cent 16–24, 27 per cent 65+) and by AB (24 per cent) and DE (34 per cent) respondents. There was slightly greater value accorded politicians by AB respondents (10 per cent difference). Similarly, celebrities were perceived a bit differently by younger and older respondents (36 per cent 16–24, 26 per cent 65+), AB (28 per cent) and DE (36 per cent) respondents, and there was slightly greater value accorded celebrities by AB respondents (10 per cent difference). Once again, those respondents less likely to watch reality TV were a bit more critical of programme makers' treatment of these groups. Those respondents who were more likely to watch reality TV placed slightly less value on fair treatment of politicians and celebrities.

Genre

Attitudes towards news and documentary ethics are very similar. To use Britain as an example, 54 per cent of respondents perceived children to be treated very well in documentaries (same as for news), 40 per cent for politicians (44 per cent for news) and 39 per cent for celebrities (42 per cent for news). There were similar attitudes towards the perception and value of fair treatment in documentary for all groups, apart from people with mental health problems or disabilities, where there was some criticism as to their treatment. For example, the perception and value of experts was 48 and 41 per cent, respectively, and the following for men (52 and 53 per cent), women (53/51 per cent), and for people with mental health problems (39 and 57 per cent) and disabilities (42 and 57 per cent). The general agreement of the perception and value of fairness highlights how viewers perceive the treatment of most participants by programme makers proportionate with the value placed on fairness. The value scales used for documentary are slightly lower than those for news (about 10 per cent less), which is in keeping with the general social value attributed to these genres (see Chapter 3).

Comparing genres, reality TV is perceived differently by viewers. Although we might expect attitudes towards fair treatment to differ according to demographic variables, there are only minor differences. The statistics paint a picture of general agreement on ethical treatment of different social groups. Rather than identifying with specific social groups, according to age, gender or socio-economic status, viewers use genre evaluation and social attitudes towards people to create a moral and social order for fairness. The key factors are an ethics of care towards vulnerable groups, a public interest defence for people in the public eye, and the motivations of ordinary people who participate in reality TV. Rather than building relationships with ordinary people in reality programming as 'people like us', viewers make clear distinctions between themselves and reality participants. As Winston (2000) argued, the fact that reality participants are in something created for television rather than naturally occurring in real life is a major factor in audience assessment of fair treatment. However, as we shall see in the next section, it is reality participants rather than programme makers who are ultimately held responsible for the representation of themselves on TV.

Contexts

There is an ideal ethical position with regard to fairness. This is a universal position, one where people have a right to be treated fairly and equally. In one sense, the results in the previous section support a universal right to fair treatment, as respondents in the surveys thought everyone deserved some level of fair treatment. The following comment illustrates an ideal ethical position: 'All human beings should be treated with the same respect. I don't think it matters that you're on TV, like, if there is a news reader, a celebrity and a homeless person, all three should be treated the same' (30-year-old female bar manager). An awareness of the contexts to participation in TV shouldn't get in the way of general principles. As this viewer explains: 'You always want to be treated like everybody else is treated' (21-year-old female student). The law of reciprocity so integral to an ethics of care is treated by this viewer as a universal value. An ethics of care is also apparent in general attitudes towards the responsibility of caring for those people perceived as more vulnerable than others: 'I think the worst thing will be someone that obviously looks like they can't speak for themselves, act for themselves, and then they're taken advantage of' (27-year-old salesman). There is a sense of the audience as looking into a mirror, and seeing the fair treatment of other people on television as a reflection of how they would like to be treated themselves. This is especially the case for ordinary people, where there is some recognition that non-professionals represent members of the public, that is to say, the audience as public: 'I think because we are ordinary people, we would like to see other ordinary people being treated good' (27-year-old female sales advisor).

An ideal notion of fairness does not take into account fundamental differences within value judgements for participants in television. The context to ethical treatment of participants matters. Winston (2000) argued against ethical systems in favour of a relativist situational ethics for journalists and documentary film makers. This kind of ethical position is based on an awareness of moral principles, such as a respect for basic rights, but at the same time an application of ethics that is situated in professional practices, and which ultimately relies on personal moral judgements as to right and wrong ways to live our lives. A similar ethical position is also adopted by audiences. There is an awareness of moral principles, such as universal humans rights, care and responsibility, but there is also an application of these principles that is situated in social and cultural values, and in the practices of participation and television viewing. As audience attitudes to fairness are so similar, personal moral judgements are bound up with social knowledge and genre knowledge, as discussed in the previous chapter. Therefore, whilst audiences generally agree that all people should be treated fairly in television, the context to participation, and the motivations of participants and programme makers, complicates matters.

News

In relation to news practices, the common understanding that people who are asked to take part in news are mainly treated fairly gives way to a more contextual position. The way journalists treat victims of tragedy, the way they investigate the private lives of celebrities, the manner in which they question politicians, all provide opportunities for viewers to reflect on particular examples of fairness. This doesn't mean to say that viewers are the best judge of journalism ethics, but it is to say that they share a similar view to many journalists, which is that ethics are situated within practices. The most common topic of discussion regarding news and fairness was treatment of victims, and ordinary people. These were people who were thought to be vulnerable, either emotionally vulnerable or open to manipulation by others. A group of male and female participants (aged 40–55) talked about the focus on emotions for victims of tragedies:

BIANCA: I hate how some of the presenters, you know, when somebody has been through quite a dramatic situation, and the presenters ask 'how do you feel?' You know.

JOSTEIN: Yeah, that is horrible.

BIANCA: And then there would be another saying 'and how did you feel?' and another and another. You know, you're not supposed to ask how people feel, you should just do a programme about that.

BETH: Also, when there was the earthquake, and I was watching it on television, on CNN, and they would exactly be like that. And they'd describe how the earthquake was, and 'what did you lose?' and 'oh, your family died.'

JOSTEIN: After they had this [story] for the London bombs: 'what do you feel after three months?' I mean, it was your son, it was your brother, what's the use of these questions? It's probably reality TV infected.

Their condemnation of this style of journalism is to do with their own responses to the emotions of the victims. The perceived intrusive questioning of people's feelings, the repetitive emphasis on emotional drama, makes these viewers feel uncomfortable. One viewer connects emotions with reality TV, seeing it as an infectious disease that has transmuted to news. Their reactions go against other research in news reportage of tragic events, where it was found that the humanizing aspects of a specific event can help audiences to connect with the people involved, such as the loss of a son during armed conflict (Philo and Berry 2004). The use of emotions in news coverage of violence has been greatly influential in public opinion about war, or natural or man-made disasters (Seaton 2005). It is a powerful communication tool, and yet here it is criticized because these viewers feel it is overused, that it is intrusive not only to the people involved but to the news genre itself.

In the Swedish survey, a series of questions were asked about the news coverage of the tsunami catastrophe on 26 December 2004. There was a high degree of trust in the general treatment of victims and their relatives and friends by the news media, with 52 per cent claiming their trust was very, or fairly high. Respondents made clear distinctions between fair treatment of the victims on SVT and TV4, the two most respected channels for public service news provision, and the tabloids. Over half the sample thought SVT and TV4 judged it right (58 and 53 per cent, respectively), but 43 per cent claimed that the tabloids were too intrusive. As this focus group participant explained, the scale of the human tragedy was sometimes too much to take: 'the crisis in Asia, how people who were in shock and got filmed close up, and all this tragedy, the media may have made a violation . . . it gets too close, so that you instead can't take it in but shut off totally' (29-year-old Swedish female clerk). The emotional coverage so common to tabloid papers would have been part of the criticism of fairness and intrusion in news reportage of the catastrophe. Tabloid journalism has been accused of 'sensationalising the news, short circuiting reason through excessive emotionality' (Glynn 2000: 7). The respondents reacted to a perceived emotional excess, and the Swedish tabloids crossed a line between acceptable and unacceptable responses to victims. These respondents already had an emotional investment in the victims and their friends and relatives, as 15 per cent personally knew victims, and 33 per cent knew of friends who had been affected by the catastrophe. With such an emotional investment already in place, sensitivity to the victims of the catastrophe was paramount, and any attempt at sensationalism roundly condemned.

Another viewer commented on the perceived formulaic journalistic techniques in the use of ordinary people in news items:

> Most normal people probably get ensnared in news coverage . . . I mean I think it's really like they've been given a short script . . . I think the news industry learns from dealing with ordinary people, and I think it's such a set agenda, probably such a winning formula for them that nothing is going to really change that (39-year-old male health psychologist).

As with the previous examples, it is the repetitiveness of these ways of treating ordinary people that is criticized. The 'set agenda', the 'scripting' of ordinary people is something news professionals are perceived to have learned. It is not the use of ordinary people in news, but the overuse of particular styles of interview that is of concern here. Similar to criticism of emotional melodrama and intrusion, the accusation of journalistic bias is something associated with tabloid journalism and its heavy emphasis on style and repetitive news agendas. It is also associated with reality TV, not a genre viewers want to see infecting news values. A comment by the following viewer on the heavy coverage of victims in news stories shows that concern for the fair treatment of victims can also be about the way viewers feel emotionally uncomfortable when watching such stories:

> I think what the news quite often does, to personalize the story, is to pick a victim and sort of follow that victim through, and that really annoys me . . . during the Iraq war, there was that young boy, who was really made the sort of focus and the symbol of the war. . . . And I don't quite know why, but there was something that was very uncomfortable for me about that. Not for him, but more for the audience . . . (36-year-old female personal assistant).

Her uncomfortable feelings are as much to do with her own interest in following the young boy as her perception of his treatment by journalists.

Professionals

Contradictory positions are at work in viewers' attitudes towards the treatment of people in the public eye. Viewers recognize that news of celebrities and public figures can be intrusive. As this discussion shows, using the public's right to know as a defence means professionals are accorded less rights to privacy:

GARETH: The problem is that they don't ever do coverage, like, an apology-coverage (21-year-old male writer).

ROSE: They always say 'oh, he's been acquitted' but they don't say 'sorry about hounding you outside your kids' school, your church, your supermarket, your restaurant' (25-year-old female photographer).

The perceived absence of an apology coverage highlights how ethical treatment of professionals is situated in common journalistic practices. The following comment is a rare example of a viewer defending people in the public eye: 'I think because they're professionals you should maybe respect their private life' (30-year-old female multimedia developer). The 'maybe' in between 'should' and 'respect' signifies ambivalence towards the rights of professionals. This Swedish viewer explained: 'Of course celebrities should have a private life as well, but if you have chosen to be a celebrity you have to put up with that people want to know what you're doing' (25-year-old female student).

With politicians, most viewers draw on the 'right to know' defence to explain their position: 'you have to be tough. You have to be like that because politicians, they have the ability to go around the subject, and around, and around, and around' (41-year-old male financial consultant). The use of spin and other political techniques means many viewers feel politicians should be given a hard time, and questioned by a professional journalist who has learned to play the political game: 'you have to push them very hard because they are professional debaters . . . which is why you think "how does he manage to sort of wriggle out of that?", but that's their job' (34-year-old male bookseller). As with celebrities, their treatment is judged in terms of their proximity to the media, and their level of media knowledge, or public relations expertise. The more professional a politician appears, the more viewers want to see journalists use professional techniques to challenge politicians. In Britain, many viewers referred to several well-known journalists, such as Jeremy Paxman, Jon Snow, or John Humphrys, as doing a necessary job in keeping politicians on their toes. Some Swedish viewers complained that journalists were too polite towards politicians and wanted a more challenging journalistic style. There is a certain satisfaction in seeing politicians given a hard time within the framework of the right to know defence, and politicians have learned to expect it, and indeed at times to use it to their advantage (see Corner and Pels 2003).

Reality performers

The motivations of participants in reality TV are also judged according to their knowledge of the format and what is expected of them as participants. The fact that many viewers lack knowledge of specific production practices in reality television does not stop them from judging participants. As this viewer points out, there is little information on what people get out of being in a reality programme: 'Does anyone know what these people get out of, like, *Wife Swap*? What do you actually get out of being part of that? That's what I don't know. Do you think they're paid? Does anyone know?' (30-year-old female shop assistant). There were no answers to her questions, and yet there were many opinions on the desires of reality participants to be famous. The phrase 'wannabe TV' came up again and again, reflecting the high level of reality gameshow and talentshow formats viewers were familiar with. It also reflected a common knowledge regarding reality participants as ambitious and hungry for fame, something regularly reinforced by interviews with ex-participants, coverage of the participants in tabloid newspapers and celebrity magazines such as *Heat*, and the media careers of participants, no matter how short lived. Holmes (2004) has reflected on the construction of celebrity 'out of the ordinary' in reality TV. In research on Norwegian popular factual television, Ytreberg points out the high degree of performance within these formats, and the level of preparation by the media production team in ensuring non-professionals give a particular performance that is relevant to the format (2004). Viewers see themselves as cynical consumers of these participants. The following comment illustrates the connections between the knowing audience and the knowing participant:

When I saw a bit of *Big Brother* recently, I didn't realize they were so, kind of, they are wannabes. I thought they were genuinely just people plucked out of nowhere. They all, like, wanted to be a presenter. . . . Reality TV is, they're more like sort of caged animals. And they're agreeing to be degraded. Whereas in documentaries I think, there is a tradition of respect and humanism in documentary making. There should be. People who want to make documentaries are different types of persons to people who'd get involved in reality TV (30-year-old male gardener).

There is the common reference to reality participants as wannabes. The comparison between genuinely ordinary people and this species of reality performers reinforces the perception that these participants will do anything in order to be on television. It also signifies a moral line being crossed, where human beings become less than human. This degradation is distinctive to reality TV, and whereas documentaries have still retained their moral values, the people who 'get involved in reality TV' willingly debase themselves.

In the above comment there is an indirect acknowledgement that the audience is complicit in the treatment of reality performers, with the reference to caged animals implying there must be visitors to this human zoo. For some viewers the fact that people may have willingly chosen to be captive does not mean that they deserve ill treatment. As this 34-year-old Swedish mother explained: 'I think for docusoaps, even if there is a contract, there has to be some kind of integrity. Even if they've got themselves to blame, it doesn't mean it is right.' Another viewer argued that participants don't necessarily know how their representations will be used:

When you apply for a docusoap and get chosen and agree to go on, then you have to take the DVD with ridiculous moments where you make a fool of yourself . . . but then, of course, there's always people who don't realize what it means . . . they understand what it means, but they don't realize what it means to them in the future, what the effects are. There I think you have a responsibility to make sure that these people who maybe haven't understood what effects this is going to have on their lives, that you help them (30-year-old Swedish male civil servant).

His comments on ethical treatment of reality performers and the responsibility of programme makers indicates an overall concern for fair treatment, and an awareness that these people are often put into challenging situations in order to make entertaining television. His concerns were echoed by a minority of viewers, such as this woman: 'I think they have a belief or a sense of what they think they're getting into but the reality is actually something quite different. And how honest are the producers, how prepared are contestants for it when they go in?' (34-year-old female teacher).

However, the majority of viewers felt that the contract between programme makers and participants was evidence that these people had given their informed consent, and therefore were mainly responsible for anything that happened to them during filming. One viewer joked that if people were unhappy with their treatment they should go to the reality TV union, implying both a professionalization of reality participants, and also their lack of rights as non-professionals. These are two examples of this common point of view:

> There is a difference between somebody who has signed a contract and somebody who didn't. If you sign a contract, if you're stupid enough to sign it, you have to live with it (21-year-old male artist).

> I think that they sort of know what they let themselves in for when they sign up for the shows, whilst I don't think it's wholly fair to really, really destroy someone and I don't like watching it (25-year-old female illustrator).

The contract becomes a get-out clause not only for programme makers but also for audiences. In the next section we shall examine how some viewers feel uncomfortable about their reactions to reality participants. Their uncomfortable feelings are partly to do with sympathy for the participants, but also with feelings of shame in their own viewing experience.

Humiliation TV

The post-war television series *Candid Camera* is an early example of reality TV, with its emphasis on hidden cameras and social drama. McCarthy traces a link between *Candid Camera* and the 'reality TV generation, where pranksters portray average citizens as mooks and buffoons, and critics bemoan the fact that people respond with homemade video pratfalls of their own' (2004: 37). The hoax was a central part of *Candid Camera*, where members of the public were set up so that viewers could observe human behaviour and laugh at the lengths people would go to fit in with others. Although the hoax has comedic value, it is also a means to humiliate or shame other people. The contemporary example McCarthy refers to is from MTV, where people were secretly filmed fishing for a $20 note in a used public toilet (*The Man Show*). Other examples relate to crime, where the comedic potential of the hoax is dropped in favour of a sting operation that exposes criminal activities (for example, *House of Horrors*). It isn't even necessary to stage an elaborate hoax in many reality series. Caught on camera footage is often used to show criminals and ordinary people in compromising situations (*Neighbours from Hell*, *America's Dumbest Criminals* are two examples). Of the many emotions that different kinds of reality programmes can produce, humiliation is one example that connects *Candid Camera* with contemporary reality gameshows, talentshows and the reality hoax. Participants in these types of reality TV can be made to feel embarrassed and humiliated, they can be shamed and also act in shameless ways. Shame is a powerful emotion in audience responses to reality participants.

The emotion of shame

There are various ways of understanding emotions. Emotions can be some-thing inherent to our bodies; we are born with a basic set of emotions and cultivate them as we grow older. Social and behavioural researchers have argued that while emotions begin with a bodily sensation, 'emotional behav-iour is mediated through judgement and context', so that ' 'humans make judgements in relation to the physical sensations they feel when deciding what emotional state they are in' (Lupton 1998: 13). Another approach to emotions suggests that they are part of social and cultural processes. Sociolo-gists have looked at 'the ways in which norms and expectations about the emotions are generated, reproduced, and operate in specific socio-cultural settings, and the implications for selfhood and social relations of emotional experience and expression' (Lupton: 1998: 15). One of the most well-known sociological studies of emotions is that of Hochschild and her research into air stewardesses. Hochschild observed how these workers had to manage their emotions, hiding their feelings of anger or resentment towards annoying travellers because it was part of their profession to be calm and in control. Hochschild called this 'emotion work', where we change and manage our emotions. She also argued that we refer to 'feeling rules' to manage our emotions, for example the way that we draw on pre-existing expectations about how to react at a wedding or funeral. Those people who do not follow 'feeling rules' stand out from the crowd, and may provoke strong emotions in others. Emotions are also personal experiences. As Denzin argues, 'emotional practices are both practical and interpretive. They are personal, embodied, situated . . . emotional practices make people problematic objects to them-selves' (1984: 89). Emotions therefore are something we feel, something we work at in social situations, and something that we personally experience in our day-to-day lives.

Shame is an emotion often thought of as negative. It literally means to cover, and the sensation of shame is about feeling uncovered, exposed and vulnerable to condemnation from others. Ahmed points out that shame is most often attributed to oneself, it is a 'bad feeling', a self-realization that we have acted wrongly, and have been found out by others (2004: 104–5). Humiliation and embarrassment are part of feeling shame. These emotions usually involve an audience of some kind, even if we are the imagined audience, reflecting on our shameful actions. Shame involves negative self-perception, and a feeling that other people will look badly on us. Shame can be managed, so that we can be made to feel ashamed either by ourselves or others. The work of shame can be used to make people feel included, just as the person shamed is made to feel an outsider. Alongside shame is the notion of shame-lessness, a condemnatory term applied to someone who acts with no awareness of shame. People who are shameless are thought to have scant regard for 'feeling rules' for specific social situations, they are unconcerned about what other people may think, they are empty of this emotion, hence the phrase 'have you no shame?'

Shame is connected to interest. Drawing on the work of Silvan Tomkins, Probyn argues that shame is a necessary emotion, one that we should not be ashamed of experiencing. Shame connects to interest because 'without interest there can be no shame, conversely shame alerts us to things, people, and ideas that we didn't even know we wanted' (Probyn 2005: 14). She claims 'shame illuminates our intense attachment to the world, our desire to be connected with others, and the knowledge that, as merely human, we will sometimes fall in our attempts to maintain those connections' (ibid.). She maintains 'when we feel shame, it is because our interest has been interfered with but not cancelled out' (ibid.: 15). Looking at shame in this way, it is not only a negative emotion, but rather an uncomfortable, sometimes hurtful, emotion, which alerts us to what is important in our lives. By that rationale, those people who are shameless lack interest in things most of us are invested in and emotionally attached to. However, our sense of shame is both personal and social, and what one person may be interested in will not necessarily be the same as others, so shame means different things to different people depending on the circumstances.

Shame and reality TV

In his analysis of crime, Gareth Palmer highlights how shame is part of the communicative form of reality TV. He shows how the shaming of others is used time and again in a variety of formats, such as *Judge Judy* and the shaming of members of the public on trial, or *Neighbours from Hell* and the shaming of antisocial behaviour. He argues that the 'spectacle of shame' is part of the reality genre. With shows such as *Stupid Behaviour Caught on Tape* or *America's Dumbest Criminals*, we can witness the shaming of others; it is the 'television equivalent of a high fat snack we should feel ashamed about enjoying because it is undoubtedly bad for us' (2003: 14). Shaming criminals is something that has been taken up by law enforcers and judges as a technique for social order and retribution. Palmer points out the connections between 'name and shame' practices for criminals in newspapers, and the use of surveillance or camcorder footage of antisocial behaviour in reality programming. In an examination of the work of shame in *Video Vigilantes*, he claims that reality television has provided ample opportunities for shaming others: 'shaming offers us membership . . . it has never been easier to share our concerns about other people's behaviour and to become active in utilising shame to express this' (2006). He argues that:

'the use of shame, the deployment of surveillance techniques, the role of the crowd-audience-community are all means of governance which find their way into our lived experience of self and others' (2003: 160). The work of shame therefore is something used to control other people and their perceptions of law and order, or discourses concerning moral values in contemporary society.

Not all reality TV is about humiliating people. In Britain, and to a lesser extent Sweden, there are a variety of categories that make up popular factual television, from health-based reality programmes about people overcoming accidents and illness, to inspiring examples of people experiencing new things, to tips and advice on gardening or buying a home, all of which can present a positive message to viewers. However, some of the most dominant types of reality TV have been the reality gameshow (*Big Brother, Survivor*) and reality talentshow (*Pop Idol, X Factor*). These formats, and their celebrity cousins, have concentrated on putting people in difficult, often emotionally challenging, situations. Audiences have come to categorize this specific type of reality TV as 'humiliation TV'. One Swedish viewer made a pun on *Expedition Robinson* (*Survivor*) by calling it *Mobinson* – mobba means bullying in Swedish. After appearing in *Celebrity Big Brother* (Channel 4 2004, UK), the feminist critic Germaine Greer called *Big Brother* a bully and left the house after the public humiliation of a celebrity contestant. On eviction night, unpopular *Big Brother* contestants are booed and jeered by members of the public outside the house. The public repeatedly humiliated the celebrity Natalie Appleton in *I'm a Celebrity . . .* (ITV 2005, UK) when they voted for her to do tasks she had little chance of completing (for example, she was voted to attempt a height challenge after she confessed she was afraid of heights). *Pop Idol* includes the regular humiliation of contestants in their auditions to be on the show. Even a reality series about business, *Dragons' Den* (BBC 2006, UK), makes the humiliation of the inventors a staple of the format.

The use of shame is apparent in the ways viewers differentiate between themselves and the 'others' who participate in reality TV. The description of reality TV as 'humiliation TV' instantly connects shame with production and reception practices. Unlike the hoax, where ordinary people are unsuspecting participants in some form of public humiliation, many reality formats rely on people to apply to take part in a programme. It is prior knowledge of a specific format, and awareness of these reality programmes as 'humiliation TV', that makes reality participants stand out from the crowd, effectively giving up their rights as ordinary people. For example, this Swedish woman explains:

> If someone's in a docusoap for the first time you could think they were naïve and thinking 'that won't happen to me.' But if you've been in a docusoap, or you've seen how it can get angled and how wrongly you can be interpreted . . . then it's like 'well you've got yourself to blame' (23-year-old female student).

Another viewer commented on how reality participants audition for parts, acting outrageously, shamelessly, in order to be selected: 'I think they have absolutely signed up for it. You know they have the audition tape and, usually the ones that get in, they show the most outrageous thing they can do . . . so they know exactly what they're getting into' (36-year-old personal assistant).

To make reality participants responsible for their own actions is a strategy that takes responsibility away from programme makers and viewers. They literally sign up for humiliation. It is a perverse type of emotional contract where the participants bind themselves to the interests of reality programme makers. Their own personal interests in being reality participants are not shared by the majority of viewers. In fact, their interest in being a reality participant marks them out and makes them open to criticism. Viewers react negatively towards many reality participants, they use negative language to convey their emotions and they physically blush when recalling embarrassing moments in reality shows. Rather than identification and shared interests, viewers often negatively identify with reality participants. The emotional work strategies used by many viewers draw on humiliation, embarrassment and shame as a means to manage their relationship with reality participants. In managing their emotional relationships with reality participants, viewers control their investment in these people and also in the reality genre itself.

Take *Wife Swap* as an example. *Wife Swap* is a format devised by RDF, an independent production company, first shown on Channel 4 in Britain in the early 2000s, and since sold to over 20 countries worldwide. *Wife Swap* is a life experiment format. The programme revolves around the idea of taking a wife from one kind of family and placing them with another kind of family; the wives experiment in being each other, and the families experiment in a different kind of family life for a period of two weeks. Usually, two quite diverse families are part of the experiment, and this can sometimes lead to conflict as the families come to terms, or resist, other values and lifestyles. In the British version, the families often don't get on, and there is usually a shouting match at the end of the programme where the wives (and husbands) accuse each other of bad housekeeping and parenting. The most dominant response to *Wife Swap* is to mirror the judgemental attitudes of the participants. This viewer judged participants in *Wife Swap* in terms of the standards of housekeeping, a common theme in the series:

> You're gonna be judging them when you're watching a programme obviously. But at the end of the day . . . there are, like, basic standards that people should live to. That's what I'm saying, everyone should be clean, more or less, and I mean not clean up, like five times a day every day, but I mean you can't have rabbits in your bedroom and, like, you know what I'm saying, like . . . dust in every corner and . . . like, some creatures growing out of that stuff (23-year-old male sales assistant).

The reference to basic standards is not only referring to standards of cleanliness, but also shared interests in how people should live their lives. Hence, this viewer thinks the lack of basic standards shameful. He also judges participants according to their willingness to sign up to being on the programme in the first place: 'What makes me laugh is when you watch *Wife Swap* and you watch all the madness that happens, and then at the end they say "call this number if you wanna be in it as well", you chose to put yourself in that position.' Another remark illustrates a common view of participants in this programme: 'I just go "look you deserve that." If you're going to sign up your kids and your family and yourself to something like *Wife Swap* then you deserve to be in tears' (22-year-old female bar staff).

Lupton points out Western societies generally discourage the display of negative emotions, such as frustration, anger, jealousy, hate, scorn or rage. The expression of inappropriate emotions is 'generally viewed as personally or socially destructive, or both', and it is 'no longer thought acceptable to display violence, to inflict humiliation or express arrogance or feelings of superiority; to do so is to risk a loss of face and status' (1998: 171). Lupton argues that the overemphasis on controlling negative emotions has social consequences. The pressures of modern life can lead to feelings of frustration, resentment, anger, and to micro manage these negative feelings all the time can lead to alienation and distress (1998: 171). According to Lupton, knowing when to express feelings and when to repress them is a condition of living in modern societies. In this respect, participants in *Wife Swap* often let their emotions out and damn the consequences. There is little attempt to manage negative emotions or to be sensitive to feeling rules. There is an attraction in watching people behave badly, express scorn, show feelings of superiority, and shout and swear at fellow participants, including the children who can swear as well as their parents. But that attraction wears thin when there is little to identify with. As this viewer explained:

> There were fifty things for each of these couples to learn, and they might learn one of them. All I learn is that there are unpleasant people and I don't understand why someone would do that when there are children involved in it. . . . I saw one episode with a boozer couple and an uptight couple, and they both had problems, you know, I sat there in my couch, judging, because that's why people watch the show. And the kids involved in it looked very confused, like, okay, I'm in my room, my mom is gone for two weeks which is a little odd, there's TV cameras and my Dad's screaming at another woman who's telling me to get up and get dressed in the morning and she's a complete stranger. I don't think that's healthy for children (38-year-old female office assistant).

In the process of judging the participants, this viewer judges the programme makers. There is also an element of judging herself, the shaming process turns inwards and she has to think about her own reasons for judging these people in the first place.

John Hartley suggests that 'television is a major source of "people watching" for comparison and possible emulation' (1999: 155). Television can be used as a resource to learn about neighbourliness and how different or similar we are to others. He points out that many reality formats rely on the assumption that audiences will have pre-existing attitudes towards neighbourliness and civility. In this way, *Wife Swap* works as a resource for learning about the differences between participants in the series and their incivility towards each other. In many ways it teaches us about negative emotions and what happens when these are not controlled or managed. It highlights how there are different feeling rules for parenting, with some parents teaching their children about emotion work, and others eschewing the management of emotions. It also allows viewers to judge participants as fundamentally different to them, not just in how they clean their grill or put their children to bed, but in how they have agreed to go on the show in the first place. The comparative strategies for watching *Wife Swap* enable audiences to distance themselves from these kinds of people, and their ethical treatment of each other and by programme makers.

Media hot

The distancing strategy is even more apparent for reality gameshows and talentshows. This involves ordinary people as reality performers; people who are perceived as deliberately wanting to take part in a reality show in order to kick-start a career in the media. Some Swedish viewers call reality performers 'media hot' (*media kåt*). This refers to the participants' intense desires to become part of the media, they are 'hot for it'. The sexual connotations suggest an element of self-exploitation. There is also an implication that to be media hot participants attract heat in tabloid papers, celebrity magazines and chat shows, they become a 'hot topic'. To be 'media hot' also signifies reality performers will eventually burn themselves out, consumed by their own notoriety. As Turner suggests, reality viewers are cynical consumers of celebrities, perceiving reality performers as 'celetoids', people whose fame comes quick and is short lived (2004). They are also people who on the whole would not take part in a reality gameshow, and who do not like any of the personal characteristics that seem common to reality performers. This viewer explains:

> It's just about how to get on TV isn't it, everyone wants, well, not everyone because I certainly don't want to be, but some people just aspire to be on the screen. However it makes them look, in whatever context, because I might then be in the public eye, appear in *Heat* magazine and all these sort of things (34-year-old female teacher).

The other common term for reality performers is 'wannabes', a pejorative term that is reflected in the above comment on extroverts who want a level of attention that many viewers find difficult to understand.

The idea of celebrity when applied to reality performers is that they are 'media hot' in a way that debases them. Some viewers make references to the pornography industry in order to emphasize their perception of reality performers as degrading themselves: 'Well, look at who they are. . . . The policy seems to be whoring themselves, probably for a potential career, to become a celebrity, whatever celebrity means these days' (33-year-old male student). Her comments suggest that reality performers do not have real star quality, that 'whoring' themselves is the only way they will get in the media as they have no obvious talent. A discussion by a group of 21–23-year-old male and female participants illustrates this meaning of reality participants as media hot:

JACK: It's all about fame, isn't it? Those images in the beginning of those people queueing in the various cities like 'We want fame! We want fame.'

RACHEL: Yeah, absolutely and the programme teaches them to be very degrading to themselves. I think, I don't know whether or not that's how the production team manoeuvre them, but they just don't respect themselves.

CHARLIE: It's probably to give yourself a place in life as well. If you can see the most prominent version, the most successful, and you can see the most tragic or least successful out of something, because it gives you a position and makes you feel comfortable and safe.

JACK: It's like 'at least I'm not that!'

Their reference to the production of fame in these reality programmes highlights the kind of fame game that is at stake here. The perception is that people who choose to play this game lack respect for themselves. For some viewers, the strategy of comparison gives them the opportunity to feel better about themselves – 'at least I'm not like that!'

Negative identification can be about the conscious and unconscious ways we recognize things in our personality or behaviour we don't like. Psychologists call this projection, or projective identification. 'Projection involves the pushing out of the "good", and more often the "bad", feelings from the inner world to something or someone in the external world' (Lupton 1998: 29). Projective identification is when we recognize the parts of the self we have externalized in someone, but are not necessarily conscious that these feelings originated within our self (ibid.: 29). Shame can be part of projective identification, as our interest in something or someone that we feel ashamed about can be externalized as a means of unconsciously protecting ourselves from self-perceived negative feelings. In the above extract, viewers discussed how, through comparison, they could identify aspects of reality performers that were both positive and, mainly, negative. To say 'I'm not like that' implies a strong recognition of certain character traits and values that are perceived as external to the self. With regard to reality performers, these viewers mainly recognize negative character traits (a lack of self-respect) and values (fame at any cost). Rather harshly, reality performers are perceived as lacking in moral judgement, in putting their self-interest above other social and moral values. Lupton suggests that in contemporary Western societies, we are expected to manage our negative feelings, to keep them in check. One way to manage negative emotions is to externalize them onto others. If shame is connected to interest, then the shame that viewers feel when watching reality performers is perhaps connected to self-interest, those character traits and values associated with extroversion, insensitivity or irresponsibility. Viewers may not recognize these aspects of the self because they have projected them onto other people. Those viewers that do reflect on the comparison between themselves and reality performers may be working through negative emotions. In the following discussion between a group of male and female viewers (32–34 years old), they reflect on the negative aspects of *Big Brother*:

MARK: Well, that's the thing, it makes the dumb public feel like they are part of a process, because then they can call in at 90p a minute. I mean the whole thing is a scam. The *Big Brother* thing is a genius idea, but it's like a McDonald's burger it doesn't mean it's good for you. It's crap, but it's undeniable crap. You know it works, it just works.

RON: I don't know though, some of these people are just kids . . .

SYLVIA: Yeah, and I think they can really be quite mean to them. But then, sometimes, I just thought, 'well, why am I watching this? I don't really want to watch it, I think it's mean', but then I just continued. It's weird, but it seems sometimes that even if there is other stuff on the telly that you actually would want to watch, or learn something from, you sometimes end up watching the trash.

MARK: But, that's what I mean, these shows, they just make you feel kind of horrible. I mean the people on the shows are horrible and the people making the programmes are horrible to them.

Rather than aspects of reality programming being about a hoax, the whole premise of the genre is a hoax. These viewers recognize the negative sides of reality TV, they perceive it is unhealthy and 'horrible' and makes them ashamed to be part of it. And yet, they watch it. There is something about the negative emotions in this kind of reality programming that these viewers recognize, even as they condemn them. There is something of interest to them, even as they are shamed by it.

The shaming process that Palmer identifies as part of crime reality programming is similar to and different from this. He argues that viewers can join in the shaming of others, without necessarily recognizing their interest in what it is that is shameful. Whilst that is apparent in viewers' discussions of reality performers, there are times when they are ashamed of watching, and in so doing are aware of their personal interests in the behaviour of others. As this viewer explained: 'you sit watching it, laughing, or feel sorry for them, it gets so wrong, I don't know, it feels like you are a bit exploited, or that they are exploited. I don't want to watch it because I almost feel sorry for them' (24-year-old female student). There is the sense that reality participants and audiences are being manipulated at the same time. There is also the self-awareness that by watching viewers are actively participating in their own humiliation. Another comment highlights this self-awareness:

> I think sometimes they are just crossing the border, the line, like when they're asking the questions to the contestants. And I think, you know, sometimes you see them crying really bad, and really feeling uncomfortable in this sort of situation. And I really feel, like, you just want to switch off and just say stop it, because this person is going to have a breakdown in a minute. And I don't understand that sometimes, because it's, like, you know, it's like, it's okay if you're watching this, but do you really want to show this to the audience? I mean, sometimes, it's just too much, and you actually feel sorry for the person, and you want somebody to turn this off (21-year-old female student).

There is an uncomfortable realization that through watching certain reality programmes viewers are giving their informed consent to behaviour they condemn. Her inability to control the situation is reinforced by her constant reference to not being able to stop it and, as in a nightmare, she sees herself saying the words 'stop it' to programme makers, to participants and to herself, and yet she doesn't stop it. In the final section, the contradictory feelings of shame and interest in reality performers are considered in relation to ethics.

Shades of ethics

In the final part of this chapter some of the ethical issues raised in the audience research on fairness are explored further. In particular, the main finding that viewers have different positions on fairness for ordinary people in news or documentary and reality TV participants is put into the context of different degrees of ethics, from shallow to deep ethical positions on fair treatment of people in factual television. This section draws on different ethical positions used within environmentalism as a means to explore viewers' responses. This is not to say that environmental ethics is the only way to interpret the research in this chapter, but to point to the suggestive possibilities of using different shades of ethics to further understand complicated responses to fairness. It is the job of a much larger study to fully examine social ethics and audience responses to factual television. What follows are some reflections on how viewers' ethical positions vary depending on the contexts to participants in various factual and reality genres.

The rise of environmentalism has been one of the hallmarks of post-war Western societies. Philosophical questions concerning what it means to be human, legal questions concerning animal and human rights, historical and social questions on our changing relationships with nature and animals, all contribute toward environmentalism. Sociological research has moved from a view of nature and society as distinct from each other, to an approach that sees 'society and nature as a complex series of culturally embedded and contested practices' (Franklin 2001: 31). As we saw in Chapter 5 on actuality, the idea of nature as performed is part of this new approach. Ecological ethics, according to Curry (2005), is a term that encapsulates the human and the non-human, and the cultures and environments within which we live. Curry outlines three kinds of green ethics: shallow ethics, intermediate ethics and deep ethics. Each type links to an ethical scale where shallow ethics is about nature and its instrumental value to humans, intermediate ethics views animals and humans as sentient beings, and deep ethics is concerned with species, ecosystems and places, where the interests of humans are not necessarily paramount.

Shallow ethics is at one position in a spectrum of environmental principles and values. Its main characteristic is anthropocentrism: 'non human beings of any kind have no independent moral status or considerability, and only merit consideration insofar as they matter to humans' (Curry 2005: 47). The main consequences for taking a shallow ethical position on ecology is that aspects of non-human nature are 'fair game' and anything that has no use value is disposable. Curry argues that shallow ethics is the most dominant in contemporary Western societies, with environmentalism perceived principally as a political economic matter. In this sense, shallow ethics is an approach that sees nature as a resource, managed to increase its use value. Curry calls this position one of enlightened self-interest. Historically, 'enlightenment practice implied the need to learn natural laws the better to exploit their benefits' (Franklin 2001: 33). Shallow ethics is a modern take on nature as resource, popular amongst politicians and corporations for its 'light touch' policy and regulatory positions. Although a shallow ethical position does not 'preclude precautionary arguments', its main concern is 'human well-being', thus the underlying moral question is 'how long can we exploit this natural resource without destroying it altogether?' (Curry 2005: 49). The dominance of this ethical position is not only apparent in government, certain aspects of science and within corporations, it is also popular with the public, as a way of connecting nature directly to human interests is something everyone can understand. The focus on nature as a resource is one only too recognizable in contemporary Western societies.

Intermediate ethics is the next position on a spectrum of environmental principles and values. As we might expect, this position draws on a human interest perspective, but modifies it so that non-human beings have some moral status and intrinsic values, and that these are relative to humans. This form of moral extensionism means that animals can be 'perceived as possessing independent moral status, and therefore as deserving protection for their own sakes, regardless of whether they matter to human beings' (Curry 2005: 56). As Curry points out, the rights of humans 'trump all other considerations' so intermediate ethics contains a great deal of debate about when the rights of non-human beings are protected and when they are set aside in favour of human interests. Intermediate ethics is a common ethical position with regard to animal welfare, where arguments about factory farmed animals are based on the assumption that if humans are to eat meat then they should ensure that those animals killed are done so in a humane manner. One of the criticisms of this position is that it focuses too much on individuals, or sentient animals, extending the individual rights of humans to animals rather than considering larger collectives that include non-sentient beings.

Deep ethics is an ecocentric ethical position, one that is Earth centred. Deep ethics is holistic: 'it must be able to recognise the value, and therefore support the ethical defence, of the integrity of species and of ecosystemic places, as well as human and nonhuman organisms' (Curry 2005: 62). Deep green ethics also allows for 'conflicts between the interests of human and non-human nature' and therefore allows that on occasion human interests will lose (ibid.: 63). Thus, this ethical position is based on the independent moral status of natural beings in the broadest sense. Ecocentrism is the least dominant ethical position within environmentalism, partly because of the assumption that our wellbeing is dependent on the health of the earth's ecosystems rather than the other way round. However, this approach is gaining ground in the arguments about global warming, and an ecocentric world view is increasingly apparent in green philosophy and activist movements.

Fair treatment is a universal value and part of the moral fabric of the media. Silverstone argues: 'the morality of the media within the environment in which they function is grounded on their singular capacity to represent and re-present the world, and in our everyday dependence on that capacity' (2007: 162). We can include in the morality of the media the representation of people and our dependence on this function of factual television. However, the ideal of universal fairness is difficult to practically apply in the multiple production and reception contexts. Once this has been acknowledged there follows a debate about the level and type of informed consent necessary for fairness. Silverstone connects the morality of the media to regulatory practices, and the legal and regulatory matters regarding informed consent are part of debates about fairness, as discussed earlier in this chapter. The relativist situational ethical position is one that acknowledges moral principles of rights and responsibility, but allows the individual journalist or film maker to judge the application of those principles within the context of professional practices (Winston 2000). The research in this chapter has shown that most viewers tend to agree with this ethical position on fairness and participation in factual television. We might usefully characterize this position as inter-mediate ethics. Individual rights are extended across all social groups, but in certain circumstances those rights to fair treatment will change. The public's right to know is one regulatory context that can 'trump all other consider-ations'. The rights of perceived 'vulnerable groups', such as children or people with mental health problems, are also relative to the contexts within which they occur, and audiences tend to agree that these groups should be given greater moral consideration than others.

The situation changes for reality TV. In some ways, viewers adopt a shallow ethical position regarding the fair treatment of reality TV participants. The following comment sums up this ethical position: 'Well, they play the game. You've got to know what you're getting yourself into' (31-year-old Swedish female system developer). Although the contexts for reality participants are quite different to those of news or documentary, it is nevertheless striking that audiences differentiate so much between factual and reality genres. I want to suggest that it is self-interest that is one of the main factors in this difference in attitudes, especially in the perception of reality gameshows, talentshows and hoax shows. First, the self-interest of programme makers is evident to audiences in the premise for many of these reality formats; they want to attract audiences, to create a viable product that can be a good resource for future revenue, and they want to do so as economically as possible which means, amongst other things, including non-professionals. Second, the self-interest of participants is evident to audiences in the audition tapes, often screened to the public, in their behaviour whilst in the programme and afterwards in various media outlets; they want to promote themselves, and establish a media persona that will also be a resource for economic and per-sonal gain. Third, the self-interest of audiences is evident to viewers in the practice of watching and discussing these programmes; they choose to watch other people put through challenging situations, experiencing a range of positive and negative emotions, and use this as a resource for, amongst other things, identity work. The self-interest of viewers in watching reality partici-pants is quite similar to the perception of participants themselves, in that at this stage in the development of the reality genre viewers also play the game and 'know what they are getting into'.

The knowledgeable position of the audience is also something shared with reality participants. They both have knowledge of the genre, and they bring this knowledge with them prior to participation or viewing experiences. They both have social knowledge as well, and use this to assess personalities and behaviours in the staged environment of these types of programmes. From the audience perspective, they are in the most powerful position; looking from the outside in they have been given a privileged view of the participants. As this viewer explained: 'You just want to look at their lives and think, well, I quite like that person, I don't like that person. In a sense it's like a huge menu of people you might get on with and people you might not get on with, but I mean, you're always in the right, judging' (39-year-old male health psychologist). As the reality genre has developed, the types of participants have become more extreme, and viewers have come to expect the reality performer. The menu of ordinary people increasingly becomes a menu of characters, the participants appearing larger than life: 'it does make you feel pretty good about yourself. You're just, like, 'I'm not that weird, and I'm not that weird' . . . you feel so normal' (19-year-old female clerk). The use of comparison becomes a strategy for identity work, where the more out of the ordinary reality performers appear the more 'normal' viewers feel. The moral and social ordering of different groups of people that is evident in the survey results is also evident in the use of comparative strategies for reality performers. When viewers categorize themselves as normal, and reality performers as weird, they places themselves in a superior position.

Much has been made of the spectacle of reality TV. Some critics have argued that reality TV is similar to tabloid journalism, with its emphasis on out of the ordinary people and situations (Glynn 2000, amongst others). There are comparisons with the working class fascination with the Victorian freakshow, where a parade of 'weird' people was thought to be entertaining for the masses, and the popularity of talk shows or reality programming (see Dovey 2000). The travelling fairs of the Renaissance period provided opportunities for the lower classes to observe and participate in out of the ordinary experiences, characterized by the playwright Ben Jonson in *Bartholomew Fair* as a world of grotesque characters who influenced members of the public to engage in extreme behaviour. Reference has been made to the spectacle of violence in Roman gladiatorial games, and representations of violence in news, or reality programmes (Seaton 2005). The fictional television programme *The Year of the Sex Olympics* (BBC 1968, UK) depicts a futuristic world where reality television is a spectacle of violence on a par with gladiatorial games. The 'Live Life Show' is a grotesque and frightening reality experiment where participants are killed for the purposes of entertainment. The representation of the audience controlled and manipulated by the programme makers is one just as frightening as the show itself, as the audience laughs at the suffering of others, feeling no empathy for the reality participants.

There are historical similarities between previous forms of mass entertainment and contemporary media. There are also themes that run through these forms of entertainment, humiliation being one emotion that connects Victorian freakshows with talk shows and reality gameshows. However, I do not wish to suggest that audiences are unfeeling or lack empathy for reality participants. Audience responses to reality participants are contradictory, containing a mixture of positive and negative emotions. The way viewers distance themselves from many reality performers, criticizing their behaviour and condemning their motivations, is negative. At the same time, their categorization of reality gameshows and talentshows as 'humiliation TV', their uncomfortable feelings and concerns for perceived vulnerable participants, all point to an awareness of people's rights to fair treatment. As reality TV has developed, it has become more extreme in its scenarios, and cast more extreme characters in the programmes. The feelings of condemnation, concern and confusion amongst viewers increase the more extreme they perceive reality TV has become. Time and again viewers reflected on their own feelings of embarrassment, humiliation and shame for watching certain kinds of reality TV. They criticized themselves for watching. They reflected on how watching reality performers could make them feel better about themselves, 'I'm not like that', and it made them feel bad about themselves, 'why am I watching this?' Sometimes viewers' lack of concern about fair treatment of reality participants translated into concern about themselves: 'I'm not concerned with the way they treat them, because people who appear on TV, on the whole, they are fairly treated. I think it's more really how they treat the viewers' (31-year-old female assistant curator).

As the above comment shows, self-interest is a factor in attitudes to fairness. Audiences think they know about how participants are treated. They base their opinions on knowledge of the reality genre, which is extensive, and knowledge of people's motivations for going on these programmes, which is limited to what the programme makers show, and what participants' present in the media. There isn't any reason why audiences should know about the professional practices of reality programme makers. Yet, by not knowing too much about the realities of filming, viewers place responsibility for ethical treatment on participants. This is a shallow ethical position because it places the interests of programme makers, participants and viewers in reality entertainment above the universal value of fairness.

This ethical position is troubling to some viewers: 'sometimes, it's just too much, and you actually feel sorry for the person, and you want somebody to turn this off.' The most straightforward and effective response would be for viewers to switch off. Why some viewers don't switch off is because of their interest in the sometimes positive but mainly negative emotions experienced by reality performers. The shame some viewers feel at watching reality TV could be interpreted as a warning sign that their self-interest in reality performers is connected to negative feelings in themselves. When viewers express guilt in the perceived humiliation of reality performers they experience deep feelings that are based on a sense of the intrinsic value of fairness, no matter what the circumstances. The shame that they feel in watching reality performers becomes something stronger, a sense of their own responsibility in the perceived exploitation of ordinary people for the purposes of reality entertainment. These guilty reality TV viewers are exploring deeper aspects of ethics, where conflicts arise between the interests of viewers and participants in television. These tensions show that conflicts will arise in the fair treatment of non-professionals in factual television, and that sometimes the interests of the viewer will not be paramount, but rather are secondary to the moral rights of people to be treated fairly. Although tensions in audience attitudes to fair treatment in other kinds of factual genres is apparent in this chapter, it is reality TV which highlights some of the greater conflicts that arise for audiences in issues concerning fairness.

Conclusion

The production and reception of factual television highlights ethical issues to do with the treatment of people by programme makers, the motivations of people to participate in programmes, and audience responses to this. Fairness is about universal rights and responsibilities. In relation to television, fairness is associated with ethical practices within professions. In particular, it is the legal and regulatory matters of 'informed consent' and the public's 'right to know' that frame ethical treatment of people in factual television. Audience attitudes towards fair treatment of people who participate in the media show an awareness of both of these matters. There is a moral and social ordering to fairness, with the perception and value of fair treatment differing according to non-professionals, public figures and celebrities. It also differs according to genre, with news and documentary scoring higher on the fairness scale than reality TV. The contexts to fair treatment matters to audiences, and they make distinctions according to the varying degrees of informed consent in different genres. Those people thought to be more vulnerable than others, for example children and people with mental health problems or disabilities, are perceived as needing greater levels of care, and programme makers are criticized for the current treatment. The degree of criticism of existing fair treatment by viewers is a signal that programme makers are being asked to be more transparent about how they look after these groups, and to engage in a public ethics of care. This is especially the case in Sweden, where viewers are more critical of fair treatment of all groups, except politicians and celebrities. These two groups are perceived as professionals, and therefore possess different motivations and skills than other groups of people.

Viewers in both countries also made a clear distinction between ordinary people in news, or documentary, and those who take part in reality TV. These participants were thought to be 'media hot', motivated by fame. Prior knowledge about a reality format was a key factor in viewers' judgement of reality participants who were thought to play the reality game and give their informed consent to be treated as reality performers. Many viewers called reality gameshows, talentshows and hoax shows 'humiliation TV'. The category sums up a general understanding that these formats embarrass, humiliate and shame participants for the purposes of entertainment. Rather than feel concern for participants in humiliation TV, many viewers felt that participants lacked self-respect and knowingly signed up to be treated this way. Audiences compared themselves to reality participants and found little to identify with, thus distancing themselves from these ordinary people. In fact, reality performers were mainly thought to be out of the ordinary, extreme characters that often lacked civility. The perceived shameless behaviour of many reality performers was part of the reason some viewers were interested in watching reality TV, and the range of positive, but mainly negative, emotions so common to the genre. However, some viewers also felt ashamed at the humiliation of reality performers, and of their interest in watching this on television.

These feelings of guilt and shame unite with other issues explored in previous chapters around the subject of reality TV. The way viewers have consistently returned to negative emotions in their reflections on reality TV highlights the tensions in dealing with this kind of factuality. The hybridity of many reality formats means that viewers are caught between responding to a programme from a factual perspective, judging the representation of reality within the context of a factual genre's truth claims, and responding from an entertainment perspective, where the driving force for the programme is quite different from factuality. The tensions between fact and fiction in reality TV are internalized by viewers, who worry over what it means to enjoy watching reality TV, whether they should take its truth claims seriously, whether reality TV is worth including in more general discussions about factuality. As reality TV has such a low cultural status, it stands to reason that reality TV viewers feel somewhat embarrassed about their preferences. Reality TV participants represent another level in cultural status, significantly one that viewers feel fairly confident in relegating to a lower position in the value chain. The moral superiority that many viewers feel in their responses to the treatment of reality performers is important in that it is an opportunity for them to feel a bit better about themselves – 'at least I'm not as bad as that'. But the tensions surrounding viewers' responses to reality TV do not stop there as, in elevating themselves above reality performers, some viewers find themselves in a moral dilemma. These viewers know that it is their own viewing practices that contribute to the perceived 'humiliation' of reality performers; if no one watched reality programmes, then there would be no need for people willing to put up with all sorts of ordinary and extraordinary demands in reality television production. To stop watching reality TV is the simplest way out of this moral dilemma for viewers, and yet not everyone takes this route. This suggests that the darker side of reality TV, its focus on negative emotions, incivilities and lack of 'feeling rules', makes for compelling viewing. If reality TV was fiction, and the people in these programmes were professional actors, then the issue of fair treatment would not be quite so pressing. Tensions arise precisely because non-professionals in reality TV are a hybrid of ordinary person and performer, hence the phrase 'reality performer'. Although reality TV may be entertaining, viewers cannot get away from the basic point that these are real people. Feelings of shame or guilt therefore get caught up in the development of the reality genre, where it is neither fact nor fiction, and therefore seems to lack a moral centre by which viewers can check their own moral compass.

Audience attitudes towards the fair treatment of social groups in various genres highlight different ethical positions, from shallow to deep ethics. Different shades of ethics have suggestive possibilities for understanding the tensions that arise from audience attitudes to fairness for non-professionals, celebrities and public figures in various different factual genres. The most common ethical position in the research in this chapter has been what we might call intermediate ethics. Individual rights are extended across all social groups, but in certain circumstances those rights to fair treatment will change. Another ethical position on fairness is shallow ethics. This specifically relates to reality TV, and places emphasis on the self-interests of audiences in reality participants being a resource for entertainment. Another position is that of deep ethics. This can be seen in some audience attitudes towards the intrinsic value of fairness for everyone, no matter what the circumstances, in no matter what genre. It can also been seen in some attitudes towards reality TV participants, where guilty viewers begin to show an awareness of the problems in the shallow ethical position and turn to ideas of universal fairness. Thus, there is a spectrum of ethics that arises from audience responses to the issue of fairness in factuality, and these variations in attitudes to fair treatment show there is no one answer to the question of fairness.

Chapter 8

Containing factuality

'It's about to go off the rails.'

Contemporary factual television is constantly on the move. This is a natural state for television to be in, as its ability to survive in a media environment is based on its adaptability and creativity. However, the impact of new broadcasting policies in the 1980s and 1990s, the rise of commercialization and the introduction of new technologies all contributed to speeding up the process. Within these policy, economic and production contexts, factual television has undergone enormous changes. The relationship between representation and reality in genres such as news or documentary has always involved a certain degree of hybridity within the confines of professional practices. Hybridity is now the distinctive feature of factuality, and the boundaries between fact and fiction have been pushed to the limits in various popular factual formats that mix non-fiction and fiction genres. Popular factual genres are not self-contained, stable and knowable, they migrate, mutate and replicate. Significantly, they cross over into existing factual genres, with the cross-pollination of styles increasing the pace of change in news and current affairs, or documentary programming.

   The changes to factual television are challenging for audiences. On the one hand, change is exciting and can provide new opportunities for representing different kinds of reality to popular audiences. On the other hand, the pace of change is unsettling and can threaten the integrity of existing factual genres. The restyling of factuality has had a disruptive influence on core issues concerning truth claims, knowledge and fairness. Viewers are forced to deal with the changes taking place and to re-evaluate their own knowledge and experiences along the way. A common strategy for dealing with the changes to factual television is to work at containing their impact, taking in these changes and managing them in various ways. Classificatory practices allow audiences to use pre-existing categories and value judgements to order a wide range of factual genres. A factual scale emerges, with public service genres at the top and popular factual genres at the bottom. It is significant that reality TV is off the scale and has been re-classified as reality entertainment by viewers. Another strategy for factuality is that of genre work, where immersive and reflective modes of engagement with factual genres allow viewers to personally respond to people and their experiences. The strategies of classification and genre work allow viewers to manage their engagement with the restyling of factuality.

Key findings

This multimethod project is based on quantitative and qualitative research in Britain and Sweden. There are four research questions. How do adult viewers understand and evaluate the changing generic environment of factual programming? How do viewers evaluate the truth claims of different types of programming? What do viewers consider they learn from different types of programmes? What attitudes do viewers have towards fair treatment of different social groups within news and current affairs, documentary and reality programmes? This is an overview of the ten key findings.

I. Factuality

Factual television is a container for non-fiction content. It also signifies social and personal values for non-fiction genres, and it is part of non-fiction production and reception practices. Factuality is understood as 'factual experiences, imagination, values, that provide settings within which media institutions operate, shaping the character of factual television processes and viewing practices' (adapted from Corner and Pels 2003: 3). Audiences use a definition of factuality that signifies factual programmes that make truth claims and are based on facts. News and current affairs are the most well-established factual genres. Audiences recognize documentary as a broad genre and classify different kinds of documentary as sub-genres with distinctive modes of address. A huge variety of other kinds of factual genres work alongside news and current affairs and documentary, some of which can be classified as hybrid genres, where one established factual genre has been merged with another fiction or non-fiction genre. Popular factual genres therefore sit at the margins of factuality. In the world of factual television, viewers do not experience genres in isolation but as part of a wide range of genres that make up factuality.

2. The restyling of factuality

Factual genres are constructed within specific production contexts, often responding to public service or commercial imperatives, and also within specific reception contexts, developing alongside genre expectations (Mittell 2004). Viewers are aware that factual television is in a state of transition. The hybridization of many factual formats, and the high degree of crossovers between different sub-genres within factual programming, ensures viewers are 'working through' factual television, questioning the blurring of the boundaries between traditional factual genres such as documentary and contemporary factual genres such as reality gameshows (Ellis 2000). The process of categorizing factual television highlights the inherent problems for television viewers in defining a genre that by its very nature is concerned with multiple generic participation and constant regeneration. Nevertheless, audiences are aware that there has been a breakdown of the boundaries between the public and popular, a focus on spectacle, emotion and personality, a new aesthetics of the real (Corner and Pels 2003). There is an understanding that reality TV has become so bloated and extreme that it has instigated its own relocation into light entertainment and drama. One of the outcomes of the restyling of factuality is a move back to reality, away from the spectacle of reality entertainment.

3. Public and popular genres

Audiences have responded to the restyling of factuality by making order out of chaos. The public/popular divide is a powerful framing device for genre evaluation. There is a social and cultural ordering to factual genres, with viewers valuing public service factual genres associated with investigations of reality more than popular genres associated with constructions of reality. Dominant cultural and social discourses surrounding public service and commercial broadcasting have a significant impact on value judgements and speak to concerns about the public role of factual television as a knowledge provider (Corner 1995). Normative ideals for factual content are rarely matched by personal experience of watching television in Britain and Sweden. This creates a contradictory position whereby public genres such as current affairs are highly valued but not watched, and popular genres such as reality gameshows are watched but not valued. There are reality refusniks who defend traditional public service factual genres, and contemporary viewers who watch a range of genres, in particular reality TV. It is these younger viewers who are deeply involved in the restyling of factuality.

4. Classificatory practices

The perception and value of factuality is framed according to pre-existing categories and hierarchical structures. Classificatory practices give viewers an opportunity to make sense of complex representations of reality. Viewers' categories critique or re-enforce factual genres. The experience of classification can highlight conceptual frameworks and social and genre knowledge shared by viewers. Classificatory practices are based on repetition and variation; there is an inherent performativity to classification that makes it flexible, adaptable and reflexive (Waterton 2003). Viewers use traditional categories to re-enforce a perceived natural order between public service and commercial broadcasting, including some genres in the scheme and excluding others, notably reality TV. However, in the act of classification viewers flexibly respond to developments within broadcasting, adapting existing categories and introducing news ones along the way.

5. Genre work

Genre work is the process of collecting generic material for viewing experiences and also reflecting on what genre means. It involves two basic modes of engagement, immersion and reflection, which are drawn from the psycho-dynamic processes of dream work (Bollas 1992). The experience of watching a factual programme can feel like being in a dream, 'working through' (Ellis 2000) what is real or not. Being a factual viewer means taking on multiple roles, as witness and interpreter, and occupying multiple spaces, between fact and fiction. Genre work allows viewers to draw on their knowledge of genres to personally respond to various programmes, highlighting the often contradictory and confusing responses that are part of dealing with the changing nature of factuality. There are distinct but related modes of engagement with news and current affairs, documentary and reality TV. Audiences are especially critical of reality TV and the strange dreamlike experience that is associated with watching this genre. Thus the restyling of factuality raises problems in that some genres have gone beyond the limits of factuality, occupying a troubling intermediate space between fact and fiction that is unsettling to audiences.

6. Feral genres

Reality TV is a feral genre. It is wildly opportunistic in its desire to attract popular viewers around the world; it is de-territorial in its ability to cross generic boundaries; it is disruptive in the production and scheduling of existing factual genres; and above all, it is resistant to containment. The construction of cultural discourses surrounding reality TV contribute to a general association that it is not natural to factual broadcasting, that it is a simulation (Dovey 2004). For some viewers, reality TV has invaded 'the knowledge project' of public service broadcasting (Corner 1998). Viewers' critical engagement with the truth claims or information in news, documentary and reality TV indicates awareness of a 'reality effect' on many aspects of factual programming. The reality genre is not a simulation but a natural development in the evolution of broadcasting and its ability to survive in the fertile environments of modern society. Reality TV highlights the natural ability of genres in making and remaking factuality. However, the lack of containment of genre experimentation has created consequences for audience trust in factuality. Viewers are critically engaged with the generic development of reality TV and its cross-pollination with other factual genres.

7. True to life

Truth claims are a defining characteristic of factuality. Audiences classify factual genres according to what they perceive to be natural, or true to life, about representations of reality. Viewers apply a 'truth rating', using a hierarchy where news is at the top and reality TV at the bottom. Such an assessment of truth claims within factual genres foregrounds the referential integrity of factual television. Viewers also apply a performance rating, with reality TV at the top and news at the bottom of the scale. A truth/performance rating is a simple and effective way for viewers to judge the nature/artifice of various factual genres. The perception of reality TV as a genre experiment in fact and fiction has meant that it has had a disruptive influence on attitudes towards actuality. The chain of trust created by news and documentary is a chain of distrust for reality TV. Discussions regarding truth claims within news and current affairs, documentary and reality TV show how audiences have to be fast on their feet if they are to take into account the changing nature of factual genres. Audiences perform factuality, repetitively responding to truth claims within factual genres and also varying their responses to deal with changes along the way.

8. Knowledge and learning

The knowledge profile of factual television is rich and complex, with various news and current affairs, documentary and reality genres bringing different kinds of knowledge to viewers (Corner 2005). One factual programme can be addressing the viewer about different kinds of knowledge at the same time. In order to make sense of this range of knowledge, viewers make distinctions between knowledge about the world, knowledge about the media, and self-knowledge. They also make a distinction between knowledge as facts and learning as experience. Viewers use classificatory practices to order factual genres according to a knowledge/learning scale. The understanding of knowledge as objective facts ensures news is at the top of the scale and reality TV at the bottom. However, audiences also reflect on traditional notions of public knowledge alongside more personal notions of learning. Viewers describe themselves riding a wave of information when watching news. Learning as getting something from a programme, something for yourself, is most commonly associated by audiences with some types of documentary and popular factual. Information can go into a learning reserve and can be drawn on when needed. Another type of learning is related to genre knowledge and shows just how resourceful the viewer is in learning about the media from the media

(Buckingham 2004; Livingstone *et al.* 2004). This 'environment of information' shows that the knowledge profile for television is contextual to viewers' understanding of factuality.

9. Fairness

The restyling of factuality highlights viewers' varying ethical positions on fairness. There is a social and moral ordering to viewers' attitudes to fair treatment. They value the fair treatment of all social groups in all genres, but they value fair treatment more in relation to children than celebrities, and in news rather than reality TV. There is no universal position on fair treatment, but rather a context specific position that draws heavily on people's motivations for taking part in factual programmes, and on the professional practices within different genres (Winston 2000). There is a clear distinction between ordinary people in news or documentary, and those who take part in reality TV. These reality performers are thought to be 'media hot', motivated by fame. The perceived shameless behaviour of many reality performers is a reason viewers are interested in watching 'humiliation TV' (Probyn 2004). Rather than feel concern for participants, many viewers felt that they lacked self-respect, and knowingly signed up to be treated this way. Other viewers also felt ashamed at their interest in watching 'humiliation TV', revealing tensions in dealing with this kind of factuality. Audience attitudes towards the fair treatment of social groups in various genres highlights different ethical positions, from shallow to deep ethics (Curry 2005). There is a spectrum of ethics that arises from variations in attitudes to fair treatment, showing there is no one answer to the question of fairness.

10. Containing factuality

The restyling of factuality is challenging for audiences. On the one hand, change is exciting and can provide new opportunities for representing different kinds of reality to popular audiences. On the other hand, the pace of change is unsettling and can threaten the integrity of existing factual genres. The more extreme reality TV becomes in its experimentation of representations of reality, the more audiences become concerned about the value of factuality as truthful and informative. There is a common perception amongst viewers that broadcasters have failed to contain the impact of reality TV on other genres. One means of containing factuality is for viewers to relocate reality TV into entertainment. The movement of reality TV to entertainment opens up opportunities for a re-evaluation of factuality. This raises further challenges and problems for viewers as they deal with a growing range of news, current affairs and investigations and documentary, as well as other kinds of popular factual, not only on television but also across an increasingly divergent range of multiplatform content. Thus, audiences are dealing with a mass of existing and new content on a day-to-day basis, finding various routes through the changes taking place in factuality.

Practices

This book has been concerned with cultural trends and viewing strategies which are so strikingly similar in Britain and Sweden they have come to form the main argument about the restyling of factuality. There are differences in the data; these are two nations, cultures and societies made up of diverse peoples. The small everyday practices of media reception are rich sites for analysis; wherever possible they have featured in the analysis and will be explored in further publications. For example, there is more detail on Swedish television viewing practices in a co-authored publication (Hill *et al.* 2005), and specific case studies on British current affairs, and lifestyle production and reception (Corner and Hill 2006; Dover and Hill 2007). Even though the data sets cover a diverse range of factual and reality genres in two countries, there are still parameters for the research that mean other issues have not been explored here. For example, the relationship between factual television and other news sources is one area that would further investigate national knowledge orders of the kind discussed in Chapter 6. Television news is the primary source for the respondents in this study, but the information is there to consider newspaper reading habits, public service and commercial news sources, and the value accorded in the two countries. Another area of interest is factual content for online or mobile users, and the different experiences for segmented and broadcast content. One issue touched on in Chapters 3 and 5 is factual television audiences in other countries, in this instance Finland, and the similar responses to social value and the question of truth claims in these Northern European countries. The possibility to conduct research in other countries with different broadcasting systems would allow other cultural trends to emerge. For example, in Portugal, the survey used in this study has been revised according to the sharp distinction between news that is an hour long and includes a combination of world/national, consumer and celebrity news, and reality TV, much of which is dominated by celebrity gameshows and talentshows (in association with the University of Lisbon, forthcoming). Such is the nature of audience research that the analysis in this book is both not detailed enough to do justice to the range of viewing practices, nor is it extensive enough to address the way media practices are embedded in every-day life. These tensions come with the territory, and this book is only one of several stories to tell about factual reception practices. This section looks at the contexts to factual television audiences and charts, in somewhat crude terms, patterns that appear distinctive in each country and which suggest wider socio-cultural trends in Northern Europe. The presence, or absence, of these trends in other countries highlights the significance of national broadcasting systems, cultural policies and shared or divergent experiences amongst audiences and publics.

Contexts

At the start of the book factuality was defined as 'factual experiences, imagination, values, that provide settings within which media institutions operate, shaping the character of factual television processes and viewing practices (adapted from Corner and Pels 2003: 3). The meaning of factual television in both countries explains an important difference that emerged in the production contexts. In Britain, factual television would mean quite a range of categories, including popular factual ones, although this would not be without debate. The answers to the open question in the British survey on defining factual television were wide ranging, but reality TV was part of it, even if only to rant against its inclusion. To say factual television in Sweden excludes 'docusoaps', the term given to reality TV. The Swedes differentiate between factual television as educational and docusoaps as entertainment, and yet the term docusoap demonstrates the connections between documentary and the evolution of docusoaps as a hybrid genre. In the Swedish study, the meaning of factual television was got around by using 'factual and reality' to show the distinction already in place for viewers.

Swedish viewers also differentiate between home and foreign factual and reality programming. In Britain, viewers expect to see home-grown factual programmes most of the time; they can watch American reality shows on digital, satellite and cable channels, but they rarely air on the main channels, which have their own formats or own versions of foreign reality shows. Not so in Sweden, where viewers expect to see foreign imports on all the channels, especially reality TV on the commercial channels. The project addressed foreign imports in the Swedish research and there was an almost virulent dislike of American reality shows, perceived as sensationalist, overly commercial and far removed from a Swedish mentality of 'down-to-earth-ness'. This viewer asked: 'Couldn't they try to make a Swedish one, something produced in Sweden and something typical of Sweden, something which we can recognize ourselves in?' There is a pleading in her voice and she speaks for many younger viewers who want to enjoy watching their own popular factual television. Various production companies have done just this, Strix being a good example of an independent company that produced *Farmen*, where Swedish participants stayed in a summer house on a lake, a typically Swedish summer activity. However, the production budget constraints in Sweden ensure these programmes are expensive and high risk, and cannot take the place of foreign imports. The international trade in formats, or the export of British factual series to Sweden, does help in shared points of reference. British and Swedish viewers know about *Pop Idol*, *Big Brother* or *Wife Swap* because all of these formats are made locally. However, the strong attitudes towards American reality programming in Sweden are a good indication that some television seems alien to particular viewers. To reinforce this point, Swedes also felt closer to Nordic factual and reality television than British or other European programmes.

This sense of culturally specific responses to factual television is also apparent in other international reception studies. Young teens in Chile felt that reality TV filled a gap in Chilean popular television in representing diverse social groups, and including ordinary young people that these viewers could identify with (Souza 2004). The reactions of Nigerian viewers to the first reality programme shown in the country suggest the representations of conflict in the survival challenges connect with the perception that Nigerians have to overcome obstacles to get on in life (Ekpabio 2004). In her analysis of ordinary television, Bonner (2004) highlights how programmes about typically Australian leisure activities, being outdoors, having barbeques, are staple to non-fiction programming. Similarly, international formats that are made in Australia will appeal more to viewers than the foreign version, so that *Big Brother* in Australia becomes something audiences can relate to as their own. In the television series *Charlie Brooker's Screenwipe* (BBC4, transmitted 18 August 2006), Brooker showed a group of Americans a scene from the series *Rail Cops* (BBC), a fly on the wall documentary series that observes the rather mundane and minor infractions that take place on trains. Needless to say American viewers thought the series was far removed from their own crime reality shows, such as *Cops* where the law enforcers are confronted with violence and gun crime on a daily basis. Indeed, they seemed to think it was some kind of mock series, a version of *The Office* (BBC) that was a comedy rather than a representation of reality.

Moran (2005: 305) calls the international circulation of format adaptations a sign of 'new television', where developments in intellectual property, and new technologies for distribution and production, have led to 'formats that are simultaneously international in its dispersal and local and concrete in its manifestation'. The number of formats distributed internationally is phenomenal, with dozens of versions of *Pop Idol*, *Big Brother* and *Wife Swap* all over the world, and specific series such as *Jamie's School Dinners* screened internationally in dozens of countries. The political economy of reality TV has been well documented, and Moran uses *Big Brother* as an example of the international reach of 'new television'. Peter Bazalgette, chief creative officer of the format house Endemol International, wrote a book about how reality formats changed the face of television, and how John de Mol turned *Big Brother* into a 'billion dollar game' (2005). On a much smaller scale, there is some evidence that the international trade in reality formats isn't always welcomed by audiences. Swedish viewers' responses to local versions of *Extreme Makeover*, for example, indicate even when translated into Swedish culture it still seems foreign. Cosmetic surgery is undertaken in Sweden, but the idea of making an entire format about its transformative powers doesn't sit well with viewers' perception of themselves and their cultural identities, with some viewers finding it difficult to relate to the concept of plastic surgery as an answer to problems of self-esteem. Another example concerns imported documentaries in Sweden. The commercial channels show imported documentary programming and Swedish viewers expect some of these to be along the lines of body horror stories common to some men's magazines and tabloid papers. One of the commercial channels imported the British documentary *The Man Whose Skin Fell Off* which, despite the sensational title, was an award winning, sensitive account of one man's fight against a fatal disease. It would be hard for Swedish viewers to differentiate between this import and others unless they watched it, once again highlighting the perception of foreign imports and the impact of channel identity on attitudes to television. The absence of such discussion amongst British viewers in the study just goes to show how many factual programmes are British in origin, or how foreign formats such as *Big Brother* have been given the full treatment by programme makers in order to ensure they work for local audiences (see Bazalgette 2005).

It is fair to say that factual and reality television doesn't mean the same thing in Britain and Sweden. And yet, it means similar things to most people in both countries. With some adjustment and sensitivity to production contexts, the project was able to proceed smoothly and the results were similar. The samples used in this study were nationally representative of the populations in both countries. The analysis of the quantitative and qualitative data incorporated looking for similarities and differences across a range of variables, including gender, age, lifestage, socio-economic status, personal income, ethnicity, education, region, newspaper readership and access to the internet. There were differences in viewing preferences, an obvious indicator of diverse tastes for diverse peoples. Minor differences in viewing preferences for men and women, people from different socio-economic groups, with different levels of education, all point to heterogeneous media preferences. The major difference in this study was age, with an older population watching news and current affairs more than younger viewers, and watching public service channels more than commercial ones. The age factor led to a marked distinction between older viewers who saw themselves as reality refusniks and younger viewers who had more contemporary tastes. British younger viewers tended to watch a range of factual and reality programmes across the schedules, although politics or current affairs was not high on their list. Swedish younger viewers tended to watch popular factual on commercial channels, similarly avoiding more traditional factual. When variations in value judgements occurred in the samples they were mainly connected to age and viewing preferences rather than other factors we might expect, such as gender or socio-economic status. For example, the high social value accorded news and current affairs by Swedish viewers may suggest the Swedes take their news seriously, which they do, but it also demonstrates how a population with a high proportion of older people will influence general social values for news.

Indeed, there were surprisingly little variations in value judgements despite some obvious trends in viewing preferences. It is the shared perceptions and value judgements for factual and reality TV that point to wider socio-cultural issues in Britain and Sweden, specifically public service broadcasting and popular culture.

Public service

The meaning of public service broadcasting is open to debate. According to Syversten, there are shifting definitions of public service; it can mean a common utility or public good, it can mean publicity or a space for the public to talk to each other, and it can mean a public's service, an option for consumers (1999, cited in Bolin 2004). For Syversten, the changes in the definition of public service have left it devoid of meaning, it is just another service amongst many. For Bolin, it is precisely because the definition of public service is open to interpretation that it still has relevancy: public service is a 'rhetorical benchmark in a battle over what our media are and should be' (2004: 285). British and Swedish audiences have grown up with public service television meaning different things to them. There is a shared sense that it represents ideal social values, that is to say, public service as a common good. This is a set of political democratic values which place emphasis on enlightenment, moral standards and public knowledge (Bolin 2004). In this respect, viewers see themselves as citizens, mainly united in their understanding that public service factual content should be for the public good. The idealized values given to factuality by viewers explicitly relate notions of truth, objectivity and knowledge to factual television as a resource for citizens. News, current affairs and documentary are genres publicly valued by viewers precisely because they are perceived to represent these ideals.

There is also a sense that public service is a service, one that people can use when it suits them. This is an understanding of public service as evidenced by viewing practices. Whilst older viewers may be more loyal to public service channels, and may prefer news to reality TV, younger viewers seem to access public service channels and genres less frequently. In discussions of news, for example, viewers all agreed news was important, that they liked to know it was there as a public resource for knowledge about the world. But some viewers also admitted they didn't really watch the news often, and if they did it was just the headlines or sports news, for example: 'I don't watch enough, I probably should, but I don't really watch news.' Hagen (1994) found similar ambivalent attitudes towards news in Norway, where viewers felt it was their civic duty to watch, but it was also boring. We should assume that people over-report their frequency of viewing for public service genres in the same way they may over-report eating fresh fruit and vegetables – as one viewer explained 'can you be bothered?' It is interesting to see how viewers call reality TV 'junk food television', and yet can't seem to change their habits, wondering out loud why they still continue to watch something they think is bad for them. Some viewers say it is because the news, or other factual programming, is boring. Others that it is boring because it feels aimed at older viewers, for example: 'They are for old people, it feels like I'm having dinner with my remote old relatives and I do that too often already as it is.' There is also a feeling that reality TV is an escape from the news, a point emphasized in Sweden by scheduling news against stripped reality shows. As one viewer explained: 'With the news sometimes when there's too much, you can just close it out, you just switch channels, that's why you watch that kind of crap because it's easy.' The level of interest in public service and commercial channels in Sweden follows age groups, with people aged over 30 far more likely to be interested in SVT, and those aged under 30 interested in TV3 and Kanal 5, two channels that have little interest in news.

The economic interests of broadcasters are at odds with a public service ethos. The privileging of programming for younger age groups as the most valuable target groups for broadcasters isn't concerned with their role as citizens but rather their levels of disposable income. The somewhat elderly profiles for public service channels in Britain and Sweden are cause for concern for broadcasters if they wish to attract the commercially valuable 16–34 age group. The commercial public service broadcaster Channel 4 claims to have the largest portion of younger adults watching its channel, and every year *Big Brother* helps the channel to maintain this position (series seven had a 40 per cent share of 16–34 year olds). TV4 claim they have the largest range of age groups watching its channel, and the results of the Swedish survey support this, alongside annual studies such as the *Media Barometer*. Public service broadcasters are increasingly under pressure to maintain commitment to public service factual content and at the same time offer popular genres. Ellis believes this kind of state-funded broadcasting will not survive unless it changes emphasis from public service as common good, to popular public service as a quality service to rival commercial channels (2000). There is a 'damned if you do, damned if you don't' characteristic to this argument, which highlights how public service broadcasters have to change and find a way to remain dominant players in the marketplace, and yet by changing risk the very qualities audiences value about the service.

There is a danger that a public/private hybrid will go the way of public/private partnerships. In Britain, these hybrid public and commercial enterprises have mainly been disastrous, significantly failing to maintain quality standards, and roundly criticized by the public for failing them as a public service. Common utilities such as trains, postal services, gas, electricity and so forth have suffered under these hybrid schemes. Healthcare services such as children's care homes, or assisted living for people with mental health problems or disabilities, have been outsourced to commercial companies. Undercover investigative programmes have targeted these public/private services to show the public how corrupt they can be, and how the welfare state is being eroded by commercial concerns. The market orientation of these public services is evidence of what is sometimes called a post welfare society. Other factors also include changes in the makeup of populations in Britain and Sweden, where it is difficult to speak of common interests, or a public as a single entity, when there is so much diversity amongst the population. In a post welfare society the emphasis on a public ethics of care changes to make room for personal interests and needs, for a private ethics of care that is focused on the self and immediate family and friends (Kittay 2001). In the same way, public service broadcasting is part of a wider structure of care, part of a public caring ethics that foregrounds social responsibility and citizenship. Popular public service broadcasting may damage the structure of care essential to the notion of public service as a common good.

There have been several arguments by scholars regarding the neo-liberal tendencies of television, in particular popular factual genres. Neo-liberalism is associated with a range of values and policies that promote the free market world view. Thus neo-liberal policies of cutting public services, privatizing state-owned services, deregulating services such as telecommunications, are policies that contribute to a post welfare society where services for the public good are replaced by private services. A political economic perspective on neo-liberal tendencies stresses the overemphasis on the media as a resource for personal profit rather than democratic potential (see McChesney 2000, amongst others). Ouellette (2004) argues that neo-liberal policies can also be interpreted as subjective power relations. She uses the work of Michel Foucault on discourse and power as a means to analyse the way neo-liberal regimes try to control the behaviour of citizens through self-training or governance. Palmer (2003) analysed crime policies and crime reality pro-grammes in relation to governance, where the inscribed meanings in policy or television content on crime work to reinforce attitudes towards criminals as outside of society, and citizens as people who need to protect their family and personal interests. In Ouellette's analysis of *Judge Judy*, she makes a similar argument to Palmer that the programme 'attempts to shape and guide the conduct and choices' of people by governing at a distance (2004: 232). This programme, along with other popular factual series, articulates 'neo-liberal templates', and constructs 'citizen subjectivities' that are based on 'personal responsibility and self-discipline' (247–8). Her point is that the way reality TV addresses the audience makes it an active agent in the transformation of society from democratic to neo-liberal world view.

This interpretation of popular factual television emphasizes the dominant discourses within certain programmes or genres. It is an approach that shows how generic discourses are constructed within wider socio-economic environ-ments, and how they can potentially influence people. The framing device of public service and popular genres used by respondents in this study is connected to generic discourses on news and current affairs, documentary and reality TV, and public debate about these genres in the press, on television, via the internet and in people's everyday lives. The power of these discourses to shape people's attitudes is a reason such discourses should be identified and critically examined. However, the focus on discourse privileges mental and cognitive constructions; it also places great emphasis on content and imagined responses to such content. The approach adopted in this book has recognized generic discourses as part of understanding factuality, but not the only, and not even the most important, part of it. Instead, greater emphasis has been placed on practices and processes. An overemphasis on the power of discourses to shape neo-liberal tendencies does not give due weight to media practices. There can be other forces at work that counteract political and social trends. Viewing practices may be positive and negative, they may be contradictory, but they are part of the development of factuality.

A counter argument to neo-liberal tendencies in the media can be found in Scannell's (1996) case that public service broadcasters help to create a shared public culture. The ideal of public service broadcasting for the public good comes into practice through the co-production between programme makers and audiences. An example of the co-production of shared public culture can be found in *Jamie's School Dinners* (Channel 4 2005). Common consensus amongst British respondents in the focus groups was that this series managed to pull off an unlikely combination of celebrity-led social change. Jamie Oliver was well known to viewers for his celebrity status and ability to use his personal and professional life to further his career. *Jamie's School Dinners* followed another series for Channel 4, where Oliver set up a training scheme and restaurant for young adults who wanted to get into catering. Viewers were therefore familiar with Oliver in the role of social actor and celebrity and came with a certain cynicism about his new personality-led series. The premise for this series was that Oliver would attempt to improve the nutrition of children's school meals which, as a result of outsourcing to private companies, were widely condemned as unhealthy, convenience foods. The food industry and vending machine companies have a tight hold on school dinners, with an estimated annual turnover of £45 million for vending machines alone (Lawrence 2006). With obesity on the rise in Britain, and claims that one in eight children was obese, Oliver had a tough job. He worked with dinner ladies to introduce healthy menus, first in one school in London and then in other schools around the country. The four-part series showed him joke, plead, fight and cry with the dinner ladies and children as he struggled to find ways to get them engaged with healthy eating. After the series aired, a petition of 271,677 signatures was sent to 10 Downing Street, the government agreed to a £220 million budget increase in children's school meals, and one borough began using his specially prepared menus in all of its schools, with others to follow (Lawrence 2006).

The series really stood out to viewers as popular factual television as public good. It was informative, moving and engaging, and it tackled a timely social problem with great success. Most significantly, viewers could get behind

Oliver, they could see he personally cared about improving school meals and was prepared to try his best to change things. As this viewer explains: 'in the beginning he comes out crying he's gonna change the government's opinion on this, and doesn't he get kicked to the curve about sixteen times? To the point where his wife is screaming at him, he tells Bill Clinton to go make your own dinner and then walks out of his restaurant.' Many viewers put their cynicism of Oliver as a celebrity chef to one side and applauded his determination to change something for the better: 'he was going out to make a change, to make a positive difference.' Watching the series made viewers feel good about themselves: 'you know that what you're watching actually is making a difference.' It was a successful hybrid of public popular content, made by a public service commercial channel, using a celebrity chef as social activist. Paradoxically, it underscored how public/private partnerships for children's school meals were at odds with the general ethos of caring for children's welfare. The shared interests and values of programme makers, participants and audiences to take responsibility for children's school meals, to re-install a sense of public interest and welfare into healthy eating, created a public popular documentary.

There are other examples of popular factual programming that audiences perceive have a positive feel to them. The BBC's *Restoration* is an interactive series where viewers can vote to restore a public building as part of Britain's national heritage. *Little Angels* (BBC) is another series mentioned by viewers as an example of pro-social television, where a child psychologist attempts to help parents improve their children's challenging behaviour. Rather than criticize the parents in their parenting skills, the psychologist supports them in their attempts to change. Viewers may agree or disagree with the cognitive behavioural approach to children put forward by the series, but what they mainly respond to is how the parents try their best, whether they succeed or not. Channel 4 scheduled a few of these more positive popular factual programmes together, hoping to build audiences on the strength of the transformative theme in the shows. For example, *You are What you Eat*, *Supernanny* or *It's Me or the Dog* all have presenters/experts who attempt to help people make their lives better, from eating healthy food, to getting children to sleep through the night, to making the dog walk to heel. *Rent-a-Granny* was a one-off life experiment programme that was part of week-long series of content addressing older age (Channel 4 April 2006). Despite the title, the programme was moving and uplifting; it showed how one grandmother whose grandchildren lived abroad could help a family whose grandparents were absent.

The relocation of reality gameshows and talentshows into light entertainment means there is room for new developments in popular factual programming. The most obvious value of popular factual genres is their ability to attract popular audiences. Not only do public service broadcasters need to find ways to make factual programmes popular, audiences need to find

ways to engage with factual content. The history of popular factual programming shows it can reach diverse viewers in ways news or documentary
struggle to reproduce on a regular basis. Joke Hermes argues that the value of
popular culture is in 'what interests us and what binds us' (2005). There are
popular factual series about everyday personal concerns, often presented in
ways that foreground consumerism or personal responsibility. There will also
be room for new generic developments of the kind exemplified by *Jamie's
School Dinners*. As one viewer explained, *Jamie's School Dinners* is 'a new style of
documentary, kind of like *Big Brother* meets *Panorama*.'

One of the most significant impacts of reality TV is that it has become
so bloated and overblown in its own attempts to play the reality game that it
has given viewers the opportunity to reflect on its value as popular culture.
The fact that viewers call it 'humiliation TV' shows a brutally honest take on
what is interesting about it in its current form. What binds viewers in Britain
and Sweden is the sense that reality TV is a form of entertainment. It may be
shameful, it may be fun, but it no longer has any claims to the real. Viewers'
classificatory practices are strategies for moving the reality genre away from
what they value about factual television. The separation between the public
knowledge project and popular culture has been, and continues to be,
important to viewers. As Hermes says, 'the public and private influence each
other' (2005: 152). Viewers have reflected on the shared social values of
factual television genres as a public good, and this has influenced their
perspective on the values of popular factual genres as entertainment. But,
as Livingstone points out in a discussion of young adults and new media,
"public" and "private" mean something different in different contexts, as part
of distinct debates, and should not be confused or conflated' (2005a: 180). In
this context, the debate about the development of the reality genre has been
understood in relation to a wider debate about the public and personal value
of factual television. This is because the reality genre has developed within
distinctive public service dominated countries and has influenced the meaning of public service factual content for audiences. The movement of reality
TV to popular entertainment opens up opportunities for a re-evaluation of
factuality.

Restyling factuality

The original idea for this research into factual television audiences is driven
by the connections between a wide range of genres, from news to documentary to reality TV. The challenge as a researcher is in trying to pin down
something so broad. When looking at audiences, they seem to have mastered
the art of plate spinning. There is some effort involved, occasionally a plate
falls, but plates of all shapes and sizes keep on spinning. As a researcher you
try to keep all the factual genres in play, but as soon as your attention turns to
one genre another drops out and you have to start again. It is possibly because

you think too much about it that the work seems full of effort, slow and clumsy indeed. When viewers deal with factual genres they make it seem easy, something instinctive that allows them to see all of it at the same time. It is the instinct of factual television audiences to see factuality all around them. They know that news is different from current affairs, and that documentary is different from reality TV, but they also know that they are linked to the processes of factuality.

It has been a common approach in scholarly research to focus on one kind of factual genre. There are people who study news, who examine the professional practices of journalists, or the cultural process of television, radio and print news. There is research in news audiences, both in terms of responses to particular world events, to certain types of news, political or entertainment, and to different news sources, such as television or the internet. These studies have shown that news is a complicated business; there isn't one kind of news but several kinds, such as financial or sports news; there isn't one kind of journalist but many, such as investigative reporters, columnists and critics; and there isn't one kind of news consumer but rather news is consumed by young people, ethnic minorities, men and women, in different ways. In short, news is a large area to study, and it raises all sorts of issues concerning history, political economy, quality, professional standards and ethics.

Current affairs has also been the subject of serious study, with research into investigative journalism, political reporting, consumer news, from the perspective of professional practices, choice of content, style of address and audience responses. Current affairs is often the study of quality standards, and the strengths and weaknesses of certain current affairs series, or stand-alone programmes, can signal the relative health of public service broadcasting. In-depth analysis of issues such as healthcare or crime illuminate dominant social, political and cultural discourses, and researchers situate the framing of current affairs in relation to policy agendas or 'state of the nation' style debates. Current affairs is therefore also a broad area of study, and there are significant historical, political and sociological findings from research in this kind of media.

Documentary studies is a well-established field, covering professional practices, historical developments, legal and ethical issues. There are so many different types of documentary that researchers have considered generic issues in some detail, and explored the implications of categorization for various documentary modes, from expository to performative modes. Much research has also been conducted in documentary film, as well as television and radio. The relationship between fact and fiction, and the referential and aesthetic qualities of documentary, has inspired sophisticated theories of documentary, both in terms of the subjects addressed in specific films or programmes and also the autobiographical, psychological and reflexive aspects of documentary itself.

Work in reality TV is also diverse, using political, economic, historical and cultural analysis to explore an emergent area that spills over into light entertainment and drama. The hybridity of reality TV has meant that researchers need to consider theories of documentary alongside performance, drama or gaming theory. There has been analysis of the surveillance properties within reality TV and the implications of this for notions of the public and private, citizens and consumers, in politics and society. There has been research on the production and consumption of celebrity in relation to reality TV. The use of convergence in many reality formats has also led to research on television and new media economies, and international production and distribution of multiplatform content. Audience research has explored the negative and positive aspects of watching reality TV, and also examined issues of quality, pleasure and the sociability of reality TV audiences.

Many of these studies have been referred to in this book, and they are important studies that need to be done in order for further understanding of specific genres within television. It is also time for research in all these genres together. It is timely because audiences don't watch news and current affairs, documentary or reality TV in isolation. All these genres appear all the time in television schedules, newspapers, celebrity gossip magazines, in discussions with friends, family and work colleagues. The ways that audiences are immersed in this world of factuality draws attention to their knowledge and awareness of different kinds of genres. They have learned to compare genres and make evaluations based on the differences and similarities of a never-ending range of programmes. As one viewer put it, there is 'crap I would never watch, crap I might watch, and then crap I would definitely watch.' So, there are fine distinctions between different kinds of factual television, where one factual programme is perceived as better than another for various reasons. Sorting factual programmes into clusters helps viewers to decide what they will never watch, might watch and definitely watch. It is a necessary move, otherwise they would be overwhelmed by the hours and hours of programming on offer.

Through looking at factuality as a whole, this research illuminates the dynamic nature of viewing practices. It demonstrates the impact of broadcasting structures, such as scheduling, on the viewing experience. It shows how genre evaluation is a powerful means to understand factual content, revealing the complex value judgements people use to work through a range of representations of reality. It underscores the presence of social and cultural discourses for factual genres, and how established discourses concerning public service broadcasting and popular culture are mapped onto current debate about 'the state of the real'. The enduring presence of binaries such as public and popular, information and entertainment, in the evaluation of factual genres suggests that these familiar categories still have relevance in contemporary broadcasting. Being able to make distinctions between public and popular factual genres allows audiences to use shared values to collectively think through the changes within factuality. As this viewer explained: 'You can categorize according to how trustworthy things are.' The more hybrid factual television has become, the more audiences draw on evaluative tools that allow them to make distinctions, to separate genres from one another in a way that is not only personal, but also social. Classificatory practices have been overlooked in scholarly research, especially when one genre or type of programme is under investigation. These practices are essential to viewers, a coping strategy for the overwhelming amount of media content available to them. In the act of classification, viewers show their knowledge of factuality and in what ways 'the state of the real' matters to them.

A picture emerges of two kinds of viewers, reality refusniks and contemporary viewers. Reality refusniks feel reality TV is a no-go area. They want to block it out of their experience of factual television, remove it from their understanding of what factual television ought to be, that is to say, factuality as truthful and informative. As one viewer put it, factual TV is based on 'real people, real events, real places'. Reality TV comes to represent a threatening presence for these viewers, and the notion of the feral genre becomes one that connects with reality TV as an unwanted presence, an environmental risk that needs to be contained. Contemporary viewers are living in a cosmopolitan factual television environment. They watch a lot of different kinds of programming, some of which will be news or documentary, but a lot of which will be from popular factual genres, such as lifestyle, life experiment or reality gameshows/talentshows. Their experience of factual television is therefore fairly hands on, and their understanding of factual television as truthful and informative works alongside a practical engagement with life on the street, so to speak. Reality TV is a constant presence, they may not always like it, or agree with what it is doing, but it is a regular feature in their viewing experiences. Reality refusniks and contemporary viewers know about each other. There is a sense of each group watching the other at work, a wary acknowledgement that both are going about their business and at some point they may have to work with each other. Although the reality refusnik is the most watchful group, wary of the impact of contemporary viewing practices on their own group dynamic, they are curiously the least engaged in what is happening around them. It is as if they have trained their sights too closely on reality TV viewers, the neighbours from hell they need to keep an eye on but also don't want to have anything to do with. Contemporary viewers therefore become the viewers who are most engaged with the restyling of factuality. How they deal with the range of genres on offer is interesting in that these viewers have to be fast on their feet, they have to keep adjusting their responses as they come up against what factual television ought to be and what it is on a daily basis. For many of these viewers, their own image of themselves working through factual genres is often a negative one, as if in the act of watching they get caught up in a complicated self-assessment. This is in part connected to the wider negative discourses of reality TV in the context of discussions regarding quality standards and factuality. But, it is also related to how contemporary viewers get caught up in the restyling process, their viewing practices contributing to changes taking place, a chain reaction which can have positive and negative consequences for factual television.

Looking at factuality as a whole also highlights the psychodynamic aspects of viewing practices. Representations of reality are psychologically weighty material for audiences. They challenge all sorts of conventions and received wisdom on the relationship between fact and fiction. As in a dream, reality appears unstable. In this research viewers consciously reflect on factual content but there is always a sense that as they talk about various representations of reality they are moving into uncharted territory, exploring more unconscious aspects of their viewing experiences. Thus, genre work becomes a distinctive feature of factuality. Viewers slip in and out of immersive and reflective modes of engagement. Watching factual content can bring about intense feelings, whether in response to people or events featured in a programme, or in the way a programme has been constructed. Viewers describe feelings of excitement, happiness and inspiration, and also feelings of sadness, resentment and anger, when watching news items, particular documentaries or participants in reality TV. In moments of recognition when they see themselves watching television some viewers are troubled by this image, unhappy with what this personally means to them. As one viewer put it: 'Where is TV going to take us?' There is light and shade to viewing experiences, and in responding to specific factual content viewers sometimes confront a dark side to themselves, bringing up feelings of shame, guilt or other negative emotions. Genre work highlights the complex psychodynamic aspects that are part of being an audience.

Viewer responses to factuality show the significance of nature as a metaphor for the real. The phrase true to life is a powerful means of understanding the role of factual television in society and culture. Audiences come to the viewing experience with an understanding that factual content should be true to life. The paradox that representations of reality are constructed in factual programmes creates a mismatch between an idealized view of factual television and what is actually on the television screen. That factual television ought to be true to life is a prevailing belief amongst audiences. As this viewer simply put it: 'If it's not true it's not factual.' Their comment signifies trust in what you can see or hear, and the value in being natural, authentic, and true to yourself and others. Nature isn't always a benign force, nor is it untouched by human activity or protected from environmental change. But, nature and the natural world is the space within which we live and co-exist with others. This metaphor suggests that audiences want to use the idea of truth as a defining characteristic of factuality. Although the ideal concept of truth poses all sorts of difficulties for evaluating factual content, and makes viewing experiences challenging on all sorts of levels, audiences want to hold onto this ideal. At a time of great change in factual television program-ming, nature as a metaphor for the real becomes a vehicle for dealing with transition, a back to basics approach where the complexity, artificiality and knowingness of factuality can work alongside more primary elements in factual television.

The knowingness of factual television is a sign of the complexity of the knowledge project of television. There is a relative separation of different kinds of knowledge, from knowledge about the world, to knowledge about the self, to knowledge about the media. One programme can contain a range of knowledge, and sorting out the facts, information and experiences into different kinds of knowledge and learning is a necessary part of the viewing experience. Some times there is just too much knowledge on offer, a sea of information that can be hard to navigate. Viewers become judges of informa-tion, questioning facts, objectivity and truth claims within various genres. They also switch off, avoiding learning, looking for something entertaining on another channel. The questioning of knowledge thus becomes part of understanding factuality. In attitudes towards fair treatment of social groups in factual television, audiences use the degree of knowledge of participants to judge right and wrong ways to treat people in programmes. The know-ingness of participants is connected to their awareness of a format, they 'know what they are getting into'. It is a curious logic of learning that implies too much knowledge is bad for you, linking with the notion of artifice associated with truth claims. If something is too tricky, too smart, it becomes questionable, something not to be trusted. This logic of learning also applies to audiences and their self-awareness. The knowingness of audi-ences is a sign of the complexity of viewing experiences. As one viewer put it: 'You learn about yourself – why do I sit here and watch?' They question themselves in the act of viewing, reflecting on what being an audience means.

The art of plate spinning implies that research into audiences reveals hidden talents, a spectacle where viewers display how clever they are in their knowledge of genres. Watching factual TV isn't so much an art as part of life. Representations of reality are all around and viewers bump up against them all the time. The restyling of factuality is also something viewers jostle with every day. They have learned to deal with this chaotic, noisy and constantly evolving world. They step out of the house every morning into a bustling city, dealing with the traffic, people, noise, smells and general mayhem as part of life at a particular time, in a specific location. There are challenges and problems for viewers as they deal with a growing range of news and current affairs, and documentary, as well various kinds of popular factual, not only on television but also across an increasingly divergent range of multiplatform content. And as new experiences, challenges and problems arise, audiences learn to deal with these as well. Audiences are living in a cosmopolitan factual television environment, dealing with a mass of programmes on a day-to-day basis, finding various routes through the changes taking place in factuality. As this viewer put it: 'You are watching life. You might not like that life, you might not like what you are seeing, but it is life.'

Appendix: Research methods

Sample and recruitment

In Britain, a quantitative survey was conducted with a representative sample of 4,516 people. The sample included people aged 16–65+ living in Britain, and was conducted during November 2003, and carried out by Ipsos RSL. The response rate was exceptionally high, with a net response rate of 95 per cent, as this was an existing sample for the Broadcasters Audience Research Board. According to Ipsos RSL, the weighting for the panel is carried out for the full panel of 4,000 continuous reporters. Individual weights are calculated to correct for regional and demographic imbalances in the panel. Five 'super-regions' are defined and targets are set which reflect the age, sex and social grade profiles of these regions. This is achieved by setting rims which combine regions with each of these variables. The regions are as follows: London, Central/Anglia, Granada/Yorkshire, Meridian/HTV/WCTV, STV/Tyne Tees/Grampian/Border/Ulster. The weekly data are rim-weighted to targets derived from the Establishment Survey, including lifestage/socio-educational matrix, ITV region, size of household, age, sex, social grade AB, C1, C2, DE, working status, method of reception (cable, satellite, terrestrial). Other variables included ethnicity, marital status, children in the home, household size, newspaper readership and internet access. The survey contained one open question, and 17 closed questions.

In Sweden, a quantitative survey was conducted with a random sample of 2,000 people. The sample included people aged 16–80 living in Sweden, including foreign citizens. The survey was conducted in co-operation with the SOM Institute, Göteborg University, and carried out by Kinnmark Information AB. Mail questionnaires were collected from 4 February to 25 April 2005. The net sample was 1,854 people, with 944 respondents and a net response rate of 51 per cent. The distribution amongst responses compared with the Swedish population as a whole, and also compared with another representative survey (National SOM study 2004). Detailed analyses of comparable questions in both surveys show a very high similarity. The questionnaire contained 12 pages of questions on TV habits and TV attitudes.

Most questions contained fixed response alternatives, requiring a single mark, but the questionnaire also included two open-ended questions. In all, the questionnaire contained 39 questions, most of them multi-item questions. The responses to both surveys were scanned optically, and produced as an SPSS data file. The SPSS data was analysed using descriptive statistics, multi-variate analysis and factor analysis. The quantitative research was conducted in association with Professor Lennart Weibull and Åsa Nilsson at the Department of Journalism and Mass Communication and the SOM Institute in Sweden (see Hill *et al.* 2005 for further details).

A series of semi-structured focus groups were conducted in Sweden and Britain during two time periods between November 2004 to January 2005 and November 2005 to February 2006. There were 24 groups, 12 in each country, with a total of 129 respondents aged 18–60. The recruitment method used was quota sampling and snowball sampling. The sample was based on the criteria of age (split into two groups of 20–30 year olds and 40–60 year olds), gender (mix of male and female), socio-economic status (working and middle class, and educational levels from school to university). In Sweden, there were 56 respondents, 34 female, 22 male; in Britain, there were 73 respondents, 31 male and 42 female. Occupations ranged from unemployed, students, administrators, teachers, sales assistants, technicians, office workers, carers, artists and retired people. In Sweden, there were no ethnic minorities present in the focus group sample, although recruitment was conducted in and around Stockholm. In Britain, there were people from White, Indian Bandladeshi, Black African, Black Caribbean ethnic groups, and foreign nationals (German, Greek, Norwegian, Polish), which was not by design but reflects the diversity of the population of London where recruitment took place. The focus groups were held in both professional market research settings (four), an educational setting (11) and informal household settings (nine).

The focus group questions provided valuable insight into general attitudes of the survey. A series of open questions were asked regarding the four key questions of genre, actuality, learning and fairness. A game was used, whereby participants were asked to group a range of programme titles into categories and to discuss their reasons for the clusters of titles. Television clips from current affairs, documentary and reality programmes were used as visual prompts. In Britain, these clips included scenes from *Tonight with Trevor McDonald, Jamie's School Dinners* and *Wife Swap*. In Sweden, these clips included scenes from *Uppdrag granskning, The Domestic Army* and *Izabellas bröllop*. The focus groups were audio-recorded, and in addition notes were taken on general group behaviour and body language. The audio recordings were fully translated (in the case of Sweden) and transcribed by the focus group moderators, and coded using the qualitative software package NVivo.

The Finnish survey was an online self-completion questionnaire, in conjunction with a national study of *Big Brother* audiences. The survey was placed online in December 2005 as a 'pop up' on the website of the MTV3 channel, the largest channel in Finland (commercial), and the website is the most visited one in Finland. The total sample was 1,745 respondents; of these, 312 respondents were male, with a disproportionate amount of females, 1,419, reflecting the popularity of *Big Brother* with Finnish female viewers. The largest group of respondents was aged 25–44. The age span was 58 male respondents and 448 female respondents aged up to 25, 177 male respondents and 756 female respondents aged 25–44, and 76 males and 213 females aged 45+. Whilst the sample is not representative of the Finnish population, the responses are illuminating regarding gender and age differences.

Quantitative research: survey design

Questions in this appendix relate to those used in both the British and Swedish questionnaire. They are reproduced in text form, not in the format used in the survey itself. Other questions specific to each survey are detailed in the relevant chapters. The categories shown here indicate those which are comparable in both countries. These categories were listed in this form next to the relevant questions:

- News (*Nyheter*), e.g.:
  - *BBC News* or ITV's *News at Ten*
  - *Rapport, Nyheterna, TV3 Nyheter*
- Current affairs/documentaries (*Samhällsprogram/dokumentärer*), e.g.:
  - *Tonight with Trevor McDonald* or *Panorama*
  - *Dokument utifrån, enskilda dokumentärer*
- Investigative journalism (*Undersökande journalistik*), e.g.:
  - *Kenyon Confronts* or *House of Horrors*
  - *Uppdrag granskning, Kalla fakta, Insider*
- Political programmes (*Politiska debattprogram*), e.g.:
  - *Question Time* or *Jonathan Dimbleby*
  - *Agenda, Debatt, Ekdal mot makten*
- Consumer programmes (*Konsumentprogram*), e.g.:
  - as *Watchdog* or *Rogue Traders*
  - *Plus, Kontroll, Motorjournalen*
- Nature programmes (*Naturprogram*), e.g.:
  - *Life of Mammals* or *Survival*
  - *Mitt i naturen, Farligt möte*
- Documentary series (*Dokumentära serier*), e.g.:
  - *Real Lives* or *Cutting Edge*
  - *Djurpensionatet, Barnsjukhuset, Veterinärerna*
- Reconstructions (*Rekonstruktioner*), e.g.:
  - *999* or *Police, Camera, Action!*
  - *Efterlyst, På liv och död*

- Lifestyle experiment programmes (*Livsstilsexperiment*), e.g.:
  - *Faking It* or *Wife Swap*
  - *Par på prov, Switched, Blind Date*
- Lifestyle programmes (*Livsstilsprogram*), e.g.:
  - *Changing Rooms* or *House Doctor*
  - *Äntligen hemma, Solens mat, Roomservice, Fab 5, Gröna rum*
- Reality gameshows (*Dokusåpor*), e.g.:
  - *Big Brother* or *Pop Idol*
  - *Big Brother, Farmen, Riket*

Question one

What do you personally consider to be a factual television programme? It may just be one type of programme or it may cover a whole range of different types. If it would help, please use examples of actual programmes to explain your personal definition.

Question two

How often do you watch each programme category on any channel? (always, most of the time, sometimes, rarely, never)

Question three

How important do you think it is that these types of programmes are shown on television? (very important, fairly important, not very important, not important at all)

Question four

How would you categorize each of the following types of programme – are they more informative programmes or entertainment programmes or are they a combination of both? (informative, informative and entertaining, entertaining)

Question five

How much do you think you generally learn from each of the following types of programme? Please only answer for those types of programmes you ever watch. (a lot, quite a bit, an average amount, only a little, nothing)

Question six

How often do you think the following types of factual programmes help you to form opinions about various subjects? Please only answer for those types of programmes that you have ever watched. (always, most of the time, sometimes, rarely, never)

Question seven

(a) How much do you agree or disagree with the following statement about different types of factual programmes? 'I think the following types of factual programmes are true to life.' (agree strongly, agree, neither agree nor disagree, disagree, disagree strongly)
(b) How important is it to you that each of the following types of factual programmes are true to life? (very important, fairly important, not very important, not important at all)

Question eight

(a) How much do you agree or disagree with the following statement about different types of factual programmes? 'I think the ordinary people shown in these programmes act up for the camera.' (agree strongly, agree, neither agree nor disagree, disagree, disagree strongly)
(b) How important is it to you that ordinary people do NOT act up for the cameras in the following types of factual programmes? (very important, fairly important, not very important, not important at all)

Question nine

(a) How much do you agree or disagree with the following statements about the treatment and portrayal of different groups of people in these different types of factual programmes? (agree strongly, agree, neither agree nor disagree, disagree, disagree strongly)
   The selected categories included young children, teenagers, men, women, elderly, ethnic minorities, people with mental health problems, people with disabilities, politicians, experts and celebrities.
   'I think the following groups of people are treated fairly in news programmes.'
   'I think the following groups of people are treated fairly in documentary programmes.'
   'I think the following groups of people are treated fairly in reality programmes.'
   (b) How important is it to you that the following groups of people are treated fairly in news programmes?
   How important is it to you that the following groups of people are treated fairly in documentary programmes?
   How important is it to you that the following groups of people are treated

fairly in reality programmes? (very important, fairly important, not very important, not important at all)

Qualitative research: focus group design

- Semi-structured, medium level of moderator involvement. Standard key topics for all focus groups, but probing questions and clips will alter with age groups.
- Basic questionnaire to be filled in by all participants.

Introduction

Welcome; summary of research topic; emphasis on hearing different points of view; on their experiences and perspectives; try to not talk all at once; ask them to introduce themselves, saying name and regular factual programme they watch.

Key topics

Viewing experience

USE LIST: Which of these programmes do you most like? Which of these programmes don't you like?
  Probe the genres of news and current affairs, documentary and reality TV.
  Probe scheduling, peaktime viewing.
  Probe debate and gossip for particular news stories or reality events.

Genre definitions

How would you define factual or non-fictional programmes?
  Probe what they think are the defining characteristics of the genres, e.g. how would you define news?
  Probe what they value about genres, based on definitions.

USE GAME, ASKING PEOPLE TO CATEGORIZE DIFFERENT PRO-GRAMMES AND TO EXPLAIN THEIR REASONS

Truth claims

Do you think the stories you see in factual programmes are true to life?
  Probe different sub-genres.
  Probe members of the public acting up for the cameras.
  Probe staged reality, and authentic reality, how then tell the difference.

SHOW CLIP FROM DOCUMENTARY PROGRAMME

Learning

What do you learn from these kinds of programmes?
   Probe learning about practical, social, emotional things, and ask for examples.
   Probe different genres.
   Probe social attitudes to learning from TV.
   Probe learning about the media.

SHOW CLIP FROM NEWS OR CURRENT AFFAIRS PROGRAMME

Participation

Are there right and wrong ways to treat people who take part in factual programmes?
   Probe different social groups, e.g. men, women, children, celebrities, etc.
   Probe perceptions of participants in reality TV compared with documentary or news.

SHOW CLIP FROM REALITY PROGRAMME

Sum up and questions

Is there anything you would like to discuss?

Bibliography

Abercrombie, N. and Longhurst, B. (1998) *Audiences: A Sociological Theory of Performance and Imagination*, London: Sage.

Ahmed, S. (2004) *The Cultural Politics of Emotion*, Edinburgh: Edinburgh University Press.

Akpabio, E. (2004) 'Reactions of Nigerian Youth's Perceptions of Reality TV', in C. von Feilitzen (ed.) *Young People, Soap Operas and Reality TV*, Göteborg: International Clearinghouse on Children, Youth and Media, Nordicom, Göteborg University, 219–26.

Andrejevic, M. (2004) *Reality TV: The Work of Being Watched*, Maryland: Rowman and Littlefield.

Aslama, M. (forthcoming) *Big Brother Finland: Production and Reception Study Report*, Helsinki: University of Helsinki.

Aslama, M. and Pantti, M. (2006) 'Talking Alone: Reality TV, Emotions and Authenticity', *European Journal of Cultural Studies*, 9: 167–84.

Asp, K. (2002) 'TV-viewers programme preferences and the 11 of September', in S. Holmberg and L. Weibull (eds) *A New Spring for Politics*, SOM Report No.30, Göteborg: SOM Institute, Göteborg University, 219–29.

Austen, T. (2007) *Watching the World: Screen Documentary and Audiences*, Manchester: Manchester University Press.

Bazalgette, P. (2005) *Billion Dollar Game: How Three Men Risked it all and Changed the Face of Television*, Britain: Time Warner Books.

BBC News (2005) 'Spoof Show to Trick Astronauts', at: http://news.bbc.co.uk/1/hi/entertainment/tv_and_radio/4442882.stm.

Beck, U. (1995) *Risk Society*, London: Sage.

Bell, D. and Hollows, J. (eds) (2005) *Ordinary Lifestyles: Popular Media, Consumption and Taste*, Maidenhead: Open University Press and McGraw-Hill.

Bengtsson, S. (2002) 'The Uncomfortable TV Viewer', in S. Ericson and E. Ytreberg (eds) *Fjernsyn mellom høy og lav kultur*, Kristiansand: Høyskoleforlaget.

Bengtsson, S. and Lundgren, L. (2005) 'The Don Quixote of Youth Culture: Media Use and Cultural Preferences Among Students in Sweden and Estonia', *Mediestudier vid Södertörns högskola*, 2005: 1, Huddinge: MKV.

Biltereyst, D. (2004) '*Big Brother* and its Moral Guardians: Reappraising the Role of Intellectuals in the *Big Brother* Panic', in E. Mathjis and J. Jones (eds) *Big Brother International: Formats, Critics and Publics*, London: Wallflower Press, 9–15.

Biressi, A. and Nunn, H. (2005) *Reality TV: Realism and Revelation*, London: Wallflower Press.

Bolin, G. (2004) 'The Value of Being Public Service: The Shifting Power Relations in Swedish Television Production', in *Media, Culture and Society*, 26: 277–87.

Bolin, G. (2007) 'The Politics of Cultural Production', in K. Riegert (ed) *Politico-tainment: Television's Take on the Real*, New York: Peter Lang.

Bollas, C. (1992) *Being a Character: Psychoanalysis and Self-Experience*, London: Routledge.

Bondebjerg, I. (1996) 'Public Discourse/Private Fascination: Hybridization in "True-life-story" Genres', *Media, Culture and Society*, 18: 27–45.

Bondebjerg, I. (2002) 'The Mediation of Everyday Life: Genre, Discourse and Spectacle in Reality TV', in A. Jerslev (ed.) *Realism and 'Reality' in Film and Media*, Copenhagen: Museum Tusculanum Press, 159–92.

Bonner, F. (2003) *Ordinary Television*, London: Sage.

Bonner, F. (2005) 'Whose Lifestyle is it Anyway?', in D. Bell and J. Hollows (eds) *Ordinary Lifestyles: Popular Media, Consumption and Taste*, Maidenhead: Open University Press and McGraw-Hill, 35–46.

Broadcast (2006) 'Creative Report', 19 May 2006: 22–35.

Broadcasting Commission (2004) 'Swedish TV Programming 2003', report series of the Broadcasting Commission, No.13.

Brunsdon, C. and Morley, D. (1978) *Everyday Television: 'Nationwide'*, British Film Institute Television Monograph 10, London: BFI.

Brunsdon, C., Johnson, C., Moseley, R. and Wheatley, H. (2001) 'Factual Entertain-ment on British Television: The Midlands TV Research Group's "8–9 Project"', *European Journal of Cultural Studies*, 4(1): 29–62.

Bruzzi, S. (2000) *New Documentary: A Critical Introduction*, London: Routledge.

Buckingham, D. (2000) *The Making of Citizens: Young People, News and Politics*, London: Routledge.

Buckingham, D. (2003) *Media Education: Literacy, Learning and Contemporary Culture*, Cambridge: Polity Press.

Bulkley, K. (2006) 'Factual Entertainment', *Broadcast*, 31 March 2006: 27–8.

Calabrese, A. (2005) 'The Trade in Television News', in J. Wasko (ed.) *A Companion to Television*, London: Blackwell, 270–88.

Caldwell, J. (2002) 'Primetime Fiction Theorizes the Docu-Real', in J. Friedman (ed.) *Reality Squared: Televisual Discourse on the Real*, Newark, NJ: Rutgers University Press, 259–92.

Carter, G. (2004) 'In Front of our Eyes', in E. Mathjis and J. Jones (eds) *Big Brother International: Formats, Critics and Publics*, London: Wallflower Press, 250–7.

Clark, N. (2003) 'Feral Ecologies: Performing Life on the Colonial Periphery', in B. Szerszynski, H. Wallace and C. Waterton (eds) *Nature Performed: Environment, Culture and Performance*, Oxford: Blackwell Publishing, 163–82.

Clifford Giles, D. (2002) 'Keeping the Public in their Place: Audience Participation in Lifestyle Television Programming', *Discourse and Society*, 13(5): 603–28.

Collins, R. (2003) 'Ises and Oughts: Public Service Broadcasting in Europe', in R. C. Allen and A. Hill (eds) *The Television Studies Reader*, London: Routledge, 33–51.

Corner, J. (1995) *Television Form and Public Address*, London: Edward Arnold.

Corner, J. (1996) *The Art of Record: A Critical Introduction to Documentary*, Manchester: Manchester University Press.

Corner, J. (1998) *Studying Media: Problems of Theory and Method*, Edinburgh: Edinburgh University Press.

Corner, J. (1999) *Critical Ideas in Television Studies*: Oxford: Oxford University Press.

Corner, J. (2001) 'Review of Seeing Things', *European Journal of Communication*, 15(4): 558–60.

Corner, J. (2002a) 'Documentary Values', in A. Jerslev (ed.) *Realism and 'Reality' in Film and Media*, Copenhagen: Museum Tusculanum Press, 139–58.

Corner, J. (2002b) 'Performing the Real', *Television and New Media*, 3(3): 255–70.

Corner, J. (2005) 'Television Documentary and the Category of the Aesthetic', in A. Rosenthal and J. Corner (eds) *New Challenges for Documentary,* second edition, Manchester: Manchester University Press, 48–58.

Corner, J. (2006) 'A Fiction (Un)like Any Other?', *Critical Studies in Television*, 1(1): 89–97.

Corner, J. and Hill, A. (2006) 'Value, Form and Viewing in Current Affairs Television', *British Cinema and Television*, 3(1): 34–46.

Corner, J., Goddard, P. and Richardson, K. (2007) *Public Issue Television: World in Action 1963–98*, Manchester: Manchester University Press.

Corner, J. and Pels, R. (eds) (2003) *Media and the Restyling of Politics*, London: Sage.

Costera Meijer, I. (2006) 'The Paradox of Popularity: How Young People Experience the News', unpublished paper presented at the RIPE Conference, Netherlands, 18–26 November.

Couldry, N. (2002) 'Playing for Celebrity: Big Brother as Ritual Event', *Television and New Media*, 3(3): 283–94.

Curry, P. (2005) *Ecological Ethics*, Cambridge: Polity Press.

Dahlgren, P. (1995) *Television and the Public Sphere: Citizenship, Democracy and the Media*, London: Sage.

Dahlgren, P. (2005) 'Television, Public Spheres, and Civic Cultures', in J. Wasko (ed.) *A Companion to Television*, London: Blackwell, 411–32.

Dahlgren, P. and Sparks, C. (eds) (1992) *Journalism and Popular Culture*, London: Sage.

De Burgh, H. (2000) *Investigative Journalism: Context and Practice*, London: Routledge.

Denzin, N. (1984) *On Understanding Emotion*, San Francisco, CA: Jossey-Bass.

Descola, P. (1996) 'Constructing Natures – Symbolic Ecology and Social Practice', in P. Descola and G. Palsson (eds) *Nature and Society*, London: Routledge.

Dover, C. and Barnett, S. (2004) 'The World on the Box: International Issues in News and Factual Programmes on UK Television 1975–2003', Report, London: 3WE.

Dover, C. and Hill, A. (2007) 'Mapping Lifestyle', in D. Heller (ed.) *Reading Makeover Television*, London: IB Taurus.

Dovey, J. (2000) *Freakshows: First Person Media and Factual TV*, London: Pluto.

Dovey, J. (2004) 'It's Only a Gameshow: *Big Brother* and the Theatre of Sponteneity', in E. Mathjis and J. Jones (eds) *Big Brother International: Formats, Critics and Publics*, London: Wallflower Press, 232–49.

Drotner, K. (1992) 'Modernity and Media Panics', in M. Skovmand and K. C. Schroeder (eds) *Media Cultures: Reappraising Transnational Media*, London: Routledge, 42–62.

Ekström, M. (2000) 'Information, Storytelling, and Attractions: TV Journalism in Three Modes of Communication', *Media, Culture and Society*, 22: 465–92.

Elias, N. (1958) *Involvement and Detachment*, Oxford: Basil Blackwell.

Elias, N. (1994) *The Civilising Process*, Oxford: Blackwell.

Eliasoph, N. (1998) *Avoiding Politics: How Americans Produce Apathy in Everyday Life*, Cambridge and New York: Cambridge University Press.

Ellis, J. (2000) *Seeing Things: Television in the Age of Uncertainty*, London: IB Taurus.

Ellis, J. (2005) 'Documentary and Truth on Television: The Crisis of 1999', in A. Rosenthal and J. Corner (eds) *New Challenges for Documentary*, second edition, Manchester: Manchester University Press, 342–62.

Feilitzen, C. von (2004) *Mer tecknat . . .? Animerade TV-program – marknad, utbud, barn, föräldrar*, Stockholm: Våldsskildringsrådet.

Feilitzen, C. von (ed.) (2005) *Young People, Soap Operas and Reality TV*, Göteborg: Nordicom Foundation Publishers.

Franklin, A. (2001) *Nature and Social Theory*, London: Sage.

Franklin, S., Lury, C. and Stacey, J. (2000) *Global Nature, Global Culture: Gender, Race and Life Itself*, London: Sage.

Freud, S. (1909) *The Interpretation of Dreams*, London: Wordsworth Editions.

Gamson, J. (1998) *Freaks Tack Back: Tabloid Tack Shows and Sexual Non-conformity*, Chicago: University of Chicago Press.

Gauntlett, D. and Hill, A. (1999) *TV Living: Television Audiences and Everyday Life*, London: Routledge.

Gauntlett, D. (2007) *Creative Explorations: New Approaches to Audiences and Identities*, London: Routledge.

Giddens, A. (1991) *Modernity and Self Identity: Self and Society in the Late Modern Age*, Cambridge: Polity Press.

Globescan (2006) *Trust in the Media*, BBC, Reuters, Media Centre Poll, at: http://www.globescan.com/news_archives/bbcreut.html.

Glynn, K. (2000) *Tabloid Culture: Trash Taste, Popular Power, and the Transformation of American Television*, Durham, NC and London: Duke University Press.

Goffman, E. (1959) *The Presentation of Self in Everyday Life*, London: Pelican Books (reprint 1969).

Goffman, E. (1981) *Forms of Talk*, Oxford: Blackwell.

Griffen-Foley, B. (2004) 'From *Tit-Bits* to *Big Brother*: A Century of Audience Participation in the Media', *Media, Culture and Society*, 26(4): 533–48.

Grodal, T. (2002) 'The Experience of Realism in Audiovisual Representation', in A. Jerslev (ed.) *Realism and 'Reality' in Film and Media*, Copenhagen: Museum Tusculanum Press.

Gustafsson, K.E. and Weibull, L. (1995) *Sweden*, in European Institute for the Media (eds) *Television Requires Responsibility*, Gütersloh: Bertelsmann Foundation Publishers.

Habermas, J. (1989) *The Structural Transformation of the Public Sphere*, Cambridge: Polity Press.

Hadenius, S. and Weibull, L. (2003) *Mass Media: A Book About the Press, Radio and TV*, Falkenberg: Albert Bonniers Förlag.

Hagen, I. (1994) 'The Ambivalences of TV News Viewing: Between Ideals and Everyday Practices', *European Journal of Communication*, 9: 193–220.

Hammond, K. (1980) 'The Integration of Research in Judgment and Decision Theory', Report No. 226), Boulder, CO: University of Colorado Press.

Hartley, J. (1999) *Uses of Television*, London: Routledge.

Hermes, J. (2005) *Re-Reading Popular Culture*, Oxford: Blackwell.

Hibbard, M., Kilborn, R., McNair, B., Marriott, S. and Schlesinger, P. (2000) *Consenting Adults?*, London: Broadcasting Standards Commission.

Hill, A. and Palmer, G. (2002) '*Big Brother*: Special Issue', *Television and New Media*, 3(3).

Hill, A. and Kondo, K. (2006) 'Barriers to Interactive Media: Report on Interactive Media Audiences and Design', unpublished, University of Westminster.

Hill, A. (2000a) 'Crime and Crisis: British Reality TV in Action', in E. Buscombe (ed.) *British Television: A Reader*, Oxford: Oxford University Press.

Hill, A. (2000b) 'Fearful and Safe: Audience Response to British Reality Programming', *Television and New Media*, 1(2): 193–214.

Hill, A. (2002) '*Big Brother*: the Real Audience', *Television and New Media*, 3(3): 323–40.

Hill, A. (2004) 'Watching *Big Brother* UK', in E. Mathjis and J. Jones (eds) *Big Brother International: Formats, Critics and Publics*, London: Wallflower Press, 25–39.

Hill, A. (2005) *Reality TV: Audiences and Popular Factual Television*, London: Routledge.

Hill, A., Weibull, L. and Nilsson, Å. (2005) *Audiences and Factual and Reality Television in Sweden*, JIBS Research Reports No. 2005–4, Jönköping: JIBS.

Hill, A., Weibull, L. and Nilsson, Å. (2007) 'Public and Popular: British and Swedish Audience Trends in Factual and Reality Television', *Cultural Trends*, 16(1): 17–41.

Hochschild, A.R. (1983) *The Managed Heart: Commercialization of Human Feeling*, Berkeley and Los Angeles: University of California Press.

Höijer, B. (1998a) 'Cognitive and Psycho-dynamic Perspectives on Reception of Television Narration', in B. Höijer and A. Werner (eds) *Cultural Cognition: New Perspectives in Audience Theory*, Göteborg: Nordicom.

Höijer, B. (1998b) 'Social Psychological Perspectives in Reception Analysis', in R. Dickinson, R. Harindranath and O. Linné (eds) *Approaches to Audiences: A Reader*, London: Arnold, 166–83.

Höijer, B. (2000) 'Audience Expectations and Interpretations of Different Television Genres: A Sociocognitative Approach', in I. Hagen and J. Wasko (eds) *Consuming Audiences? Production and Reception in Media Research*, CressKill, NJ: Hampton Press, 189–208.

Holmes, S. (2004) 'All you've got to worry about is the task, having a cup of tea, and doing a bit of sunbathing': Approaching Celebrity in *Big Brother*', in S. Holmes and D. Jermyn (eds) *Understanding Reality Television*, London: Routledge, 111–35.

Holmes, S. and Jermyn, D. (2004) *Understanding Reality Television*, London: Routledge.

Independent Television Commission (2003) 'Factual Programming for ITV and Channel 4', unpublished material.

Jensen, K.B. (1986) *Making Sense of the News*, Arhuus: Arhuus University Press.

Jensen, K.B. (ed.) (1998) *News of the World: World Cultures Look at Television News*, London: Routledge.

Jerslev, A. (ed.) (2002) *Realism and 'Reality' in Film and Media*, Copenhagen: Museum Tusculanum Press.

Johansson, S. (2006) 'Reading Tabloids: A Study of Readers of the *Sun* and the *Daily Mirror*', doctoral dissertation, University of Westminster.

Jost, F. (2004) '*Big Brother* France and the Migration of Genres', in E. Mathjis and J. Jones (eds) *Big Brother International: Formats, Critics and Publics*, London: Wallflower Press, 105–22.

Jung, C.G. (1974) *Dreams*, from *The Collected Works of C.G. Jung*, Volumes 4, 8, 12 and 16, translated by R.F.C. Hull, Princeton, NJ: Princeton University Press.

Jung, C.G. (1978) *Man and His Symbols*, London: Picador.

Kilborn, R. (2003) *Staging the Real: Factual TV Programming in the Age of Big Brother*, Manchester: Manchester University Press.

Kittay, E.F. (2001) 'A Feminist Public Ethic of Care Meets the New Communitarian Family Policy', *Ethics*, 111(3): 523–47.

Lawrence, F. (2006) 'Junk Food Banned in Schools from September', *Guardian*, Friday, 3 March: 6.

Lewis, J. (2004) 'The Meaning of Real Life', in S. Murray and L. Ouellette (eds) *Reality TV: Remaking Television Culture*, New York: New York University Press, 288–302.

Littleton, C. (2004) 'Dialogue with Producer Mark Burnett', *Hollywood Reporter*, 26 May, at: http://www.hollywoodreporter.com/thr/article_display.jsp?vnu_content_id=1000518943.

Livingstone, S. (1998) *Making Sense of Television: Psychology of Audience Interpretation*, second edition, London: Routledge.

Livingstone, S. (2002) *Young People and New Media: Childhood and the Changing Media Environment*, London: Sage.

Livingstone, S. (2005a) 'On the Relation Between Audiences and Publics', in S. Livingstone (ed.) *Audiences and Publics: When Cultural Engagement Matters for the Public Sphere*, Bristol: Intellect Books, 17–42.

Livingstone, S. (2005b) 'In Defence of Privacy: Mediating the Public/Private Boundary at Home', in S. Livingstone (ed.) *Audiences and Publics: When Cultural Engagement Matters for the Public Sphere*, Bristol: Intellect Books, 163–86.

Livingstone, S. and Lunt, P. (1994) *Talk on Television: Audience Participation and Public Debate*, London: Routledge.

Livingstone, S. and Thumim, N. (2003) *Assessing the Media Literacy of UK Adults: A Review of the Academic Literature*, report commissioned by the Broadcasting Standards Commission/Independent Television Commission/National Institute of Adult and Continuing Education.

Livingstone, S., Van Couvering, E. and Thumim, N. (2005) *Adult Media Literacy: A Review of the Research Literature*, report commissioned by the Office of Communication.

Lunt, P. and Stenner, P. (2005) '*The Jerry Springer Show* as Emotional Public Sphere', *Media, Culture and Society*, 27(1): 59–81.

Lupton, D. (1998) *The Emotional Self*, London: Sage.

McCarthy, A. (2004) 'Stanley Milgram, Allen Funt, and Me', in S. Murray and L. Ouellette (eds) *Reality TV: Remaking Television Culture*, New York: New York University Press, 19–39.

McChesney, R. (2000) *Rich Media, Poor Democracy: Communication Politics in Dubious Times*, New York: New Press.

MacNaughton, P. and Urry, J. (eds) (2001) *Bodies of Nature*, London: Sage.

Maley, J. (2006) 'Britons Lead Spending on Culture and Recreation', *Guardian*, Friday, 31 March: 15.

Mannheim, K. (1936) *Ideology and Utopia*, London: Routledge and Kegan Paul.

Mathijs, E. (2002) 'Big Brother and Critical Discourse', Television and New Media, 3(3): 311–22.

Mathijs, E. and Hessels, W. (2004) 'What Viewer? Notions of the Audience in the Reception of Big Brother Belgium', in E. Mathjis and J. Jones (eds) Big Brother International: Formats, Critics and Publics, London: Wallflower Press, 62–76.

Mathjis, E. and Jones, J. (eds) (2004) Big Brother International: Formats, Critics and Publics, London: Wallflower Press.

Media Barometer 2003 (2004) Nordicom, Göteborg University.

Mepham, J. (1990) 'The Ethics of Quality in Television', in G. Mulgan (ed.) The Question of Quality, London: British Film Institute, 50–70.

Messinger Davies, M. and Mosdell, N. (2001) Consenting Children? The Use of Children in Non-fiction Television Programmes, London: Broadcasting Standards Commission.

Mittell, J. (2004) Genre and Television, London and New York: Routledge.

Moran, A. (2005) 'Configurations of the New Television Landscape', in J. Wasko (ed.) A Companion to Television, Maldon, London and Victoria: Blackwell, 291–307.

Morley, D. (1986) Family Television: Cultural Power and Domestic Leisure, London: Routledge.

Murray, S. and Ouellette, L. (eds) (2004) Reality TV: Remaking Television Culture, New York: New York University Press.

National Statistics (2005) UK 2005 Yearbook, Office of National Statistics, at: http://www.statistics.gov.uk.

Neale, S. (2001) 'Studying Genre', in G. Creeber (ed.) The Television Genre Book, London: British Film Institute, 1–3.

Nichols, W. (1991) Representing Reality: Issues and Concepts in Documentary, Bloomington and Indianapolis, IN: Indiana University Press.

Nichols, W. (1994) Blurred Boundaries: Questions of Meaning in Contemporary Culture, Bloomington and Indianapolis, IN: Indiana University Press.

Nichols, W. (2001) Introduction to Documentary, Bloomington, IN: Indiana University Press.

Nilsson, Å. and Weibull, L. (2005) 'Medier eller innehåll?', in S. Holmberg and L. Weibull (eds) Lyckan kommer, lyckan går, Göteborg: SOM-institutet, Göteborg University.

Nordström, B. (2001) 'The Strong and Weak Sides of Public Service Television', in S. Holmberg and L. Weibull (eds) Country, the Blessed?, SOM Survey 2000, SOM Report No. 26: 237–56.

OECD (2006) Organisation of Economic Co-operation and Development Factbook 2006: Economic, Environmental and Social Statistics, at: http://www.oecd.org.

Ofcom (2006a) The Communications Market 2006, London: Office of Communications.

Ofcom (2006b) The Provision of Current Affairs, London: Office of Communications.

Ouellette, L. (2004) 'Take Responsibility for Yourself', in S. Murray and L. Ouellette (eds) Reality TV: Remaking Television Culture, New York: New York University Press, 231–50.

Paget, D. (1998) No Other Way to Tell It, Manchester: Manchester University Press.

Palmer, G. (2003) Discipline and Liberty, Manchester: Manchester University Press.

Palmer, G. (2006) 'Video Vigilantes and the Work of Shame', Jump Cut, at: www.ejumpcut.org.

Philo, G. and Berry, M. (2004) Bad News from Israel, London: Pluto Press.

Power, R. (2000) A Question of Knowledge, Harlow: Prentice Hall.

Private Eye (2005) 'Space Cadets', December: 8.

Probyn, E. (2005) *Blush: Faces of Shame*, Minneapolis, MI: Minnesota University Press.

Reevell, P. (2006) 'Top 100 Shows of 2005', *Broadcast*, 6 January: 16–17.

Roscoe, J. (2001) '*Big Brother* Australia: Performing the 'Real' Twenty-four-seven', *International Journal of Cultural Studies*, 4(1): 473–88.

Roscoe, J. and Hight, C. (2001) *Faking It: Mock-documentary and the Subversion of Factuality*, Manchester: Manchester University Press.

Rosenthal, A. and Corner, J. (eds) (2005) *New Challenges for Documentary*, second edition, Manchester: Manchester University Press.

Scannell, P. (1996) *Radio, Television and Modern Life*, London: Blackwell.

Schlesinger, P. (1978) *Putting 'Reality' Together*, London: Constable.

Schudson, M. (1995) *The Power of News*, Cambridge, MA and London: Harvard University Press.

Seaton, J. (2005) *Carnage and the Media: The Making and Breaking of News about Violence*, London: Penguin.

Seymour, E. and Barnett, S. (2005) *Bringing the World to the UK: Factual International Programming on UK Public Service TV*, CMRU, London: University of Westminster.

Silverstone, R. (1994) *Television and Everyday Life*, London: Routledge.

Silverstone, R. (2007) *Media and Morality: On the Rise of the Mediapolis*, Oxford: Polity Press.

Social Trends (2005) *Social Trends*, 33, London: Office of National Statistics, at: http://www.statistics.gov.uk.

Souza, M.D. (2004) 'Chilean Tweens and Reality Soaps', in C. von Feilitzen (ed.) *Young People, Soap Operas and Reality TV*, Göteborg: International Clearinghouse on Children, Youth and Media, Nordicom, Göteborg University: 169–80.

Swedish Statistics (2006) *Annual Report 2006*, at: http://www.scb.se/statistik.

Syversten, T. (1999) 'Hva Kan "public service" Begrepet Brukes Til?', in U. Carlsson (ed.) *Nordiska Forskare Refleterar: Public Service-TV*, Göteberg: Nordicom.

Syvertsen, T. (2001) 'Ordinary People in Extraordinary Circumstances: A Study of Participants in Television Dating Games', *Media, Culture and Society*, 23(3): 319–37.

Syvertsen, T. (2004) 'Citizens, Audiences, Customers and Players: A Conceptual Discussion of the Relationship Between Broadcasters and Their Publics', *European Journal of Cultural Studies*, 7(3): 363–80.

Szerszynski, B., Heim, W. and Waterton, C. (eds) (2003) *Nature Performed: Environment, Culture and Performance*, Oxford: Blackwell.

Szerszynski, B. (2003) 'Technology, Performance and Life Itself: Hannah Arendt and the Fate of Nature', in B. Szerszynski, H. Wallace and C. Waterton (eds) *Nature Performed: Environment, Culture and Performance*, Oxford: Blackwell, 203–18.

Turner, G. (2004) *Understanding Celebrity*, London: Sage.

Turner, G. (2006) *Ending the Affair: The Decline of Television Current Affairs in Australia*, Sydney: University of New South Wales Press.

Van Leeuwen, T. (2001) 'What is Authenticity?', *Discourse Studies*, 3(4): 392–7.

Van Zoonen, L. (2005) *Entertaining The Citizen: When Politics and Popular Culture Converge*, Lanham, MD: Rowman and Littlefield.

Wadbring, I. and Grahm, S. (2001) 'How we watch TV', *JMG Surveyor*, Göteborg University: 4–5.

Ward, P. (2005) *Documentary: The Margins of Reality*, London: Wallflower Press.

Waterton, C. (2003) 'Performing the Classification of Nature', in W. Szerszynski and C. Waterton (eds) *Nature Performed: Environment, Culture and Performance*, Oxford: Blackwell Publishing, 111–29.

Westlund, O. (2006) 'Medieförtroendets mening', in S. Holmberg and L. Weibull (eds) *Du stora nya värld*, Göteborg: SOM-institutet, Göteborg University.

Winston, B. (1995) *Claiming the Real: The Documentary Film Revisited*, London: British Film Institute.

Winston, B. (2000) *Lies, Damn Lies and Documentaries*, London: British Film Institute.

Wollaston, S. (2005) 'In a Galaxy Not that Far Away', *Guardian*, Thursday, 8 December, at: http://media.guardian.co.uk/site/story/0,14173,1661949,00.html.

Wollaston, S. (2006) 'Forget *Big Brother* and *Love Island*', *Guardian*, Wednesday, 2 August, at: http://environment.guardian.co.uk/conservation/story/0,,1846765, 00.html.

Ytreberg, E. (2004) 'Formatting Participation within Broadcast Media Production', *Media, Culture and Society*, 26(5): 677–92.

Index

Abercrombie, N. 20
Abyss, The 80
accuracy of information (news) 25, 99, 112, 115
actors 11, 15–17, 20, 30, 48, 88, 141, 173–4, 178, 210, 225; non professional actors 117, 119, 140, 154
actuality 113–19; critical engagement 133–4, 136, 140, 142; feral genre 129, 143; Finland (perception and value of factual TV) 126; learning and genre work 156–7; looking through 114–16; nature and artifice 116–19, 144; performance 126, 144; research methods 20, 25; shades of ethics 204; true to life 120–1; 123–4, 143, 216; truth claims 28, 112–19, 143
age: viewing preferences 65–8; fairness 185–7; public value 71–2
Agenda 54, 236
Ahmed, S. 195
Airline 35, 54, 80, 132
Aktuellt 41, 77
America 9–10, 13, 32, 46, 55, 128, 156, 174
American Family, The 15, 177
American TV (imports to Sweden, audience attitudes) 37, 124, 128–35, 184, 219–20
America's Dumbest Criminals 194, 196
Andrejevic, M. 49
Antiques Roadshow 95
Äntligen hemma 41–2, 54, 237
apathy 167–8
Apprentice, The 5, 7, 9–10, 41, 93, 104, 106
Are Your Kids on Drugs 48
Armstrongs, The 1, 15

Aslama, M. 73
Austen, T. 47
authenticity 11–12, 16, 89, 113–19, 139, 141–3, 185
avoiding learning 166–9

Barnett, S. 33
Barnsjukhuset 54, 236
Bazalgette, P. 9–10, 220–1
BBC 7–9, 15–17, 23, 32–6, 44–8, 50–3, 55, 65, 77, 91, 95, 98–101, 132, 156, 166, 168, 174, 179, 207, 220, 226; BBC1 6, 34–6, 44–6, 48, 50–3; BBC2 6–7, 17, 34–5, 46, 51; BBC3 51; BBC4 48, 220
BBC 6 O'Clock News 44
BBC News 16, 36, 44, 53, 91, 95, 236
Beck, U. 117
Bell, D. 68, 160
Bengtsson, S. 82, 96
Berry, M. 44, 136, 149, 189
Big Brother 6, 9–10, 13, 15, 17–18, 21, 30, 33, 35–6, 38, 52–4, 61, 65, 73, 78, 80–1, 93–5, 105, 107–9, 115–16, 128, 132–3, 140–1, 154, 174, 179, 192, 197, 202, 219–20, 221, 223, 227, 235–7
Big Brother's Big Mouth 10
Big Brother's Little Brother 10
Biltereyst, D. 97, 132–3
Biressi, A. 49
Blind Date 54, 237
Blue Planet 48, 55, 65, 156
Bolin, G. 13, 39, 222
Bollas, C. 84, 87–8, 92, 94, 96, 109, 215
Bonner, F. 160, 178–9, 220
Boy Whose Skin Fell Off, The 15

Breakfast with Frost 45
British broadcasting 32–6
British Isles 7
British schedules and ratings 33–6
British Seaside, The 48
British television 6–9, 23–4, 27, 40, 47,
  54, 57, 132, 164, 218, 221; British
  broadcasting 32–6; *see also*
  broadcasting structures; commercial
  television; reality TV
Broadcast (television industry magazine)
  6, 17, 24
Broadcasting Commission 37–8
broadcasting structures 31–43; British
  broadcasting 32–6; British schedules
  and ratings 33–6; Swedish
  broadcasting 36–43; Swedish
  schedules and ratings 39–43
Brunsdon, C. 34, 134, 142, 144, 161
Bruzzi, S. 47, 124
Buckingham, D. 146, 151, 164, 217
Bulkley, K. 7–8

Calabrese, A. 11, 15
Candid Camera 17, 194
Carter, G. 114, 128
Cavemen see Walking with Cavemen
CBS 10, 32
celebrities: broadcasting structures 36;
  critical engagement 139, 141; factual
  categories 45, 47, 49, 51–3; factuality
  2, 5; fairness 180–2, 185–9, 209;
  genre work 111; humiliation TV 197,
  200–1; key findings 217–18; learning
  from factual TV 154; participants and
  audiences 178–9; participation 28,
  172–4; practices 225–6; production of
  30, 229; professionals 191–2;
  restyling (of) factuality 11, 16–17;
  shades of ethics 211; truth and
  performance 124; viewing modes 104,
  106–7; *see also I'm a Celebrity Get Me
  Out of Here; Celebrity Big Brother;
  Celebrity Love Island*
Celebrity Big Brother 15–16, 106, 141,
  197
Celebrity Love Island 33, 94, 104–5, 116,
  141
celebrity profiles 49, 51, 154
celebrity reality gameshow 2, 52, 111;
  see also reality gameshow
Celebrity Shark Bait 106–7

chain of distrust 140–3, 216
Changing Rooms 17, 36, 51, 54, 80, 93,
  95, 140, 237
Channel 4 6–8, 16–17, 23–4, 32–3,
  35–6, 44, 47, 50–3, 77, 91, 95,
  100–1, 132, 177, 197–8, 223, 225–6
Channel 4 News 6, 77, 91, 95, 100–1
Channel Five 23, 32, 34–5, 44, 46,
  48–9, 51, 77, 106
Charlie Brooker's Screenwipe 220
Children of Beslan 7
Children's Hospital 15
citizenship 12, 14, 151, 167, 224
civic cultures 13–14, 168
Clark, N. 117–18, 127, 143
class 185–187
classification: by audiences 4, 27, 58, 63,
  67, 76, 85, 89, 91, 94, 103, 120, 127,
  133, 143, 157, 165, 169, 213–15,
  230; in factual television 5, 6–11; in
  sociology of nature 62, 75
classificatory practices 214–15; *see also*
  classification
Clifford Giles, D. 179
CNN 8, 32, 189
Cold Feet: the Final Call 51
Collins, R. 60
commercial television 7, 12–13, 30–2,
  58, 60–2, 68–71, 75, 81–2, 85, 144,
  169, 214–15, 226; British 6–7, 15,
  23–4, 53–6, 64, 77, 128, 132, 168;
  British broadcasting structures 32–6;
  Finnish 73; Swedish 23–4, 53–6; 77,
  100, 124, 128–31, 137, 168, 219,
  221, 223, Swedish broadcasting
  structures 36–43
commercialization 12, 32, 137, 144,
  212
consumer programmes 45–7, 50–51,
  54–6, 65–70, 80, 126, 158; *see also*
  lifestyle programmes
containing factuality 212–33; key
  findings 217–18
Contender, The 10
contemporary viewers 79–81
contexts (participation): 188–94; news
  189–91; professionals 191–2; reality
  performers 192–4
contract of trust 137, 143
Cops 220
Corner, J.: actuality 114; avoiding
  learning 170; critical engagement

133–4; current affairs 218; fact and
fiction 87; factual categories 44–5, 47;
factuality 3–5, 213, 218–19; feral
genres 215; knowledge and learning
145, 150; learning from factual TV
155–6; performative factuality 143;
politicians 192, 198; public and
popular genres 60, 214, 216; restyling
(of) factuality 11–14, 214; viewing
modes 101; working through 90
Costera Meijer, I. 70, 82, 149, 156
Couldry, N. 13
Countdown 80
Countryfile 80
Crimewatch 80, 95
critical engagement 133–42;
documentary 137–9; news 134–7;
reality TV 140–2
cultural citizens 12, 14, 151
cultural discourses 20, 63, 65, 68, 70,
73, 82, 90, 98, 117–18, 123, 215,
228–9
current affairs: actuality 112–14;
broadcasting structures 31–3, 36,
39–41; contemporary viewers 79–80,
83; critical engagement 133–4; fact
and fiction 85; factual and reality
trends 10; factual categories 43–7, 53,
55, 56; factuality 5–8; genre work 27;
information and entertainment 74;
key findings 212–17; learning and
genre work 159, 169; learning from
factual TV 154–6, 158; participants
and audiences 174; practices 18,
221–2, 224; restyling factuality 2,
12–14, 228–9, 232; public and
popular genres 59; public value
69–72; 'reality refusniks' 77–9, 82;
research methods 25; traditional
viewers 77; truth claims 28; truth and
performance 119–20, 123, 127;
143–4; understanding learning
145–7, 151–2; viewing modes 96,
101; viewing preferences 64–7;
working through factuality 90–1, 93
Curry, P. 204–5, 217
Cutting Edge 54, 236

Dagens Nyheter 38
Dahlgren, P. 13–14, 150
Daniella Westbrooke Story, The 45
data analysis 21, 26, 63, 119, 221

dating gameshow 52, 178; *see also* reality
gameshows
David Letterman Show 54
Day Today, The 46
Debatt 41, 54, 77, 236
De Burgh, H. 115
defining factual TV 75–81;
contemporary viewers 79–81;
idealistic viewers 76–7; 'reality
refusniks' 77–9; traditional viewers
77
Denzin, N. 195
Desperately Seeking Sheila 8
Diet or Die 39
Discovery (US) 8, 81, 94
Djurpensionatet 54, 236
documentary: critical engagement
137–9; documentary aesthetics 90,
114; documentary genre 74, 86, 102,
123–4, 139, 156; documentary modes
5, 11, 101–4, 123, 139, 156, 160,
228; documentary series 7–9, 15,
32–3, 36, 39, 54–5, 65, 69, 220;
factual categories 47–8;
history/science documentary 7, 35,
54, 56, 123–4, 154, 156; mock
documentary 1; natural history
documentary 20, 31, 35, 47–8, 102,
117, 124, 157; observational
documentary 5, 20, 30, 35, 36, 47–8,
54, 56, 66–67, 101–2, 117, 123–34,
154, 156, 177; viewing modes 101–4
documentary aesthetics 90, 114; *see also*
documentary
documentary genre 74, 86, 102, 123–4,
139, 156; *see also* documentary
documentary modes 5, 11, 101–4, 123,
139, 156, 160, 228; *see also*
documentary *and* viewing modes
documentary series 7–9, 15, 32–3, 36,
39, 54–5, 65, 69, 220; *see also*
documentary
docusoaps: contemporary viewers 79–80;
critical engagement 140, 142; factual
categories 47, 49; factuality 5;
humiliation TV 197; learning and
genre work 163; learning from factual
TV 156; 'reality refusniks' 78;
participants and audiences 177;
practices 219; public and popular
genres 60; reality performers 193;
Swedish broadcasting 38–9; truth and

performance 124, 132; working
through factuality 94
Dokument utifrån 54, 236
Domestic Army, The 2
Dover, C. 33, 43, 75, 160, 218
Dovey, J. 15, 116, 128, 207, 215
Dragons' Den 197
Drastic Plastic 106
dream work 84, 87–9, 92, 96, 108–10,
215
Driving School 132
Drotner, K. 61
dumbing down 150, 156, 168

editorial processes (news) 100, 136
education: viewing preferences 65–8,
public value 71–2
Efterlyst 54, 137, 236
Ekdal mot makten 54, 236
Ekström, M. 99
Elias, N. 147, 149, 153, 159, 169
Eliasoph, N. 156, 166–8
Ellis, J.: British schedules and ratings
34; broadcasting structures 31; critical
engagement 138–9, 141–2; fact and
fiction 84–7, 89; genre work 84, 109,
215; learning from factual TV 156;
performance 124; practices 223;
public and popular genres 214;
restyling (of) factuality 12, 16;
working through 91
emotion of shame 195–6
Endemol 6, 9, 10, 16, 115, 132, 220;
Endemol International 10, 115, 220;
Endemol UK 6
Enskilda dokumentärer 54, 236
entertainment 28–9, 56, 81–2, 144,
209, 210–11; actuality 116;
broadcasting structures 31–2, 37;
critical engagement 137, 140;
entertainment news 11, 44, 49, 51,
100, 137; factual and reality trends
8–9; factual categories 50; factual
entertainment 7, 16, 48, 80, 107; key
findings 217; learning from factual
TV 154; light entertainment 3, 30,
40, 43, 49, 52–3, 175–8, 214, 226,
229; participants and audiences 174,
176; popular entertainment 13, 85,
227; practices 219; public and popular
genres 61; reality entertainment 2–10,
17–18, 38–39, 48, 89, 94, 115, 128,

208, 213–14; 'reality refusniks' 78;
restyling (of) factuality 12–13, 227–9;
shades of ethics 207;
sports/entertainment news 44, 100,
222, 228; truth and performance
119–20, 123, 126, 128;
understanding learning 152–3;
viewing modes 97, 104–6; working
through factuality 93; *see also*
information and entertainment *and*
information
entertainment genre 7, 12, 178
entertainment news 11, 44, 49, 51, 100,
137; *see also* entertainment *and*
information and entertainment
Equinox 47
ethical treatment of people in
programmes *see* fair treatment *and*
perception and value of fair treatment
ethics 24, 172, 174–5; deep ethics 28,
174, 203–6, 208, 211, 217; ethics of
care (public and private) 175, 184–5,
187–8, 209, 224; and fairness 217;
green ethics 204–5; intermediate
ethics 204–5, 211; professional
journalistic/documentary ethics 175,
177, 187–9, 228; shades of ethics
203–9, 211; shallow ethics 28, 174,
203–4, 211; and shame 203; social
and rights ethics 175, 204
Expedition Robinson 38, 94, 128, 184, 197
Extreme Makeover 41, 128, 220

Fab 5 41, 54, 237
fact and fiction 85–90
factual and reality trends 6–11
factual categories 43–53; current affairs
and investigation 45–7; documentary
47–8; news 44; non-fiction genres
(other) 53; popular factual 48–52
factual entertainment 7, 16, 48, 80, 107;
see also entertainment *and* information
and entertainment
factual television 26–31, 82–3, 142–6,
169–72; actuality 112–14, 116, 118;
avoiding learning 165; broadcasting
structures 34–6, 40–2; contemporary
viewers 80–2; critical engagement
144; defining factual TV 75–6; fact
and fiction 85; factual and reality
trends 7, 10–11; factual categories 43;
factuality 3–5; fairness 185;

humiliation TV 197; idealistic viewers 76–7; key findings 212, 214, 216; learning and genre work 164; learning from factual TV 153, 158–9; participants and audiences 174–5; practices 218–19, 220–4; programme categories 53, 55; public and popular genres 59–62; reality performers 192; 'reality refusniks' 78–9; research methods 22, 24; restyling (of) factuality 1–3, 11–13, 16, 18, 227–33; shades of ethics 203–9; traditional viewers 77; truth and performance 119–20, 123, 127–33; viewing modes 95–7, 111; viewing practices 20–1; working through factuality 90, 94–5

factuality 3–5; actuality 113, 115–16, avoiding learning 168; book outline 21–6; classification 1–6, 212; contemporary viewers 83; critical engagement 133–4, 143–4; defining factual TV 75–6; fact and fiction 90; genre work 85, 111; information and entertainment 75; key findings 213–18; learning from factual TV 153; participation 172; performative factuality 115, 143; practices 219, 222, 225, 227; public and popular genres 59, 62; public value 69–70; 'reality refusniks' 79, 82–3; research methods 22–6; restyling of 10–18, 110, 227–33; truth and performance 117–20, 124, 131; truth claims 112–13; viewers understandings of 170, 210–11; viewing modes 95, 103, 111; viewing practices 19–20; viewing preferences 63, 67, 82; working through factuality 90–5

fair treatment (audience attitudes towards): of children 173, 180–2, 184, 187, 206, 209, 217, 223; of celebrities 180–2, 185–87, 189, 191–2, 209, 211, 217; of men 180–2, 187, 221, 228; of ordinary people 149, 175, 188–90, 203, 208; of people with disabilities 180–2, 184, 187, 209, 223; of people with mental health problems 180–2, 184, 186–7, 206, 209, 223; of politicians 173, 175, 178, 180–2, 185–7, 189, 191–2, 209; of teenagers 180–2, 184, 186; of

the elderly 180–2, 184–5, 223; of the Royalty 180–2; of women 180–2, 187, 221, 228; see also perception and value of fair treatment

fairness 25, 107, 172–3, 175, 180–7, 184–90, 203, 205–9, 211–12, 217; age, gender and class 185–7; genre 187; perception and value of fair treatment 181–5; see also fair treatment

Faking It 6, 50, 54, 93–4, 161–2, 237

Fame Academy 6, 52, 80

Farligt möte 54, 236

Farmen 38–9, 41–2, 54, 131, 163–4, 219, 237

feral genre 112–13, 118, 127–33, 143, 230; key findings 215–16

Finland 21–2, 82, 143, 218; public value 73–4; truth and performance 126–7

Flog It 80

focus group design 239–40; see also research methods

Franklin, A.18 117, 204

Franklin, S. 18

Freud, S. 86–7

gameshows 15, 52–3, 55, 78, 128, 178; see also reality gameshows

Games, The 53

Gamson, J. 53

Gardeners' World 51

Gauntlett, D. 96

gender: fairness 185–7; public value 71–2; viewing preferences 65–8

genre: documentary genre 74, 86, 102, 123–4, 139, 156; entertainment genre 7, 12, 178; fairness 187; feral genre 112–13, 118, 127–33, 143, 215–16, 230; genre experiment 112, 143, 216; genre work 84–111; learning and genre work 159–66; news genre 70, 97, 100, 134, 165, 189; non-fiction genres 3–4, 49, 53, 213; popular genre 2, 32, 58–62, 65, 68–70, 85, 103, 153, 159, 168, 214, 223–4; populist genre 39; public and popular genres 59–62, 65, 69, 153, 159, 214; sub-genre 3–5, 49, 55–6, 213–14; tabloid genre 128; traditional genre 67, 70, 72; see also popular factual genre; reality genre; hybrid genre

genre evaluation: as a strategy 81; critical engagement 133; fairness 181, 184, 187; information and entertainment 75; learning from factual TV 153, 155; public and popular genres 58, 61, 214; research methods 24, 27–8; restyling factuality 229; traditional viewers 77; truth and performance 119, 121, 124
genre experiment 112, 143, 216
genre work 84–111; critical engagement 133; fact and fiction 85–90; key findings 213, 215, 231; learning 151, 159, 164–5, 168, 170; looking through 114; viewing modes 95–109; working through factuality 90–5
Germany 7–10
Giddens, A. 96, 116
Globescan 8, 26
Glynn, K. 190, 207
Goffman, E. 11, 19, 149
Going Tribal 8
Grahm, S. 37
Greatest Reality TV Moments 49
Griffen-Foley, B. 174
Grodal, T. 3, 113–14
Gröna rum 54, 237
guilty viewers 96, 104, 111, 174, 208, 211
Gustafsson, K.E. 37

Habermas, J. 13, 60, 168
Hadenius, S. 37–8
Hagen, I. 82, 222
Hartley, J. 12, 151, 154, 200
Heather Mills: the Real Mrs McCartney 51
Hell's Kitchen 6
Hermes, J. 12, 20–1, 227
Hibbard, M. 175–6
High School Reunion 39, 41
Hight, C. 21, 74
Hill, A.: British schedules and ratings 34; contemporary viewers 81; critical engagement 141; factual categories 45; factuality 4–5; feral genre 128, 132; information and entertainment 74–5; learning and genre work 160–1, 165; learning from factual TV 154, 156; looking through 115; nature and artifice 118; performance 126; public and popular genres 61; public value 69; 'reality refusniks' 79; research

methods 21, 24, 26; restyling (of) factuality 13, 15; viewing modes 96, 104–5; viewing practices 218; viewing preferences 63
History of Britain 54
history/science documentary 7, 35, 54, 56, 123–4, 154, 156; see also documentary and natural history documentary
Hochschild, A.R. 15, 195
Höijer, B. 90, 99
Holiday 35–6, 46
Hollows, J. 68, 160
Holmes, S. 31, 132, 186, 192
Honeymoons from Hell 50
Horizon 47, 93, 95, 101
House Doctor 51, 54, 237
House of Horrors 47, 54, 194, 236
Human Body, The 47
humiliation TV 194–203; emotion of shame 195–6; media hot 200–3; shame and reality TV 196–200
hybrid genres 3–5, 30, 32, 49, 85, 94, 112, 124, 165, 170, 177, 213, 219; factuality 3–5; broadcasting structures 30, 32; factual categories 49; fact and fiction 85, 94, truth claims 112, 124, knowledge and learning 165, 170; participants and audiences 177; key findings 213, practices 219

I Shouldn't be Alive 8
idealistic viewers 76–7
Idol 9, 42, 94, 128
I'm a Celebrity, Get Me Out Of Here 6, 33, 36, 45, 52, 80–1, 94, 105, 154, 166, 197
impartiality 112, 135
Independent Television Commission 21, 33, 175
information: avoiding learning 166–71; broadcasting structures 31–2; critical engagement 133, 136; fact and fiction 85–6; factual and reality trends 8, 12–13; factual categories 44–5, 47–8, 51–3; factuality 3, 5; fairness 180; idealistic viewers 76; information and entertainment 12, 32, 61, 74–5, 81, 91, 229; key findings 215–18; learning and genre work 162–3, 165; learning from factual TV 28, 153–9; participants and audiences 176; public

and popular genres 61; public value 68; reality performers 192; 'reality refusniks' 78; research methods 25; restyling factuality 229, 232; truth and performance 123; truth claims 112; understanding learning 146–53; viewing modes 96–7, 99–100, 106, 109; working through factuality 91, 93–4; *see also* entertainment

information and entertainment 12, 32, 61, 74–8, 81, 91, 229; *see also* entertainment *and* information

informed consent 172, 175–8, 180, 194, 203, 205, 209

Insider 54, 236

interactive television 5, 10, 24, 93, 226

intermediate space 27, 110–11; fact and fiction 88–9; key findings 215; working through factuality 94; viewing modes 102, 108

International Emmy Awards 6, 10

investigation 45–7

investigative journalism 5, 45, 54–6, 69, 70, 101, 115, 154, 177, 228; *see also* documentary

It's Me or the Dog 226

ITV 6–8, 23–4, 32–6, 45, 47–8, 50–3, 55, 77, 100–1, 197; ITV1 6, 34–6, 45, 47–8, 50–2

ITV News 45, 101

Izabellas bröllop 2

Jamie's School Dinners 7, 9, 93, 95, 101, 139, 160, 220, 225, 227, 235

Jensen, K.B. 44

Jermyn, D. 31, 49, 132, 186

Jerry Springer 14

Johansson, S. 14

Joe Millionaire 52

Johansson, S. 14

Jonathan Dimbleby 54, 236

Jones, J. 162

Judge Judy 169, 225

Jung, C.G. 85, 87, 108

Kalla fakta 54, 77, 236

Kanal 5 10, 23–4, 37–8, 41–2, 223–42, 223

Kenyon Confronts 54, 236

key findings 213–18; classificatory practices 214–15; containing factuality 217–18; factuality 213; fairness 217; feral genre 215–16;

genre work 215; knowledge and learning 216–17; public and popular genres 214; restyling (of) factuality, the 213–14; true to life 216

Kilborn, R. 4, 118, 132

Kittay, E.F. 175, 224

Kondo, K. 24

Kontroll 54, 236

knowledge and learning 145–71; avoiding learning 166–9; learning and genre work 159–66; learning from factual TV 153–9; understanding learning 146–53

knowledge as facts 28, 145, 166–7, 169–70; key findings 216; learning and genre work 159; understanding learning 146, 149; *see also* learning

Lawrence, F. 225

learning: avoiding learning 146, 150, 166–70, 232; classification of learning 146–53; as contributing to cultural citizenship 151; as different from knowledge 152; emotional learning 145, 147, 159, 161, 200; formal and informal learning 145–6, 152, 167–8, 170; information transformed into learning 151–2, 171, 216; knowledge and learning 28, 145–71, 216–17; knowledge as facts 28, 145–6, 149, 159, 166–7, 169–70, 216; learning about the media from the media 146, 164–5, 216; learning as experience 146–9, 161, 169; learning from different factual genres 154–60, 163, 165, 168, 216; learning from factual TV 153–9; nature and artifice 117; objective and subjective learning 147, 153, 159; opinion formation and learning 158; personal learning 146, 148–9, 159, 161, 167–70, 216; practical learning 147, 152; research questions 24–5; self-reflexive learning 163, 232; social learning 145–7, 152, 154, 162–3, 170; understanding of learning (by audiences) 153–5, 157–8, 165, 169

Lewis, J. 138

life experiment programmes 5, 33–9, 49–50, 54, 56, 65–9, 71–2, 123–8, 158–61, 198, 226, 230

Life Laundry 51

Life of Grime 48, 80
Life of Mammals, The 47, 54, 80, 102, 236
lifestyle: broadcasting structures 33–6, 39, 40–2; entertainment and information 74–5; factual categories 46, 49, 51; factuality 5–7; humiliation TV 198; key findings 218; learning and genre work 159–66; learning from factual TV 153–9; lifestyle experiment programmes 54; lifestyle programmes 46, 51–5, 65–9, 75, 126; participants and audiences 177–9; programme categories 54–6; public value 69–72; restyling factuality 230; truth and performance 123, 126; viewing preferences 67; working through factuality 93, 95; *see also* consumer programmes
lifestyle programmes 46, 51–5, 65–9, 75, 126; *see also* consumer programmes
light entertainment 3, 30, 40, 43, 49, 52–3, 175–8, 214, 226, 229; *see also* entertainment *and* information and entertainment
Little Angels 226
Littleton, C. 10
Livingstone, S.: programme categories 53; public and popular genres 61; critical engagement 133; knowledge and learning 146, 217; learning and genre work 164; practices 227; understanding learning 151
Longhurst, B. 20
London bombings, July 7th, 2005 (news coverage) 97, 99–100, 136–7, 150
looking at and looking through 21–2, 102–4, 113–16, 133–4
Love Island 18
Lundgren, L. 82
Lunt, P. 14, 53
Lupton, D. 85, 195, 199, 201–2

McCarthy, A. 194
McChesney, R. 224
McIntyre Undercover 46
MacNaughton, P. 18, 117
makeover programmes 35–6, 41, 51, 55, 75, 79–80, 126, 128, 160–1, 179, 220
Maley, J. 23
Man Show, The 194
Man Whose Skin Fell Off, The 221

Mannheim, K. 147
mapping factual TV 30–57; broadcasting structures 31–43; factual categories 43–53; programme categories 53–5
Mark Burnett Productions 7, 10
Match, The 6
Mathjis, E. 61, 162
Media Barometer 223
media hot 28, 173, 180, 209, 217; humiliation TV 200–3
media literacy 133, 146, 164–6
media panic 61, 67, 97, 132
melodrama 49, 190
Mepham, J. 114
Messenger Davies, M. 174, 185
methods *see* research methods
Mitt I naturen 54, 236
Mittell, J. 4, 30, 59, 61, 213
mock documentary 1; *see also* documentary
modes of engagement: actuality 113–15; critical engagement 133–42; fact and fiction 88–90; genre work 27, 84–5; key findings 213, 215, 231; learning and genre work 159–65, 169; restyling factuality 2, 231; truth claims 28; viewing modes 95–109; *see also* viewing modes
Moran, A. 9, 220
Morley, D. 96, 142, 144
Mosdell, N. 184
Motorjournalen 54, 236
multimethod research 2, 20, 26, 175, 213
Murray, S. 32, 49, 61, 186
Mythbusters 8

Nanny-akuten 80
National Statistics 23
natural history documentary 20, 31, 35, 47–8, 102, 117, 124, 157; *see also* documentary *and* history/science documentary
nature and artifice 116–19
nature and performance 18–19, 112, 117, 134
Neale, S. 4
Neighbours from Hell 50, 194, 196, 230
news: 9/11 (news coverage) 15, 100, 150; accuracy of information 25, 99, 112, 115; critical engagement 134–7;

editorial processes 100, 136;
entertainment news 11, 44, 49, 51,
100, 137; factual categories 44;
London bombings, July 7th, 2005
(news coverage) 97, 99–100, 136–7,
150; news contexts 189–91; news
coverage 6, 93, 99–100, 136, 150,
189, 190; news genre 70, 97, 100,
134, 165, 189; participation contexts
189–91; sports/entertainment news
44, 100, 222, 228; viewing modes
97–101; see also BBC News; Sky News;
Ten O'Clock News
News at Ten 52, 236
news coverage 6, 93, 99–100, 136, 150,
189, 190
news genre 70, 97, 100, 134, 165, 189
Newsnight 35, 91, 95
Nichols, W. 4, 19, 43, 47, 102, 114, 139
Nightmare before Christmas, A 1
Nilsson, Å. 63, 70
non-fiction genres 3–4, 49, 53, 213
Nordström, B. 37
Nunn, H. 49
Nyheterna 41, 53, 236
999 15, 50, 54, 132, 236

observational documentary 5, 20, 30,
35, 36, 47–8, 54, 56, 66–7, 101–2,
117, 123–34, 154, 156, 177; see also
documentary
Odyssey of Life 7
OECD 22–3
Ofcom 7–8, 32–3, 35, 45, 164
Office, The 1, 220
opinion formation: and learning 158,
165; audience attitudes towards
153–9; political 13; public opinion
153, 159, 189
ordinary and celebrity 178–80
Ouellette, L. 32, 49, 186, 224

Palmer, G. 15, 196, 202, 224
Panorama 44–5, 54, 79–80, 93, 95, 101,
227, 236
Par på prov 54, 237
participants and audiences 174–80;
informed consent 175–8; ordinary and
celebrity 178–80
participation 172–211; contexts
188–94; fairness 180–7; humiliation
TV 194–203; participants and

audiences 174–80; shades of ethics
203–9
Pels, R. 3, 11, 14, 143, 192, 213–14,
219
perception and value of factual TV:
public value 68–74; truth and
performance 119–33
perception and value of fair treatment
181–5; see also fair treatment
Perfect Vagina, The 39
performance 124–6; as spectacle 20;
nature and performance 18–19, 112,
117, 134; of
participants/actors/personalities 16,
20, 52–3, 117, 141, 154, 192; of
politicians 11–12, 14–16, 74, 120,
126, 143, 156, 185;
truth/performance judgements 28,
112, 115–17, 119–34, 142–4, 169,
185, 216; see also truth and
performance
performative factuality 115, 143
performative politics 11–12, 143
personalities 15–16, 52, 141, 173, 206
Pet Rescue 93, 95, 140
Philo, G. 44, 136, 149, 189
Planet Earth 15–16
Planet's Funniest Animals, The 50
Plastic Surgery Live 95, 107, 161
Plus 54, 236
Police, Camera, Action 54, 236
Police, Stop 50
political apathy 167–8
political culture 11–12, 143
politicians: as participants in factual
programmes 30; distrust in 123, 156;
fair treatment of 173, 175, 178,
180–2, 185–7, 189, 191–2, 209;
performance and authenticity 11–12,
14–16, 74, 120, 126, 143, 156, 185;
in Question Time 46; shallow ethics 204
politics programmes: factual categories
45–6, 56; viewing preferences 65;
public value 68, 72; 'reality refusniks'
79; truth and performance 120, 123,
126, 143; learning from factual TV
155–6, 158–9
Politics Show, The 45
Pop Idol 6, 52–53–4 78, 80, 103, 178,
197, 219–20, 237
popular culture: factual categories 43,
49; public and popular genres 60–2,

82; public service 222; value of
12–13, 227, 229; viewing practices
20–1
popular entertainment 13, 85, 227; see
also entertainment and information
and entertainment
popular factual genres: avoiding learning
168, 170; contemporary viewers 79,
80, 82; factual categories 48–52;
factuality 2, 4; key findings 212–13;
knowledge and learning 146; learning
and genre work 162, 165–6; learning
from factual TV 154, 157–9;
participants and audiences 177–8;
practices 224, 226–7; programme
categories 54; public and popular
genres 61; public value 69, 70, 72;
restyling (of) factuality 12–14, 27,
229–30; truth and performance 121,
125, 127–8; viewing preferences
62–4, 67
popular genres 2, 32, 58–62, 65, 68–70,
85, 103, 153, 159, 168, 214, 223–4
popular television 153–4, 220; factual
and reality trends 10; humiliation TV
197; learning and genre work 165,
171; mapping factual TV 30;
participants and audiences 174;
practices 219, public service 224–5;
reality performers 192; truth and
performance 120, 132; truth claims
112; see also reality TV
Power of Nightmares, The 8
Power, R. 147
practices 218–27; contexts 219–22;
public service 222–7; restyling
factuality 227–33
Private Eye 17
Probyn, E. 196, 217
professionals: participation contexts
191–2
programme categories 53–5
Property Ladder 80
psychodynamic viewing practices 84–5,
90, 133, 215, 231
public and popular 58–83; defining
factual TV 75–81; information and
entertainment 74–5; public and
popular genres 59–62; public value
68–74; viewing preferences 62–8
public and popular genres 59–62, 65,
69, 153, 159; key findings 214

public figures 28, 172–4, 178, 180, 182,
191, 209, 211
public knowledge project, the: avoiding
learning 166, 168, 170; fact and
fiction 85; key findings 215; learning
from factual TV 158; public and
popular genres 60, 82; restyling (of)
factuality 12, 13, 227, 232;
understanding learning 145–6,
150–1; viewing modes 97; viewing
preferences 63
public service 222–7
public service broadcasting (PSB) 56,
82–3; avoiding learning 168;
broadcasting structures 31–2, 36–7,
41; critical engagement 135; defining
factual TV 75; fact and fiction 87;
factual categories 45; factuality 4; key
findings 215; participation 173;
practices 222, 224–5; public and
popular genres 60–2; public value
68–70, 73; understanding learning
145; restyling (of) factuality 12,
228–9; traditional viewers 77; truth
and performance 127; restyling
factuality viewing preferences 64
public sphere: and PSB 60–1, 168; in
Habermas's sense 13, 60, 85, 145,
168; multiple 14, 167
public value 68–74; age, gender and
education 71–2; Finland 73–4

qualitative research 24–6, 37, 62, 75,
96, 134, 159, 167, 213, 221, 239–40;
see also research methods
quality: in audience research on reality
TV 229; dreamlike quality of
watching 104, 114, 136; in factual TV
production 6–7, 9–10, 12–13, 37, 39,
223; as informative/entertaining
58–9, 62, 77; as issue in media
debates (fall of standards) 61, 70, 132,
136, 150, 223, 231; judgements
about different factual
genres/programmes 67–9, 124, 128,
130, 156, 228; of trashing reality TV
104–5, 107; truth and performance
119
quantitative research 236–9; 24–6,
62–3, 119, 213, 221; see also research
methods
Question Time 46, 54, 236

Rail Cops 220
Rapport 40–2, 53, 77, 236
Ready Steady Cook 80
Real Life 48
Real Lives 54, 236
realism 112–16, 142–3
reality entertainment 2–10, 17–18, 38–9, 48, 89, 94, 115, 128, 208, 213–14; *see also* entertainment *and* information and entertainment
reality event 5, 9
reality formats: actuality 118; critical engagement 141–2; fact and fiction 89; factual and reality trends 9–11; fairness 184; humiliation TV 197, 200; participants and audiences 178, 180, 209; practices 220, 229; public and popular genres 61; restyling (of) factuality 15; shades of ethics 206, 210; truth and performance 128–9, 131–2; viewing modes 103, 108; viewing preferences 65; working through factuality 93
reality gameshows: classification 5, 30, 37, 49, 52–6, 60, 74, 80; personalities 15; public value 59, 70; schedules and ratings in Britain 33–6; schedules and ratings in Sweden 39–42, 55; viewing preferences 64–5, 67–70
reality genre: avoiding learning 169; broadcasting structures 32, 38, 40–2; critical engagement 140–3; factual categories 49; fairness 181–2, 184; humiliation TV 196, 198; key findings 215, 216; knowledge and learning 146; mapping factual TV 27–8; participants and audiences 174; participation 173; practices 218; programme categories 57; public value 69, 73; research methods 21–2, 24; restyling (of) factuality 16, 18, 227; shades of ethics 204, 206–8, 210; truth and performance 120, 126–8, 131–2, truth claims 112; viewing modes 104–7, 109, viewing preferences 62, 67; working through factuality 91, 92; *see also* reality formats
reality hoax 5, 49, 52, 194
reality modes of engagement: fact and fiction 85; looking through 115; viewing modes 104–8, 110; *see also*

modes of engagement *and* viewing modes
reality performers 28, 193, 197, 200, 207, 209–10, 217; fair treatment of 149, 175, 188–90, 203, 208; motivations to take part 187; other non-fiction genres 53; in reality hoax 49, 197; reality viewing modes 104; viewing preferences 68
reality refusniks 77–9
reality talentshows 56, 226, 230; British broadcasting 33; factual categories 49; humiliation TV 194, 197, 200; practices 218; reality performers 192; shades of ethics 206, 208–9; Swedish broadcasting 39; working through factuality 93
reality TV: actuality 113–19; avoiding learning 166–9; broadcasting structures 31–43; contexts 188–92; critical engagement 140–2; defining factual TV 75–81; fact and fiction 85–90; factual and reality trends 6–11; factual categories 43–53; factuality 3–6; fairness 180–8; humiliation TV 194–203; information and entertainment 74–5; key findings 213–18; learning and genre work 159–66; learning from factual TV 153–9; participants and audiences 174–80; practices 218–27; programme categories 53–5; public and popular genres 59–62; public value 68–74; research methods 234–40; restyling (of) factuality 11–18; 227–33; shades of ethics 203–9; truth and performance 119–33; viewing modes 104–9; viewing preferences 62–8; working through factuality 90–5; *see also* reality genre *and* reality formats
reconstructions: contemporary viewers 81; critical engagement 137; factual categories 46, 48, 50; information and entertainment 75; knowledge 171; learning from factual TV 158; mapping factual TV 30; programme categories 54–6; public value 69–72; restyling (of) factuality 15; truth and performance 124, 126; viewing modes 102–2; viewing preferences 65–7

Rescue 911 15, 123
research design 21, 24–5, 147
research methods 21–6, 234–40;
    quantitative research, survey design
    236–9; qualitative research, focus
    group design 239–40
research questions 24–25, 213
research sample 2, 24–5
Restoration 226
restyling (of) factuality 1–29; factual and
    reality trends 6–11; factuality 3–5;
    key findings 213–14; practices
    227–33; research methods 21–6;
    viewing practices 18–21
Reevell, P. 6
Riket 54, 131, 237
Robinson 38, 41, 80, 108, 162, 164
Rockstar: INXS 10
Rogue Traders 54, 236
Roomservice 54, 237
Roscoe, J. 21, 74, 141

Salon, The 80
Scannell, P. 98
Schudson, M. 4, 44, 97–8, 115
Seaton, J. 4, 14, 189, 207
Second World War in Colour, The 8
Secret History 47
Secret Policeman, The 46
Sen kväll med Luuk 54
September 11th (news coverage) 15,
    100, 150
Seymour, E. 33
shades of ethics 203–9; *see also* ethics
shame: emotion of shame 195–6; shame
    and reality TV 196–200
Silverstone, R. 98, 205
Simon Schama's History of Britain 47
simulation 116–17, 132, 215,
Sky News 6, 32, 80, 95, 99, 101
soap opera 49, 55, 86, 94, 124
Social Trends 22
socio-economic status: fairness 185–7;
    public value 71–2; viewing
    preferences 65–8
sociology of nature 112, 134
Solens mat 54, 237
South Bank Show, The 47
Souza, M.D. 220
Space Cadets 16–17, 52, 141, 177
Sparks, C. 150
sports 6, 10, 49, 81, 91, 141, 173;

sports/entertainment news 44, 100,
    222, 228
Springwatch 17–18
Star Trek 15
Stenner, P. 14
Strictly Come Dancing 6
Stupid Behaviour Caught on Tape 169
sub-genres 3–5, 49, 55–6, 213–14
Supernanny 93, 95, 105, 161, 226
Supervolcano 6–7, 11
survey design 236–9; *see also* research
    methods
Survival 54, 164, 220
Survivor 10, 13, 15, 115, 128, 184, 197
SVT 23–4, 37–43, 77, 124, 128–9,
    131–1, 158, 168, 190, 223; SVT 1
    38–42, 124; SVT 2 38–42
Swedish broadcasting 36–43
Swedish public service broadcasting
    36–43
Swedish schedules and ratings 39–43
Swedish Statistics 22
Switched 54, 237
Syversten, T. 83, 222
Szerszynski, B. 18–19, 112, 117, 134

tabloid genre 128
tabloid journalism 190, 207
tabloidisation 123
Tall People 39
taste and decency 107, 111
Tate Modern 47
television genre 4, 30, 55, 59, 68, 178,
    227
television production 4, 21–2, 24, 27,
    58, 109, 178, 210
television trends 6–11, 16, 24, 26, 33,
    38–9, 47, 63–4, 127
Ten O'Clock News 6, 98
There's Something About Miriam 52
Timeteam 54
Timewatch 47
Tonight with Trevor McDonald 33, 45, 54,
    95, 101, 236
Top of the Pops 53, 94
Top Model 80
Touching the Void 103
traditional viewers 77
true to life 3, 20, 113–14, 120–4,
    143–4, 216, 231; perception and
    value of factual TV 117–30
Truman Show, The 17

truth and performance 119–33; feral genre 127–33; Finland 126–7; performance 124–6; true to life 120–4
truth claims 112–44; actuality 113–19; critical engagement 133–42; truth and performance 119–33
Turner, G. 5, 45, 156, 179, 185, 200; traditional genre 67, 70, 72
TV3 23–4, 37–8, 40–1, 53, 55, 73, 100, 124, 137, 223
TV3 Nyheter 41, 53, 236
TV4 23–4, 37–42, 77, 131, 190, 223
TV-huset 54

uncomfortable viewer 89, 96–7, 108, 110, 189, 191, 194, 196, 203, 208
understanding learning 146–53
University Challenge 80
Uppdrag Granskning 41, 54, 77, 235–6
Urry, J. 18, 117

Veterinärerna 54, 236
Vets in Practice 54
viewing modes 95–109; documentary modes 101–4; news modes 97–101; reality modes 104–9; see also modes of engagement
viewing practices 2–3, 18–21, 82, 85, 210; avoiding learning 169; critical engagement 134; learning and genre work 164; key findings 213, 218–19, 222, 229–31
viewing preferences 62–8; age, gender and education 65–8
viewing strategies 2, 27, 30, 218; see also modes of engagement and viewing modes

Wadbring, I. 37
Walking with Cavemen 95, 103

Walking with Dinosaurs 102
Walking with Monsters 7
Ward, P. 47
Watchdog 46, 54, 236
Waterton, C. 62, 75, 169, 215
Weibull, L. 37–8, 63, 69–70
Westlund, O. 69
What Not to Wear 51, 93, 95, 178
What the Victorians Did for Us 95, 102
What the World Thinks of America 46
Who Do You Think You Are 17
Who Wants to be a Millionaire 45
Wife Swap 6, 50, 54, 78, 80, 105–6, 128, 153, 161, 192, 198–200, 219, 220, 235, 237
Wildlife on One 47
Winston, B.: factual categories 47; factuality 4; fairness 187–8, 217; looking through 114–15; nature and artifice 118–19; participants and audiences 176–8; public and popular genres 61; shades of ethics 206; viewing modes 104
Wollaston, S. 17–18
working through: avoiding learning 168; and dream work 88–9, 110; Ellis's concept 84, 86–7, 89, 215; genre work (working through factuality) 85, 87, 90–5, 214; news viewing modes 95; self-assessment 230; reality performers 202
World Idol 9

X Factor, The 5–7, 9, 93, 104–7, 197

Year of the Sex Olympics, The 207
You are What you Eat 226
Ytreberg, E. 192

Zoonen, L. van 12
Zoo Quest 48

Related titles from Routledge

Introduction to Television Studies
Jonathan Bignell

'A wonderfully ambitious and clear introduction to television studies for the undergraduate reader.' – *Gill Branston, University of Cardiff and co-author of* The Media Student's Book

In this comprehensive textbook, Jonathan Bignell provides students with a framework for understanding the key concepts and main approaches to television studies, including audience research, television history and broadcasting policy, and the analytical study of individual programmes.

Features include a glossary of key terms, key terms defined in margins, suggestions for further reading at the end of each chapter, activities for use in class or as assignments, and case studies discussing advertisements such as the Guinness 'surfer' ad, approaches to news reporting, and programmes such as *Big Brother*, *The West Wing*, *America's Most Wanted* and *The Cosby Show*.

Individual chapters address:

- Studying television
- Television histories
- Television cultures
- Television texts and narratives
- Television and genre
- Television production

- Postmodern television
- Television realities
- Television representation
- Television you can't see
- Shaping audiences
- Television in everyday life

ISBN13: 978–0–415–26112–8 (hbk)
ISBN13: 978–0–415–26113–5 (pbk)

Available at all good bookshops
For ordering and further information please visit:
www.routledge.com

Related titles from Routledge

The Television Studies Reader
Edited by Robert C. Allen and Annette Hill

The Television Studies Reader offers a roadmap to contemporary issues in the expanding and dynamic field of television studies. Thirty-eight cutting-edge essays lay out a wide array of approaches to the study of the changing phenomenon that is 'television' around the world.

The Reader pushes television studies well beyond the traditional equation of 'television' with terrestrial broadcasting, showcasing exciting new work on the wide variety of ways that television is experienced around the world and addressing issues of technology, industry, genre, representation, circulation, reception and audiences, production and ownership. It brings together contributions from leading international scholars to provide a range of perspectives on current television forms and practices, acknowledging both the status of television as a global medium, and the many and varied local contexts of its production and reception. A General Introduction situates these important scholarly contributions to our understanding of contemporary television within the history of the academic study of television.

ISBN13: 978–0–415–28323–6 (hbk)
ISBN13: 978–0–415–28324–3 (pbk)

Available at all good bookshops
For ordering and further information please visit:
www.routledge.com